PENGUIN CANADA

RETURNING TO THE TEACHINGS

RUPERT ROSS has been an Assistant Crown Attorney for the District of Kenora since 1985, responsible for criminal prosecutions on over twenty remote Cree and Ojibway First Nations. He began his exploration of Aboriginal approaches to justice—and life itself—in his first book, *Dancing with a Ghost*, a national bestseller.

ALSO BY RUPERT ROSS

Dancing with a Ghost

RETURNING TO THE
TEACHINGS

EXPLORING ABORIGINAL JUSTICE

RUPERT ROSS

PENGUIN
CANADA

A Note on the Cover

It was the turtle who offered his back when a foundation was needed to re-create Mother Earth. At the beginning of time, the Anishinabe (the original people) had ways of dealing with justice within the community. The circle was known to be the place of no end. It created a space where one's voice could be heard—where the capacity, the connection, the creativity of the community found a place of being, by bringing people together to repair the harm that had been done. A victim's voice, an offender's voice, the community's voice, no longer ignored, shamed or victimized. A place of compassion, connection, sacredness, voice and truth.

The painting featured on the cover, by Randy Charboneau / Waywaymegwun, is titled *Restorative Justice and Transforming Society*. For more information about the artist, visit **www.swayingfeather.ca**.

PENGUIN CANADA

Published by the Penguin Group

First published in Penguin Canada paperback by Penguin Group (Canada),
a division of Pearson Penguin Canada Inc., 1996
Published in this edition, 2006

11 12 13 14 15   (WEB)

www.penguinrandomhouse.com

To Patricia Gill Ross
with so many reasons for thanks

Contents

Acknowledgments

I want to thank all the Aboriginal people from so many places who not only opened their good hearts to me, but also shared much more of their sane, humble and truly vibrant world than I have been able to absorb.

In particular, I want to first thank elders Alex Denny (Eskasoni, Nova Scotia), Charlie Fisher and Alex Skead (Kenora, Ontario) and Walter and Marie Linklater (Saskatoon). Then, in alphabetical order: Danny Moonhawk Alford (Hayward, California), Marie Battiste (Eskasoni, Nova Scotia), Cathy and Mide Migwun Bird (Peguis, Manitoba), Burma and Joyce Bushie (Hollow Water, Manitoba), Les Couchie (North Bay, Ontario), Pat Danard (Emo, Ontario), Evelyn Gilles (Rat Portage, Ontario), Louise Halfe (Skydancer) (Saskatoon), Eber Hampton (Regina), Marcel Hardisty (Hollow Water), Sákéj Henderson (Eskasoni), Maggie Hodgson (Edmonton), Basil Johnston (Richmond Hill, Ontario), David Keenan (Teslin, Yukon), Tobasonikwut Kinew (Kenora, Ontario), Amethyst First Rider and Leroy Little Bear (Calgary), Cathy Louis (Vancouver), Murdena and Albert Marshall (Eskasoni), Patricia Monture-Angus (Saskatoon), Wilson Plain (Sarnia, Ontario), Inspector Jim Potts (Ontario Provincial Police), Valdie Seymour (Hollow Water), Murray Sinclair (Winnipeg), Georgina Sydney (Teslin, Yukon), Rosemary Traherne (Ottawa) and Robert Yazzie (Arizona).

And then there are all my non-Aboriginal friends and colleagues who took the risk of setting me free to pursue this learning path.

Those include three people from the Ontario system who agreed to relieve me of my prosecution duties and wished me well: Richard Cummine (Crown Attorney, Kenora), Dan Mitchell (Acting Regional Director of Crown Attorneys, Thunder Bay) and Michael Code (Assistant Deputy Minister, Criminal Law, Ministry of the Attorney-General, Toronto). They also include two people who have served as the Directors of the Aboriginal Justice Directorate of Justice Canada, Ottawa, during my secondment: Judge David Arnot and, before him, Don Avison, who left to become Deputy Minister of Justice in the Northwest Territories. Don was the one who initially invited me aboard, and gained Departmental support in Ottawa for this strangest of projects.

I also wish to give a special thank you to Clare Brant, who passed away during the preparation of this manuscript, but whose heart will always remain an inspiration to me.

I must also mention that I have been inspired by the pioneering work of a great many non-Aboriginal judges, all of whom have encouraged me to listen to, and work with, Aboriginal people, just as they have done for many years. They include Judges Barry Stuart and Heino Lilles from the Yukon, Doug Campbell from British Columbia, Claude Fafard from Saskatchewan, Gerry Michel from northeastern Ontario, Don Fraser and Judyth Little from northwestern Ontario and Jean-Charles Coutu from Quebec. I know there are many others as well, men and women whom I hope to meet in the years to come.

Thank you all. My family and I have been enriched by the experiences of the past three years.

A Note on Presentation

As I have discovered in my exposure to Aboriginal peoples, there are many different ways to approach, understand and talk about the world. What feels "natural" to one group will often seem "odd" to another. In writing this book I have tried my best to respect the ways of sharing information that my Aboriginal teachers have used with me. Because they are different from the ways I grew up with, a few words of explanation may be helpful at this early stage.

You will find, for instance, that I often say something like "An old man told me such-and-such," without ever naming him or detailing when and where he said it. There is also a section at the end of the introduction where I thank my many teachers by name, without being precise about what it was they said or did to assist me. This is not the way of Western scholarship, which looks to attribute words with great precision to each particular speaker. It is, however, the way that feels proper to me in the unique context of this difficult book.

Part of it has to do with something an old Cree man (here I go!) told me: "You cannot pass along what another person 'really' told you; you can only pass along what you heard." That is one reason I often decline to name people as I go along, to avoid embarrassing them by using their words in ways that they may never have intended.

But it goes much deeper than that. There seems to be a widespread Aboriginal understanding that thought or information must be shared in ways that leave it open to the listeners to take whatever meaning they wish to find in what they have heard. That is the premise of storytelling, where the storyteller will never say, "That's not what I *meant.*" The Western preoccupation with such questions as "What did Shakespeare really mean in *Hamlet?*" is nothing more than our preoccupation; the pertinent question for most Aboriginal peoples seems to be something like "What did *Hamlet* cause *you* to think, feel or do?"

There is, for instance, sacred ground outside Saskatoon known as Wanuskewin. Cree elders have approved and guided the construction of an interpretive centre on that site. Part of its program includes a short film during which the regular narration is joined by a deep Aboriginal voice slowly asking, "What does Wanuskewin mean ... to *you?*"

In other words, there seems to be an understanding that education should focus on presenting events or experiences in ways that encourage others to find their own significance. As a result, neither the identity nor the intent of the teacher occupies centre stage. At the same time, there is a clear expectation that different people will react to "what was said" in very different ways. In fact, discussions become almost a celebration of the rich diversity of life, thought and feeling, rather than a contest between opposing views about what we "ought" to think or feel.

That is how I offer this book, and all the thoughts, feelings and experiences I've tried to express in it. They are personal to me, representing nothing more than how *I* experienced my exposure to Aboriginal peoples, their teachings and their dreams for tomorrow. I cannot tell you about Aboriginal reality, only about how I have come to understand my own exposure to small parts of it. As an old Ojibway man once told me, "All I can tell you about ... is me. All the rest is guesswork."

I also hope it can be understood that when I discuss two (or more) ways to do, say or understand things, such comparisons are not invitations to come to judgments about which way is better or worse than another. I compare only to illustrate that there *are* profound differences, and that different ways may be equally deserving of respect.

At the same time, I freely acknowledge that I have found myself strongly attracted to certain Aboriginal approaches, especially in the context of healing. I do not, however, expect everyone else to feel the same way. In fact, I expect the opposite!

So I have one request to make: read what follows in the same way you would pick up a strangely shaped piece of driftwood. Hold it for a while in your hands, glance over its knots and swirls and shadows and see if it "says" anything to you. If it does, you are free to use it as you will. If it does not, leave it where you found it, just in case it is capable of touching the next unique human beings who come along. What means little to you may mean much to them—and vice versa—and that in itself is cause for celebration.

Introduction

*R*eturning to the Teachings was first published in 1995, and I'm very grateful to Penguin Canada for reissuing it.

When I began to write this book in the 1990s, my plan was to describe some emerging First Nations justice processes in the hope that other Aboriginal communities might be inspired to begin their own journeys towards individual, family and community healing. As I wrote, however, it became clear that it was not only justice processes that called out for a reassertion of traditional teachings but most other aspects of life as well. I found myself being drawn into discussions about how a reclaiming of traditional perspectives would fundamentally re-inform parenting, politics, education, governance, health care and most other aspects of community life. I explored language differences, metaphysics and spirituality, gaining a sense of how each of them changes community perspectives and opens up community choices.

The deeper I was taken into traditional ways of seeing, the more dislocated I felt. While I sensed myself moving towards a better appreciation of many Aboriginal peoples' assertion that their cultures cause them to see the world in a different way, I was finding it increasingly difficult to let go of my own way of seeing. I never felt I had been able to escape my own paradigm enough to begin functioning freely in the other.

In the ten years since, some of those perspectives seem to have settled in around me, causing me to come at many aspects of existence with different questions, to respond in a different fashion to what I was saw as "everyday" events. I wish I could offer a simple illustration of the difference, one that might be easily grasped, but cross-paradigm discussions don't seem to work that way. I think I'll need many stories to carry readers out of one place, into the unknown and then back to the original location with brand new eyes.

And that leads me to a choice I had to make when Penguin Canada approached me about reissuing *Returning to the Teachings*. If I wanted to, I could expand upon it, trying to bring it forward to my present interpretations. As I explained in the introduction to the new edition of *Dancing with a Ghost*, I've chosen to leave the original text just the way it was, with the promise that I'll get myself into a third work as quickly as I can. That's not meant as a teaser but as a reflection of my sense that I need to reinterpret almost everything contained in both earlier books in light of my growing sense of shifting paradigm. Nothing in *Dancing* or *Returning* is "wrong"; it's just that almost everything I spoke of is either much more—or much less—than what I initially understood it to be, and it will take a comprehensive third work to convey what I mean.

I do, however, want to make some observations about what has happened—and what has not—in the fields of Aboriginal and restorative justice since *Returning to the Teachings* was first published. In some respects, there appears to have been rather incredible progress made, but I'm beginning to wonder if we can really take advantage of the restorative opportunities now being presented to us.

First, the good news: the Canadian criminal justice establishment seems prepared to acknowledge the benefits of including restorative justice processes within the system itself. In 1995, the Parliament of Canada enacted section 718 of the Criminal Code, which requires that "all available sanctions other than imprison-ment that are reasonable in the circumstances should be considered for all offenders, with particular attention to the circumstances of aboriginal offenders." Then, in 1999, the Supreme Court of Canada delivered its judgment in the *Gladue* decision, requiring the courts to make section 718 a "meaningful" provision and thus fundamentally altering sentencing law in Canada. In 2004, Parliament enacted the Youth Criminal Justice Act, which specifically encourages restorative justice processes such as conferencing. Section 38 requires the courts to consider "all available sanctions other than custody … with particular attention to the circumstances of aboriginal young persons." Section 41 states that "the court may convene or cause to be convened a conference" to make sentencing recommendations, and section 18 authorizes the creation of youth justice committees, which may, among other things, facilitate "the reconciliation of the victim and the young person."

In short, the law of the land has been changed, approving the efforts of communities to create a wide variety of restorative processes tailored to local perspectives. Criminal law, for good reason, will likely remain monolithic in its definitions of what is and is not criminal behaviour, but it is beginning to recognize that productive *responses* to criminal behaviour can show great variety. Different communities may well design different restorative responses to reflect and take advantage of their unique circum-stances; we do not have to remain trapped in a one-response-fits-all mentality. Some parts of the country are responding to the encouragement of Parliament and the Supreme Court by funding alternate processes and encouraging justice professionals to get involved with creative community justice proposals, while others are not. I guess that's to be expected. There really has been a sea change in justice thinking since 1997, and it will take time to explore it.

I am increasingly concerned, however, that the task may be more daunting than it first appears. Restorative justice processes require such a fundamentally different way of thinking that even the best-motivated people seem to be having problems escaping the preconceptions and commandments of our western way of seeing. Too frequently, the result is a wholly unsatisfactory mix of two approaches that results in the mangling of both.

Suppose, for example, that a teenager walking down a lane spots a bottle of rum on a table just inside someone's house, breaks a window, reaches in and steals it. If he has no criminal record, a court might well *impose* a sentence requiring payment for the damage and loss and perhaps require some community service work. If the case is "diverted" to a restorative justice process such as a family group conference, the offender will have to meet with the homeowners to give them a chance to speak about how they were affected by his actions and to see if a mutually agreeable resolution can be achieved. More often than not, such resolution involves the same kinds of compensation and free work that the court might have imposed, though more often the work is done directly for the victims.

The problem with many restorative justice processes as they are operated now is that they seem to focus primarily on achieving that agreement. Some programs even train their conference facilitators in mediation, a process designed to settle business disputes, where most issues can ultimately be reduced to money and where "values" and "personal relations" are seen as somehow getting in the way of achieving "win-win" agreements. When transferred into the criminal context, mediation thinking centres on material concerns such as compensation and restitution and on achieving agreements about "how much" is appropriate. It is a "stuff"-centred perspective, aimed at getting at a fair settlement for the cost of the broken window and the lost bottle of rum, together with some recognition that the peace of the victims was disturbed.

That is not, however, the focus of restorative justice processes that remain faithful to their originating visions, whether they emerge from Aboriginal, Quaker, Mennonite or other perspectives. To them, the harm done is only peripherally about "stuff." Instead, the harm is understood in the *relational* realm. How has the relationship between the homeowners and their *home* been changed? Is it still their sanctuary, or has that been altered? Do they now wake up with every noise in the night? Do they double check every door before going to bed, find themselves peering out into the night with every footfall? Has their relationship with their *neighbourhood* been changed? Do they see strangers as possible threats? Do they avoid going out alone? Do they think about moving somewhere else? How do they now feel about the teenagers they see on the street?

In the relational way of seeing, the homeowners must be helped to explore the depth and range of the relational injuries they have suffered, for that is where the crime has taken place. Until that exploration occurs, they will go away believing that they have not been heard—that their victimization has not be acknowledged. Of equal importance is bringing the offender to that same kind of understanding. He may walk into the conference believing that he "only took a bottle of rum, 20 bucks, big deal, here's your 20, stop complaining." Unless he leaves the process with a completely different understanding of the damage, he has not taken responsibility in any meaningful way—or even understood his own crime. Until he does, he has little incentive to change, and the personal empathy that is necessary to *inspire* change has not been created.

In too many restorative justice processes, the focus I just described is sacrificed to expediency. Victims are not taken beyond their anger, offenders know they should apologize and offer compensation, the hour is almost up and it's time to quantify the loss, get an agreement signed and get back to the "thing" world in which we're comfortable.

So I'm at a strange point in all of this—restorative justice is *apparently* flourishing, but it's not the restorative justice I glimpsed at Hollow Water, where the relational world is defined as the *real* world and where "stuff" is peripheral to the real concerns. The more I watch restorative justice processes turn into stuff-centered mediation (why would anyone think that crime should be the subject of mediation anyway?), even with people who are keen to bring hurt feelings into the process, the more my pessimism deepens. It's almost as if we cannot escape our technology-obsessed world where product rules over process, quantity over quality, speed over thoroughness, contract over caring—and where we focus on stuff rather than relationships. These are the cultural commandments that seem to control our lives and institutions, and maybe it's too much to expect that we could suddenly turn ourselves into different people just by sitting in a circle and talking the language of restoration. I've even seen Aboriginal justice groups send their people off to mediation courses and have them come back with the language of "win-win" and "getting to agreement," where values, insult and "personal issues" are to be carefully kept out of the discussion!

But perhaps I'm being unduly pessimistic here. Perhaps it will just take a while for the differences to be understood and for western-educated people to begin to feel comfortable working in the un-boundaried relational realm, where tears and hugs, not money and hours worked, are the true currency. And perhaps, by pointing to this challenge at the outset of *Returning to the Teachings,* the issue can be highlighted in advance.

In any event, as the Elders suggest, all that any one person can do is tell his or her own stories and share his or her own understandings of the day, always acknowledging that tomorrow will bring new shades of significance and new directions for exploration. I'm grateful that Penguin has decided that these "old" stories of mine are still worth telling—and I look forward to putting my newer ones into words in the not-too-distant future. Meanwhile, here's to all the people who are trying to move our social institutions in more productive, human-centred directions. I have been honoured to meet you, watch you at work and listen to your dreams. Each of you has changed not only my thinking but my living, and my family and I are richer for it. Thank you all.

Rupert Ross
November 2005

P.S. I hope you can understand how powerfully inspirational it has been to meet Randy Charboneau, to hear his story (which I'll let him tell) and to find that my own life and work has been so intimately intertwined with his—even though we didn't meet until the summer of 2005! The world is indeed full of wonders, and this has been one of the happiest.

CHAPTER 1

THE MOVEMENT TOWARDS TEACHING AND HEALING

Probably one of the most serious gaps in the system is the different perception of wrongdoing and how to best treat it. In the non-Indian community, committing a crime seems to mean that the individual is a *bad person* and therefore must be punished....The Indian communities view a wrongdoing as *a misbehaviour which requires teaching or an illness which requires healing.* (emphasis added)

T hat paragraph came from a justice proposal prepared in 1989 by the Sandy Lake First Nation, a remote Oji-Cree community in northwestern Ontario. I quoted it towards the end of my first book, *Dancing with a Ghost*. In the three and a half years since its publication, I have heard almost identical statements in Aboriginal communities from one coast to the other.

I remember, for instance, meeting with a chief, his young council and some elders at a remote Cree First Nation in north-western Ontario. At one point I asked what the community used to do in traditional times, before the courts came, to those who misbehaved. An old lady (and I adopt that phrase as a term of respect common with Aboriginal people) answered immediately. Through the interpreter she said, "We didn't do anything *to* them.

We *counselled* them instead!" Her emphatic Cree suggested that she couldn't understand why I would ask such a question. At the same time, the hand-covered grins of the councillors told me that they had regularly felt the power of her certainty about the wisdom of the old ways.

For the longest time, I didn't fully believe pronouncements like that. I suspected that people were giving me romanticized versions of traditional justice, with all of the punishments removed to make things look rosier than they really were. The more I looked, however, the more I saw how widespread this preference towards teaching and healing—and away from punishment—really was.

It wasn't until a few years ago, however, in a remote, fly-in Cree community of five hundred people that I understood on an emotional level how deep the commitment to teaching and healing really was. It is a story that will take a while to tell, but it is important that the full setting be understood.

The Three Cree Women

As the Crown Attorney, I had flown into the community several days before court for what we called our "Advance Day." With me was another lawyer, the Duty Counsel, whose job was to act as a public defender of sorts. Together, we were to prepare for the court day by interviewing witnesses and examining how accurate and necessary the charges were. In the majority of cases, such advance work weeds out improper charges, reduces the need for trials and helps all parties come up with sentencing proposals for the judge that seem most realistic in the circumstances.

The community's solitary policeman met us at the gravel airstrip, then drove us into the community over snow-packed roads. The temperature was about −30°C, it was still and sunny, and woodsmoke rose straight up from the hundred or so chimneys of the village. We dropped the Duty Counsel off at the Band Office and carried on to the policeman's office. It was a tiny, plywood-floored hut with a woodstove, a metal desk, a single filing cabinet, a one-bunk holding cell and an outhouse. He had put a fire in the woodstove some hours earlier, so I no longer had to wear my mitts. I unzipped my parka but kept it on.

As he filled me in on the dozen or so cases on the court list, I began to breathe a small sigh of relief. None of them looked serious enough that I would feel obliged to ask the court to impose a jail term. That meant that we were unlikely to have any contested trials, for nothing inspires pleas of "Not Guilty" like the news that the Crown is looking for jail. We quickly settled into some small talk, chatting about things like problems in the community, the extent of the drinking, what kind of hockey team was being assembled for the upcoming tournament down in Sioux Lookout, whether the kids here were sniffing gasoline, and so forth. It was at that point, almost casually, that he mentioned that the community had formed a "Police Committee" of six men and six women, and that they had been working with each of the people charged, as well as their families. In fact, he told me, they had prepared detailed recommendations for all the cases and would appear at court to ask the judge if they could speak. When I asked what kinds of recommendations to expect, he answered something like "Oh, just probation and counselling, that kind of stuff."

A few days later, we returned to the community for the actual court.

There is something about northern courts they neglected to tell us in law school: one of the more important jobs of the Crown Attorney involves getting to the local school, hall, gymnasium, church, office or other makeshift courthouse as early as possible, then locating and setting up just the right number of trestle tables and stacking chairs to accommodate the likely turnout. That was how I began that court day, for the police officer was out at the airstrip waiting for Judge Fraser's plane. Both of our local judges, Don Fraser and Judyth Little of the Ontario Court (Provincial Division), prefer putting those tables in a "circle" shape, hoping that this will reduce the adversarial nature of the process. Instead of having the accused and his lawyer sit directly opposite the Crown and the police like boxers on opposite sides of the ring, they are spread around the circle together with probation officers, translators, alcohol workers and anyone else who might have a contribution to make. My own impression is that such an arrangement does make people feel more comfortable and also contributes to a fuller community participation. Perhaps people feel better joining as equals a group discussion aimed at finding solutions than they do making formal and solitary suggestions to an all-powerful judge.

As time passed that morning, people filed into the gymnasium and milled about, helping themselves to coffee provided by the band. The Duty Counsel was scurrying about doing last-minute checks with various people. When the police officer returned with Judge Fraser, his court clerk and reporter, they took their seats and the court was opened. I advised him of the existence of the Police Committee, and he invited them to come forward. Instead of twelve people, as I had expected, three women emerged from the group at the back of the room. Judge Fraser gave them seats just to his right, directly opposite me. One of them looked to be in her sixties or seventies, another in her forties and the third in her twenties.

I should have said that there were *four* of them, because they had brought an infant along, snugly wrapped in its *tikinagan*, or cradle board. They laid the *tikinagan* flat on the trestle table in front of them, where all three could watch, touch, feed, coo and tickle. The baby stayed there through the entire court, causing no commotion at all. I should mention that in northern courts Judges Fraser and Little not only tolerate but welcome such additions.

While we've never really talked about it, I suspect that they too see it as a reminder of something Aboriginal communities always stress whenever we come into them: that we are all assembled to help make life better for the next generation. Having some of that generation actually present often proves to be a valuable reminder when we start to get caught up in our self-important roles!

One of the cases on the list, the one that makes me remember that day, concerned a man who had assaulted his wife. It was not, in strictly physical terms, a serious assault, for it involved "only" a couple of slaps. There had been no bruising or other injury. The police officer expressed his concern, however, that violence might have been used before and might be escalating. The court shared his concern, for the accepted wisdom in urban Canada is that by the time a woman reports an assault by her partner, it's the thirty-fifth time, on average, that he's done it to her.

The charge of assault was read out. The husband, a man in his twenties, entered his guilty plea. Because of that, I was permitted to "read in" a short summary of the events, instead of making witnesses give evidence themselves. It sounded like so many other summaries I had read in over the years: he had been drinking that evening, an argument had developed over some minor matter and he had slapped her twice. She had taken their two small children to her family's house overnight, returning in the morning after he had sobered up. End of story. In normal circumstances, this would have been followed by a short lecture on using violence, a sentence imposing a fine or community service work and a Probation Order requiring (I can hear the chant so clearly!) that for six months the accused must "keep the peace and be of good behaviour and abstain absolutely from the consumption of alcohol or attending at premises where alcohol is sold or dispensed. That means no house parties either. If anyone starts drinking, you leave. Do you understand?"

Except that in this case the Police Committee had their own ideas. They were put before the judge by the Duty Counsel, and they were far more complex than I was expecting them to be.

As the first stage of their proposal, they suggested that the offender go out of the community to attend a thirty-day alcohol treatment program in the distant urban centre of Thunder Bay. It was their understanding, however, that the drinking was just a surface problem that could not be solved on its own. If the reasons for the drinking were not looked at and dealt with, it would continue—course or no course. We were told that certain things had happened to the man as a boy, things he had never talked about until now. They didn't give us any more details, except to say that the elders were once again coming forward to help the young people learn what they needed to know to "live a good life" and that the young man was beginning to open up to them.

Next, they recognized that there was a serious lack of communication between husband and wife. They felt that both of them were carrying burdens alone, and that neither had really understood what was going on with the other. For that reason, they recommended that they both go the following week to a neighbouring community to attend a three-day series of workshops being held on family violence and family communication. Further, when those workshops were repeated a week later in their home community, they had to attend them as well. In that way, perhaps they could begin to break down the silences that had come between them.

At that point, I felt I was hearing one of the most thorough assessments possible. They were not, however, finished.

They told us that the children still had to be considered. Those children had seen the violence at home and were confused by it. The committee felt that if the children were not involved in understanding things, talking about them and helping to turn them around, they would grow up to repeat their father's behaviour themselves. The last recommendation therefore involved having the whole family attend a month-long family healing program available at another neighbouring community once all the other steps had been carried through.

After the Duty Counsel finished summarizing the plan and explaining that the offender would be a willing participant, Judge Fraser turned to the three women. He asked them if they wished to speak to the court themselves, instead of through the Duty Counsel. As I recall, it was the woman in her forties who spoke to us, in Cree. The transcript records the interpreter as saying the following (with the real name of the offender removed by me):

> She stated that she feels [the offender] is very sincere in his desire to seek help and treatment, and after deliberations of the other committee members they set a plan for him. That the problems [the offender] has stem from his childhood and are finally surfacing. And also that [the offender] has indicated a desire to seek help. And also that it's a good sign that he included his wife and his whole family in that process. And she feels, you know, that healing will come, that all of them seek help.
>
> In the past this was not the case, but we're getting more organized at the community level. And trying to find ways of trying to help people in our community setting, rather than have the people that are charged be taken away. They come back with the same problems, too, so the band is trying to take a different approach.

Judge Fraser included all their recommendations in the Probation Order. He also reminded the offender that it wasn't just the promises in the Probation Order that were important, but the fact that he had made the promises to his own community and to the Police Committee, which was trying to help him. The offender nodded that he understood.

At the end of the day, when all the cases had been heard, something else happened. The three women turned to Judge Fraser and, through the interpreter, thanked him for giving them the chance to give their thoughts to the court. Judge Fraser seemed to be as moved as I was, not only by the depth of their concern and the thoroughness of their analysis throughout the day, but by the fact that they should be extending their thanks to him at the end of it. As best I recall, he replied that he should be thanking *them* instead. He also said something to the effect that, in his view, their approaches to problems in their community could help show the way to the rest of Canada.

A number of things struck me at the time.

One was the fact of that "thank you." I know that very formal expressions of appreciation before and after speaking are common, for respect must always be shown to other people, whether a consensus has been reached or substantial issues remain unresolved. In my view, however, there was something else at work that day, an extra emphasis in that "thank you," as if it had been a *special* privilege to be able to give the community's perspective to the court. That, in turn, made me wonder how excluded they must have felt from the court up to that day. When they thanked Judge Fraser for "giving" them the opportunity to speak, I wondered once again what it must be like to suspect, from past dealings, that the outsiders who possess all the power don't really want to hear a single thing you have to say. For how many decades had they been hearing that kind of a message, and in how many ways?

In the face of that history, I once again marvelled at the immense respect they continued to show us as we kept flying in to do "our" business with them, using only "our" ways, then flying back out the very same day. There is one remote community in northwestern Ontario that prepares a feast for the court party each court day, with pots of wild rice, bannock, fish and game stew carried into the schoolhouse where we hold court. Those feasts take place despite the fact that, as I hope to demonstrate in the pages that follow, almost every aspect of our Western approach to justice breaks traditional Aboriginal law.

But it was not just their continuing respect for us that struck me that day. I was also inspired by the thoroughness and sophistication of their analysis. There were no Western Ph.D.'s in that group, but their knowledge of the ways in which dysfunctions—or "disharmonies"—spread and multiply within families and from generation to generation could have stood up against the best material I have seen come out of Canadian universities. That day, when I compared the sophistication of their recommendations to our usual courtroom response of "probation, abstention from alcohol, and fine or community service work," I felt just the way Judge Fraser did—that we should be thanking them instead.

I was also struck by the fact that punishment did not even seem to be an *option* that day, even amongst the women on that Police Committee—despite the fact that the victim was a woman and family violence seemed to be a major concern in the community. Why were they not saying the kinds of angry things I was used to hearing from the victims of family violence elsewhere in Canada? Their position reminded me of the old Cree lady who was so perplexed when I asked what they'd "done to" people who'd misbehaved in traditional times. The approach they seemed to take went beyond a belief that punishment wasn't necessary in that particular case, for punishment simply didn't seem to be an option in the first place.

Listening to how they approached the problem was a turning point of sorts for me. I had been hearing Aboriginal people talk about "justice-as-healing" a great deal, but I still had some doubts about how deep-rooted that approach really was. It almost seemed as if everyone had attended the same lecture somewhere and had decided to dress themselves up in the same philosophical clothes, just to look superior to the Western system. What I saw from those three women in that tiny Cree community ended my doubts about such things. What they offered was not an imported response designed to support some romantic reinvention of traditional approaches. Instead, as I felt it then and know it now, it came from the hearts of all of them and from the accumulated understandings of centuries.

I acknowledge that I shared the scepticism of many observers about how "traditional" such healing approaches really are. I have found, however, that my scepticism just couldn't survive the eyes and voices of so many old people, men and women alike, speaking only their own ancient languages, all looking dumbfounded (or outraged!) at my suggestion that punishment might be used to make things better. Nor could it withstand sitting in the sexual abuse healing circles at Hollow Water, an Ojibway community east of Lake Winnipeg, where the ancient teachings of the medicine wheel come to life to move victims and offenders forward out of their hurt and anger. As a result, my scepticism has gone into a complete meltdown. I now see teaching and healing as corner-stones of traditional Aboriginal thought.

In saying that, I want to be careful about a number of things.

First, what I have said does not mean that traditional responses to dangerous individuals were so generous in every case. Community welfare had to come first, and if a particular individual resisted (or was beyond) community efforts aimed at healing, then banishment to the wilderness was a viable, if regretted, option. I have never heard an Aboriginal community say that healing can work with everyone; what I have heard, however, is that it is short-sighted to offer healing to no one at all and to rely entirely on deterrence and jail instead.

Second, what I have said does not mean that traditional responses to dangerous individuals cannot contain elements of pain. As I will later explore, some teaching is indeed painful, and some healing is much more painful than simply hiding from the truth in a jail cell. I am saying instead that imposing pain for its own sake, strictly as punishment, unaccompanied by efforts to move people forward out of their problems, seldom seems to be an option. An eye-for-an-eye approach, I am told, leads only to the blindness of all (a phrase which suggests an alternate explanation for why the Statue of Justice is blindfolded as she holds up her scales!).

Third, I don't mean to suggest that healing is the central goal of every Aboriginal community—or even the numerical majority—at this particular point in history. A great many focus on punishment instead, and some propose punishments that are more severe than those of the Western courts. Many traditional people suggest, however, that such perspectives are simply the inevitable result of generations of imposed Western approaches, including the use of corporal punishment in residential schools. They point, for instance, to the fact that the Navajo are now moving away from their once-famous Western-based tribal courts and reinvigorating traditional peacemaking processes instead. Colonization strategies, they say, have touched everything, including dispute resolution, and are making it difficult for many communities to break free of punitive approaches and re-root themselves in restorative approaches instead.

Fourth, I don't mean to suggest that all Aboriginal leaders who now speak the language of healing are doing so out of an honest commitment to the betterment of their communities. Sadly, there are many dysfunctional communities where the groups in power promote "traditional healing programs" for one reason only: to prevent their abusive friends from being truly called to account in *anyone's* justice system, Western or Aboriginal. It is not the teachings themselves that are responsible for such abuse; it is their misuse by desperate people in desperately ill communities.

After my experiences of the last several years, I now hold the view that there is one best way for communities to deal with the problems that show up as charges in criminal courts: the traditional teachings need to be brought back to prominence once again, rather than being discounted as inadequate relics of a simpler past. In a number of communities, this has already been done: the teachings have been brought forward into full twentieth-century flower by good people determined to replace silence and suffering with honesty, hope and health.

So I offer my own conclusion: the three Cree women were not a fluke or an oddity, or a special case. Instead, they spoke from an ancient conviction shared by a great many Aboriginal peoples, a conviction that the best way to respond to the inevitable ups and downs of life, whether defined as "criminal" or not, is not by punishing solitary offenders. The focus must be shifted instead towards the teaching and healing of all the parties involved, with an eye on the past to understand how things have come to be, and an eye on the future to design measures that show the greatest promise of making it healthier for all concerned.

The past three years have shown me this preference is not unique to the Cree and Ojibway of my small part of the globe. To close this chapter, I'll take you on a short tour of some other places where Aboriginal people are bringing traditional healing and teaching back to centre stage again, including stops in the Yukon, New Zealand and Arizona/New Mexico, before returning to the Ojibway First Nation of Hollow Water in Manitoba. I have selected them primarily because I have met and learned from people involved in them, and because I sense a similarity in philosophy which is all the more striking, given their geographical separation.

First stop, the Yukon.

A Tlingit Perspective

Teslin is a Tlingit community of some 450 people in the Yukon. In 1991 I had an opportunity to hear its chief at the time, David Keenan, and the woman responsible for community justice initiatives, Georgina Sydney, when they spoke at some justice workshops in Alberta. After learning about their plans to deal in their own way with community offenders, I was not surprised to find that a case from Teslin was soon reported in the law books.

The judge who wrote the decision was Chief Judge Lilles of the Yukon Territorial Court (for lawyers' reference, the case was reported as *R.v. P.* (J.A.) (1991) 6 C.R. (4th) 126). It involved a man of forty-two who pleaded guilty to the sexual assault of his thirteen-year-old daughter, to indecent assault of another daughter in 1980 and to having sexual intercourse with a thirteen-year-old girl who was his foster child. Psychological reports on the children made it clear that they suffered psychological harm, using such words as "confused," "fearful," "shame," "guilt," "helplessness," "anger" and "distrust." After disclosure, the offender took treatment for his alcohol problems, joined educational sessions on sexual abuse as far away as Winnipeg and attended a weekly "teaching circle" run by the community of Teslin. His wife, herself a victim of earlier sexual abuse, was described as having feelings of anger, betrayal and guilt once she became aware of her husband's behaviour.

When it came time for sentencing (or "disposition," as the lawyers call it), something unusual happened: only the Crown Attorney asked for punishment.

In the case report, Judge Lilles wrote the following about the position taken by the offender's wife:

Mrs. P. gave evidence of how the disclosure affected her, but also her observations of the changes in her husband during the past year. They have talked openly about the problem, including the need for both of them to get alcohol treatment. They went to treatment together and both of them, along with the eldest daughter, C., attend the "healing circle" on a weekly basis. She described the positive changes in their relationship since the disclosure, including open communication, honesty and truth in their relationship and the courage to stand up and admit that he is an offender. Both mother and daughter support the clan recommendation for a community disposition, feeling that "jail will stop the healing that has been going on," and that the father is an "integral part of the healing process for herself."

The reactions of Mrs. P. and her daughter confirmed the need for all the parties to be involved in healing processes if *any* are to be healed. After learning that the community supported the resolution, Judge Lilles made the following comments in his judgment:

It is of interest that it has been only relatively recently that professional psychologists and social workers have begun to fully appreciate the devastating impact of this cycle of abuse. Tlingit custom and tradition have apparently recognized it for centuries. Moreover, as our criminal law focuses primarily on the offender, it is unable to effectively deal with victims, family or the community of the offender ...

The judge agreed with the community request for a healing disposition, and in doing so had this to say:

In this case I heard evidence about the humiliation which accompanies disclosure of an offence like this in a community the size of Teslin. "First, one must deal with the shock and then the dismay on your neighbours' faces. One must live with the daily humiliation, and at the same time seek forgiveness not just from victims, but from the community as a whole." For, in a native culture, a real harm has been done *to everyone*. A community disposition continues that humiliation, at least until full forgiveness has been achieved. A gaol sentence removes the offender from this daily accountability, may not do anything towards rehabilitation, and for many will actually be an *easier* disposition than staying in the community. (emphasis added)

I asked Georgina Sydney (the woman responsible for community justice initiatives) about the impact of their healing approach to sexual abuse, and she said one thing in particular that struck me: since they had begun to deal with things in that way, they had had offenders come forward and disclose their abusive behaviour *on their own*, asking for help for everyone. As a Crown Attorney, I can honestly say that no one has ever walked into my office and said, "I want to confess that I sexually abused my stepdaughter; please prosecute me." To the extent that sexual abuse spreads from one generation to the next as long as the silence is maintained, her comments suggested that our emphasis on punishment, by contributing to the silence, may also be encouraging the continuation of abuse. It was a sobering thought, and I am hearing it with increasing frequency.

Teslin, then, is one Aboriginal community in Canada that has taken the healing philosophy and begun to construct an actual program faithful to it. They are putting their healing words into healing acts, and they are doing so even in cases of incest, which represent perhaps the most horrendous breaches of human trust and the most intense degradation of victims.

I now want to take that side trip down to New Zealand. Their approach to young offenders not only demonstrates the healing focus, but also touches upon something else that Judge Lilles raised in his judgment: the deterrent power that "daily humiliation" can have over offenders when they have to openly face everyone who knows them well. At one time I suspected that such approaches were probably restricted to small communities like Teslin, but the New Zealand program suggests the contrary.

New Zealand's Family Group Conference Approach

In 1989 the government of New Zealand took a radical step with the passage of the *Children, Young Persons and Their Families Act*. It created a new process called the Family Group Conference (FGC) and extended it to all youngsters aged fourteen to sixteen charged with criminal offences other than the most serious, or purely "indictable," ones. The only condition for participation is that the offenders accept responsibility for what they have been charged with. While FGCs are based on the teachings of the Maori, the Aboriginal people of New Zealand, they are used with all young offenders, Aboriginal or not, urban or not.

As Judge F.W.M. MacElrea of the Auckland District Court described it in a 1994 article, four elements of pre-European Maori society inspired the creation of the FGCs:

> First, the emphasis was on reaching consensus and involving the whole community; second, the desired outcome was reconciliation and a settlement acceptable to all parties, rather than the isolation and punishment of the offender; thirdly, the concern was not to apportion blame but to examine the wider reasons for the wrong…; and fourthly, there was less concern with whether or not there has actually been a breach of the law and more concern with the restoration of harmony.

The FGC brings the offender, his family and his supporters together with the victim and his family and supporters. The offender's supporters can include anyone who cares for the youngster and has an interest in his or her life, whether it be a coach, teacher, older friend or neighbour down the block. What this process suggests is the possibility that no matter how large a city we live in physically, we still live emotionally and psychologically in small communities of our own making. Those communities are composed of family, friends, employers and other significant people—everyone who means something to us. In other words, the "daily humiliation" that Judge Lilles spoke about as a powerful force in Teslin could be just as powerful in an urban setting, provided the justice system brought each individual's "personal community" into the process. As I will later discuss, traditional approaches require that this public condemnation of the act be accompanied by an equally public assertion that the offender, as a person, remains a valued member of the community. The challenge involves finding ways to shame criminal acts while retaining respect for the actors and their potential to turn their lives around.

The surface purpose of the FGC is to see whether all those people can come together to design a "sentence" that responds properly to the crime. If they can't come to an agreement, the matter goes back to court for a judge's sentencing. In 80 percent of the cases handled in the first five years, a consensus has been reached. Sometimes the "sentence" is passed by the FGC itself, and sometimes it goes back to court for a judge to review and, in most circumstances, endorse.

Beneath this surface purpose, however, are a number of other intents, and I think they may be the most significant. One deeper intent is to help people see others as complex, many-sided and "whole" creatures—not just as "offenders" or "victims." Another is to give offenders a graphic demonstration of the degree to which their actions touch others, both positively and negatively, and that nothing they do is *without* consequence to others. Another aims at convincing victims and offenders and their families and friends that between them they have the wisdom to design changes in their relationships with each other that will help everyone move towards a better life.

It is important to note that while the FGCs are organized and facilitated by trained coordinators and may include people like alcohol counsellors or community work sponsors, such professionals are not supposed to control or direct the resolution. Instead, they help the parties achieve their *own* consensus, thus allowing for an improvement in their relationship to each other. The purpose is healing, not punishment—a healing accomplished by the full range of people who were affected by the original event.

How have the judges reacted to this alternate process? Judge MacElrea reports this response from New Zealand's Principal Youth Court Judge, Michael J.A. Brown:

> …The primary objectives of a criminal justice system *must* include healing the breach of social harmony, of social relationships, putting right the wrong and making reparation, instead of concentrating on punishment. The ability of the victim to have input at the family group conference is, or ought to be, one of the most significant virtues of the youth justice procedures. On the basis of our experience to date, we can expect to be amazed at the generosity of spirit of many victims and (to the surprise of many professionals participating) the absence of retributive demands and vindictiveness.

Two Australian criminologists, John Braithwaite and Stephen Mugford, had been reviewing the FGC process in New Zealand and in the Australian community of Wagga Wagga, where a pilot project is underway. One of the things they noticed was the capacity of FGCs to soften or prevent stigmatizing or degrading attacks on the offender *as a person*. Great care was taken to shame the act itself, but not the offender as a person. Instead, offenders were shown that people in the community valued and respected them, despite their wrongdoing. One actual event reveals the dynamic:

The worst stigmatic attack we observed arose when the mother of a fourteen-year-old girl [the offender] arrived at the conference. She told the coordinator that she was unhappy to be there. Then when she saw her daughter, who [had] preceded her to the conference, she said: "I'll kill you, you little bitch." A few minutes into the conference, the mother jumped from her seat, shouting: "This is a load of rubbish." Then, pointing angrily at her shaking daughter, she said: "She should be punished." Then she stormed out. These events might have created a degradation sub-ceremony of great magnitude. Instead, the other participants in the room were transformed by it and developed quite a different direction. Victim supporters who had arrived at the conference very angry at the offender were now sorry for her and wanted to help. They learned that she was a street kid and their anger turned against a mother who could abandon her daughter like this.... The more serious the delinquency of the young offender, the more likely it is to come out that she has had to endure some rather horrible life circumstances. Rather than rely on stereotypes, they see the offender as a whole person ...

And what of the victims themselves? After observing victims' reactions in the Australian FGCs, Braithwaite and Mugford made comments similar to those of Judge Brown in New Zealand:

... In Wagga, a standard question to the victims is: "What do you want out of this meeting here today?" The responses are in sharp contrast to the cries for "more punishment" heard on the steps of more conventional courts. Offered empowerment..., *victims commonly say that they do not want the offender punished; they do not want vengeance; they want the young offender to learn from his mistake* and get his life back in order. Very often they say they want compensation for their loss. Even here, however, it is surprising how often victims waive just claims for compensation out of consideration for the need for an indigent teenager to be unencumbered in making a fresh start.

If judges have been supportive of FGCs, the police have shown even greater enthusiasm. In the past, officers have been a discouraged group, seeing all their hard work come to nought in a clogged and complex legal system, where the trial and punishment of young offenders have done little to increase community safety. The FGC process, by contrast, does offer the promise of improved community security—especially in Australia, where the police become FGC coordinators as well.

And what are the real-life results of the New Zealand approach thus far? Judge MacElrea reports that the number of children admitted to Social Welfare Department residences (equivalent to youth custody facilities in Canada) dropped from 2712 in 1988 to 923 in 1992/93. As a result, half of all young-offender custody facilities in New Zealand have been closed. Even more telling, in my view, is the fact that the number of prosecuted cases against young people aged seventeen, eighteen and nineteen has dropped by 27 percent over the five years from 1987 to 1992. As Judge MacElrea expressed it, "This would tend to suggest that *the new Youth Court is producing young adults less likely to be prosecuted in adult courts.*" In other words, if the justice process looks at the forces in a young person's life in a wider, supportive and restorative way, there is a better chance of helping him or her stay out of trouble in the future as well.

This restorative approach to young offenders is now demonstrating a success rate that, to my knowledge, is unmatched in the Western world. In fact, the Western world's general determination to "get tougher" instead seems to be taking us even further away from the goal of creating respectful and peaceful young adults.

Judge MacElrea was so impressed with the results of the FGC process that he wants to see it extended to adults as well. He acknowledges that adults may have different family relationships than children, often lacking parents and grandparents, but he points out that since "very few people have no family of any sort, it would be wrong to base a model of justice on those few." He also notes that adults develop "relationships of respect" outside the family which could act as a substitute for family relationships: "Our needs for acceptance, self-affirmation, social involvement, friendship, fun and spiritual sustenance do not evaporate with adulthood or 'independence'; they all require that we are in meaningful relationships with others. *Indeed, some would say that 'to be, is to be in relationships.'*"

Even as I write this book, Aboriginal groups in Canada are showing a strong interest in the FGC approach. Representatives of the Nishnawbe-Aski Nation communities in northwestern Ontario have travelled to the United States to meet with FGC coordinator-trainers from New Zealand. Representatives of an Aboriginal child-care agency in northern Manitoba have actually travelled to New Zealand, met with various players (including Judge MacElrea) and have returned with a determination to bring similar approaches to their communities. In September of 1995 they hosted a conference in Manitoba at which Judge MacElrea and others shared their experiences. In short, the Maori-inspired FGC process seems to respect many of the central teachings of Aboriginal peoples in North America.

On that note, let's return to North America (though not quite to Canada) and quickly look at something I referred to earlier: the movement of Navajo people towards the restoration of traditional peacemaking processes.

Peacemaking in Navajo Teachings

The Navajo Tribal Court has been recognized for many years as a leading justice institution among Aboriginal peoples. Complete with its own lawyers and judges, its reliance on Navajo common law, its Navajo tribal codes and its *Navajo Supreme Court Digest,* many observers offered it as a model for self-government in the justice area. In recent years, however, some changes have been taking place. The tribal court was centred primarily on Western justice values, including adversarial processes and punishment. The use of those values causes problems—as two observers, Philmer Bluehouse and James Zion, have pointed out in an article entitled "The Navajo Justice and Harmony Ceremony." This article appeared in a special issue of *The Mediation Quarterly,* dedicated to Aboriginal peacemaking. Bluehouse, himself Navajo, is the coordinator of the recently formed Navajo Peacemaker Court, and Zion is a solicitor to the Courts of the Navajo Nation and married into a Navajo family. They have had this to say about the use of Western justice in Navajo courts: "... Navajo culture approaches justice processes with different values and procedures from mainstream American society.... Navajos are still coping with a century of coerced law—law that makes individual acts criminal and subject to punishment, rather than emphasizing restoration to harmony with others and the community...." Bluehouse and Zion go on to tell us about the Navajo Peacemaker Court, created by the Navajo Nation Judicial Conference in 1982:

> This unique method of court-annexed "mediation" and "arbitration," they write, uses Navajo values and institutions in local communities. Today, it struggles to overcome the effects of adjudication and laws imposed by the U.S. government. The alien Navajo Court Of Indian Offenses (1892–1959) and the Bureau Of Indian Affairs Law And Order Code ... made Navajos judge each other, using power and force for control. That arrangement is repugnant to Navajo morals.

One of the leading supporters of the move towards peacemaker courts is Robert Yazzie—despite his training as a lawyer and his position as Chief Justice of the Navajo Nation Judicial Branch. "In the traditional Navajo way ..." he has written, "the people involved in the dispute make the decisions.... Navajo wise persons are called *naat'aanii*. Others call them elders. They use their wisdom to counsel and provide guidance; they encourage parties to talk about their problems, not make decisions for others. They help plan decisions through guidance, but they don't make the decision."

This may make the peacemaker's role sound like that of a Western mediator or arbitrator—but there are important differences. While mediators and arbitrators are trained to think of the final agreement between the parties as a purely private matter, the peacemaker does not work in this "value-neutral" role. Instead, he or she is required to be active in teaching and promoting traditional values. According to Navajo law, the parties must be guided back into thoughts and behaviours that reflect those values, and any agreements they reach should reflect traditional understandings about proper relationships. Bluehouse and Zion describe the difference this way:

The English words *mediation* and *arbitration* do not accurately reflect how Navajos feel about their justice ceremony.... The peacemaking ceremony has stages and devices to instruct and guide disputants.... There is a stage where the peacemaker explores the positions of the parties in the universe, verifying that they are in a state of disharmony, deciding how or why they are out of harmony.... It is similar to diagnosing an illness to find causes. There are lectures on how or why the parties have violated Navajo values, have breached solidarity, or are out of harmony. Lectures are not recitations or exhortations of abstract moral principles, but practical and pragmatic examinations of the particular problem in light of Navajo values. The peacemaker then discusses the precise dispute with the parties to help *them* know how to plan to end it. (emphasis added)

This emphasis on harmony "in the universe" is important, for it means that part of the investigation in every case will involve looking into the mental, emotional, physical and spiritual dynamics of each of the parties—as well as the nature of the relationships that surround, sustain and, in a very real sense, define them as human beings. The peacemaker is thus an investigator, a teacher and a guide. His primary responsibility is to help each person come to understand that life *is* relationship, and that a healthy life requires constant effort to provide as much nourishment as possible to every relationship that engages you.

The best expression of this approach that I have come across was given by Diane LeResche. A university lecturer in conflict resolution and a tribal peacemaking consultant, she edited the special issue of *The Mediation Quarterly* that contained the Bluehouse-Zion article mentioned earlier in this chapter. Her view has proven invaluable to me, although I have had to return to it several times before its real significance began to sink in:

Peacemaking is generally not as concerned with distributive justice or "rough and wild justice" (revenge, punishment, control, determining who is right) as it is with "sacred justice." Sacred justice is that way of handling disagreements that helps mend relationships and provides solutions. It deals with the underlying causes of the disagreement.... *[S]acred justice is found when the importance of restoring understanding and balance to relationships has been acknowledged.*

A peacemaking process tends to be viewed as a "guiding process," a *relationship-healing* journey to assist people in returning to harmony ...

As I have come to see it, the focus of peacemaking, of teaching and healing, is not so much on the events that occurred between the parties, nor even upon achieving detailed agreements between them about what they should all do to sort things out for the future. While such issues will obviously form *part* of the discussion, the major emphasis seems to be upon creating healthy relationships instead. By this I mean relationships of two sorts: between all the people involved (including relatives and friends) and between the mental, emotional, physical and spiritual dimensions of each of them. Nourishing those relationships, the teachings seem to suggest, is the best way to help the parties create both their own solutions to the immediate problem and their own capacities for avoiding or settling disagreements in the future.

There is a strong temptation to look at the success of peacemaking processes like New Zealand's Family Group Conference and decide that they are not open to the more serious offences or offenders. It would be easy to conclude that restorative approaches can be effective only with those who are not "too far gone." Challenging that assumption is the experience of the Hollow Water First Nation, for their focus has been on adult offenders with long histories of sexual abuse, often of children. The more I become familiar with how they see such offenders and the dynamics of their offences, the more I see similarities to the tactics and philosophies behind the Navajo and FGC approaches. Perhaps more importantly, Hollow Water's experience has caused me to suspect that there may be very *few* situations in which our common justice goals would not be better served by taking a restorative approach.

A word of encouragement: while the next chapter delves into the ugly realities of sexual abuse, it also begins the uncovering of processes capable of lifting individuals, families and whole communities out of that abuse and back into health again. So, while it is indeed the "low point" of this book, it is also the place where something vibrant, strong and full of hope begins to emerge. Let's go, then, to the province of Manitoba, and the Ojibway community of Hollow Water. Of all the healing approaches I have encountered, it has touched me most deeply.

CHAPTER 2

HEALING INSIDE THE WHIRLWIND OF SEXUAL ABUSE

The Community Holistic Circle Healing (CHCH) Program at Hollow Water

H ollow Water is a village of some six hundred people on the east shore of Lake Winnipeg, almost at the end of the physical road—but significantly out in front when it comes to building traditional values and teachings into effective, modern-day justice processes. In tackling the most taboo subject of all, sexual abuse within families, the Hollow Water healing team has had to immerse itself totally in relationships, and in all the illnesses that can pervert them through the generations. It has proven to be a painful, often tortuous, process for all concerned.

It began in 1984, when a group of people got together to discuss community problems, especially concerning youngsters. Many of them were "social service providers" such as the child protection worker from the Manitoba Children's Aid Society, the community health representative, the nurse in charge and the NADAP (Native Alcohol and Drug Addiction Program) worker, together with people drawn from the RCMP, the Frontier School Division of the Manitoba Department of Education and community churches.

The majority of the team members were Aboriginal women from the community, many of whom were volunteers, but the team included non-Aboriginal people as well.

Their concern at the time was the level of substance abuse, vandalism, truancy, suicide and violence involving community children. The more the team worked with them, however, the more their attention turned to the kinds of homes those children returned to each day. Over time, they came to face the reality that those homes were often plagued by high levels of alcohol and drug abuse, as well as family violence. The violence in those homes was seldom acknowledged in the community, much less dealt with.

When the focus shifted from the children to the behaviour of their parents, however, things took another turn, this one more disturbing still. In looking for the causes of the substance abuse and violence among the adults, the team came to confront a frightening possibility—the possibility that underneath everything else lay generations of sexual abuse, primarily within families and involving children, that no one wanted to admit, even to themselves.

One of their first decisions as a group was to break down the professional barriers between them. They found that they each operated in separate chains of command, reporting to separate agencies. Just as importantly, they were each controlled by confidentiality rules that kept them from sharing information with each other, even when they were dealing with the same "clients" or families. They were all working in isolation, often dealing with separate aspects of each troubled person. As long as that continued, they predicted that the result would be a further splintering of those people—exactly the opposite of their shared goal of creating "whole" people.

As a result of this discovery, one of their earliest accomplishments was the creation of a true team approach of sharing their information fully with each other. Outside professionals, highly regarded by the team for their knowledge and experience, were seen from the outset as important to the project's success, but they were required to "sign on" to the team approach. They also had to permit a "lay" member of the team to be with them at all times, so their skills could be learned by community members. This pairing was also a way for team members to help train the professionals to work within a holistic framework. Partnership was, and remains, the model. Having sat in some healing circles at Hollow Water, I can say that there are no colours or races or genders in those circles—only people committed to helping others.

Team Training

They also embarked on a lengthy process of training themselves to work as a team. The more they came together, the more they were surprised to find they had been trained in different, sometimes contradictory, methods of intervening with troubled people. It all depended on whether the issue was defined as "suicide prevention," "substance abuse," "mental health," "child protection" or whatever. Each "problem" had its own separate "solution" in the compartmentalized approach of outside agencies. The more they shared information with each other, the more they realized that the dysfunctional people they dealt with were very good at telling each worker just what they wanted to hear and manipulating all the systems at once to their own advantage!

The need for common training was apparent, and over the course of five years they created over twenty different training programs for themselves. Many of them were based on Western models for intervention and healing, but others included reaching out to Aboriginal communities outside Hollow Water to explore traditional ways and teachings. At every step, they took the best from everything they explored, creating a comprehensive program that reflects both traditional Aboriginal and contemporary Western approaches.

When their attention was inevitably drawn to the issue of sexual abuse, however, they hit a snag. This had to do with the fact that the majority of the team members were members of a severely "ill" community. As such, they had not escaped the intergenerational chains of sexual abuse that were pulling everyone else down. Many of them were victims too, but they had never acknowledged that fact to anyone. As time went by, their commitment to helping their community forced them to confront their own secrets, first in their own hearts and minds, and then in the presence of other team members. It was a turning point for them, for their program and for their community. The healers came to the open acknowledgment that they too needed healing and that they would have to move some distance along their own healing paths, as individuals and as a group, before it would be safe for them to reach out to others.

I don't know how they accomplished what they did, both with and for each other. I have been with them in their healing circles as they reached out to other people, sharing their own stories of abuse, helping sketch the pathways that lead both victims and abusers out of self-hatred, alienation, anger and despair. I do know that their stories are still accompanied by vibrant pain and tears and that it is understood their healing path will require time and attention, likely for the rest of their lives. I also know that, thanks to many of the teachings they have sought out and restored, they now operate within complex and formal processes designed to take away as much of the pain as possible.

When they began to be honest with each other for the first time, however, they were largely on their own, separated from many of those teachings by generations of Western church workers intent on the complete disappearance of the sweat-lodge, the sacred fire, the shaking tent, the talking circle and all the other cleansing resources developed over the course of centuries. These traditions are coming back to Hollow Water now, for those who choose to use them, but they were not at hand when those first disclosures between team members were made. I marvel at the strength, commitment and determination of all of them in those early days. No army unit in any war has undergone a more daunting trial by fire nor built a greater sense of common spirit and dedication.

Healing Strategy

The community strategy the team developed involves a detailed protocol leading all the participants through a number of steps or stages. They include the initial disclosure of abuse, protecting the child, confronting the victimizer, assisting the (nonoffending) spouse, assisting the families of all concerned, coordinating the team approach, assisting the victimizer to admit and accept responsibility, preparing the victim, victimizer and families for the Special Gathering, guiding the Special Gathering through the creation of a Healing Contract, implementation of the Healing Contract and, finally, holding a Cleansing Ceremony designed, in their words, to mark "the completion of the Healing Contract, the restoration of balance to the victimizer, and a new beginning for all involved."

The Healing Contract is similar to the "sentence" created by Family Group Conferences. Designed by all the parties involved in, or personally touched by, the offence, it requires that they each "sign on" to bring certain changes or additions to their relationships with all the others. Such contracts are never expected to last for less than two years, given the challenges of bringing true healing in the context of sexual abuse. One of them is still being enforced six years after its creation.

This community healing takes place outside the normal criminal justice process—although links to the system are maintained. When someone alleges that they have been abused, the CHCH assessment team evaluates the complaint as quickly as possible. If it appears to be valid, the team swings into action. I was present at one such organizing session and found myself comparing it to a complex military operation. After selecting two team members to make the initial confrontation with the victimizer (instead of the police, but with full police backup if necessary), other team members "fanned out" to be with all the others who would be affected by the disclosure. That meant that the nonoffending spouse, brothers and sisters, grandmothers and grandfathers, aunts and uncles—everyone affected—would have a helper at their side to explain what had been alleged, the processes that were to be followed and the help that might be made available to everyone. No one would be left either in the dark or in their own painful isolation.

The victimizer is approached by two members of the team at a time and place most likely to permit the best atmosphere for honesty and progress. They communicate the allegations and listen to the response. They do not expect immediate acknowledgment, for their own experience with sexual abuse has taught them to expect denials, minimizations, victim blaming, hostile manipulations and the like. When they tell the victimizer that criminal charges are about to be laid, they also say that they are available to accompany him or her through the criminal justice process as long as sincere efforts are being made to accept responsibility and go through the healing process. If that is not agreeable, the victimizer is on his own. Out of forty-eight cases dealt with through to the spring of 1996, only five have failed to enter into—and stay with—the program.

The victimizer is then accompanied to the police station where he or she is formally charged and asked to provide a statement. While that statement would probably not be admissible in court, it is seen as a first step in the long process of accepting responsibility. The team then requires the victimizer to enter a guilty plea to the charges in court as quickly as possible.

The team then asks the court to delay sentencing for as long as possible. Experience has taught that they need a great deal of time to work with the victim, the offender, the families of each and the community as a whole before they can provide the court with a realistic assessment of the challenges and possibilities each case presents. Ideally, the team would like to see sentencing delayed until the Special Gathering has produced the Healing Contract. Unfortunately, that complex process often takes much more time than the courts permit, and sentencing often takes place before real commitments to sustained healing can be expected.

When the community healing process was first established, the team restricted its in-court activities to the preparation of a Pre-Sentence Report. This was a large document, analysing everything from the offender's state of mind, level of effort and chance of full rehabilitation, to the reactions, feelings, plans and suggestions of all people affected. Special attention was paid to the victim, the nonoffending spouse and the families of each. The report also detailed a proposed plan of action, stated whether or not the parties themselves had achieved a Healing Contract and requested that any Probation Order require the offender to continue to cooperate fully with the team's healing efforts. If a jail sentence was imposed, they did what they could to arrange regular work with the offender while in custody and to prepare everyone for the day of release.

More recently, however, the team has moved its processes into the courtroom itself. In December 1993, after months of separate healing circles with all the people affected by the case, a man and his wife came before the Associate Chief Judge of Manitoba's Provincial Court, Judge Murray Sinclair, for sentencing. They had jointly been involved in the sexual abuse of their three daughters, had pleaded guilty and had worked with the team. This was the first time the team had organized its own process to complement that of the court.

Since then, an elaborate sentencing protocol has been established, using a circle format. There are actually two circles, one within the other. The inner circle is for those who wish to speak, the outer one for those who wish to observe and listen. About two hundred people attended that first in-court circle, and over ninety-five attended the second one, held in August 1994.

Before court opens in the morning, the community conducts a pipe ceremony, hangs the flags, smudges or purifies the court buildings with the smoke from smouldering sweetgrass, places the community drum and eagle staff in the courtroom, serves breakfast to people from outside the community and offers an elder tobacco as a request for a prayer to guide the sentencing circle.

The sentencing proceeds according to a number of steps agreed to with the presiding judge: personal smudging (usually with sage or sweetgrass); an opening prayer; court technicalities like confirming the guilty plea; an outline of the ground rules by the presiding judge; a first "go-round," where the participants say why they came to be in the court that day; a second go-round, where all the participants are given the chance to speak directly to the victim; a third go-round, where all the participants are allowed to speak to the offender about how the victimization has affected them, the families and the community at large; a fourth go-round, where the participants outline their expectations to the offender and give their views about what needs to be done to restore balance; the passing of sentence by the judge; and a closing prayer. Following that, the participants may stay to use the circle for sharing or "debriefing" purposes. I will speak later of the rules that govern how each person is required to participate in such circles, for they are integral parts of the healing strategy.

Out of forty-eight offenders in Hollow Water over the last nine years, only five have gone to jail, primarily because they failed to participate adequately in the healing program. Of the forty-three who did, only two have repeated their crimes, an enviable record by anyone's standards. Of those two, one reoffended at a very early stage, before the sentencing had actually taken place. The second reoffended when the program was in its infancy. Since that reoffending, he has completed the formal healing program and is now a valuable member of the team, given his personal knowledge of the ways victimizers try to avoid responsibility.

More recently, after sentencing has taken place, the team requires that the process be repeated publicly at six-month intervals, without the court party, to reaffirm the promises of all, to honour whatever healing steps have been taken and to maintain community expectations of offenders.

At all times, from the moment of disclosure through to the Cleansing Ceremony, team members have the responsibility to work with, protect, support, teach and encourage a wide range of people. It is their view that since a great many people are affected by each disclosure, all of them deserve assistance. Just as importantly, all must be involved in any process aimed at creating healthy dynamics and breaking the intergenerational chain of abuse.

I indicated that many of the team members from the community are themselves victims of long-standing sexual abuse. Even former victimizers who have completed the formal healing process successfully are being asked to join the team. The personal experience of team members in the emotional, mental, physical and spiritual complexities of sexual abuse gives them an extraordinary rapport with victims and victimizers alike. I sat with them in circles as they shared their own histories as a way to coax others out of the anger, denial, guilt, fear, self-loathing and hurt that must be dealt with if health is to be re-established. Their personal experience also gives them the patience needed to stay with long and painful processes, and to see signs of progress that might escape the notice of others. It also gives them the insight to recognize who is manipulating or hiding in denial, and the toughness to insist that they keep moving towards greater honesty. The word "healing" seems such a soft word, but, as I will show later, Hollow Water's healing process is anything but soft. In fact, jail is a much easier alternative, because it does not require the victimizer to face the real truths about abuse.

Crimes Too Serious for Jail?

While the Western justice system seems to have forged an unbreakable link between "holding someone responsible for their crime" and sending them to jail, the Community Holistic Circle Healing Program (CHCH) at Hollow Water fiercely denies the wisdom of that connection. In 1993 they drafted a "Position Paper on Incarceration," in which they discuss their objections, as well as their reasons, for choosing the healing and teaching path instead. It stands as the most eloquent plea I have come across thus far.

They described, for instance, two realizations which caused them to abandon their initial support for using jail in cases which were felt to be "too serious" for a strictly healing approach. To use their words, they realized:

(1) that as we both shared our own stories of victimization and learned from our experiences in assisting others in dealing with the pain of their victimization, it became very difficult to define "too serious." The quantity or quality of pain felt by the victim, the family/ies and the community did not seem to be directly connected to any specific acts of victimization. Attempts, for example, by the courts—and to a certain degree

by ourselves—to define a particular victimization as "too serious" and another as "not too serious" (eg. "only" fondling vs. actual intercourse; victim is daughter vs. victim is nephew; one victim vs. four victims) were gross over-simplifications, and certainly not valid from an experiential point of view; and

(2) that promoting incarceration was based on, and motivated by, a mixture of feelings of anger, revenge, guilt and shame on our part, and around our personal victimization issues, rather than in the healthy resolution of the victimization we were trying to address.

Incarceration, they concluded, actually works against the healing process, because "an already unbalanced person is moved further out of balance." The team also came to believe that the threat of incarceration prevents people from "coming forward and taking responsibility for the hurt they are causing. It reinforces the silence, and therefore promotes rather than breaks, the cycle of violence that exists. In reality," the team wrote, "rather than making the community a safer place, the threat of jail places the community more at risk."

The position paper goes on to speak of the need to break free of the adversarial nature of Western courts, the barrier to healing that arises when defence lawyers recommend complete silence and a plea of "not guilty" and the second "victimization" that occurs when victims ate cross-examined on the witness stand. In their view, the "courtroom and process simply is not a safe place for the victim to address the victimization—nor is it a safe place for the victimizer to come forward and take responsibility for what has happened."

Noting that this acceptance of responsibility is more difficult yet more effective than a jail sentence, the team concluded:

Our children and the community can no longer afford the price the legal system is extracting in its attempts to provide justice in our community.

The need to break the silence is great. The Hollow Water team presently estimates that 80 percent of the population of their community, male and female alike, have been the victims of sexual abuse, most often at the hands of extended family members and usually for long periods of time. Just as shockingly, they now estimate that a full 50 percent of the community's population, male and female, has at one time or another sexually abused someone else.

In fact, many knowledgable Aboriginal people tell me that there are hundreds of such communities across Canada, all of them stuck in the silence and denial that characterized Hollow Water only nine years ago. The program director of an Aboriginal treatment program for substance abuse told me that 100 percent of the people coming to her centre have been the victims of sexual abuse. Another prominent Aboriginal woman told me that she does not have one close Aboriginal woman friend who has escaped sexual abuse.

In the next chapter, I will begin my exploration of where the healing perspective comes from, what sustains it and how it can penetrate even the most pain-filled relationships. First, however, I'd like to tell a story, one which gave me my first clues as to how abuse gets passed from generation to generation, multiplying as it goes, until entire communities become engulfed by it. Of all the stories I know, it gives the clearest picture of the incredible whirlwinds of anger, guilt and denial which communities like Hollow Water must ultimately confront. Until we gain some understanding of how this state of affairs came into being, mapping a way out of it remains almost impossible.

Carl and the Cancer of Abuse

This story is about a boy from another community, a boy I will call Carl, though that is not his real name. When he first came to the attention of the justice system at age fifteen, Carl stood charged with forcible confinement and with the sexual abuse, both anal and vaginal, of two girls. They were four and six years old.

Carl was one of five children growing up in a remote reserve of some four hundred people. His community had no airstrip, no sewer system, no running water, virtually no employment—and only one telephone.

In his first five or six years, a number of events began to shape him. He saw his Dad repeatedly beat and rape his mother in drunken rages. He, in turn, was regularly beaten by his father, sometimes for trying to protect her. His mother also beat Carl, on orders from his father. She did it, he believed, only to keep from being beaten herself. His Dad also forced him into oral and anal sex with him, then forced his mother to join in or be beaten herself.

While these acts were being repeated, Carl learned a number of things. He learned how his Dad blamed his Mom for his own rages, screaming that it was always her fault. He learned that his father justified his anger by pointing to her "failures" as a wife, mother, housekeeper, cook and so on. Carl began to see things in the same way, to believe that the violence was all her fault, that she "deserved" it.

More than that, he learned how to endure all the violence within his family in total silence. In the words of the probation officer, he "lived in dread of what would happen if he ever told or shared the family secret." At the same time, Carl began to develop a real anger towards his neighbours and his community because, as he phrased it, "They didn't see, and thought Dad was so nice."

Unable to reach outside the family for help, he came to rely on his brothers. On one occasion, they all joined together in attacking their father to rescue their mother from another brutal assault.

It should come as no surprise that they all began to sniff solvents, especially gas. It was the only way to escape.

When Carl was five or six, it became known to outsiders that his Dad was sexually abusing one of his older brothers. As a result, a child protection agency placed Carl with his grandparents in another reserve community. He stayed there until he was eight or nine, separated from his brothers and sisters, his only allies. Unfortunately, living with his grandparents did not result in an end to the abuse. A male cousin some six years older than Carl forced him into oral and anal sex on a regular basis, often bribing him with cigarettes and drugs. That abuse continued sporadically until his final arrest in 1992, at age fifteen.

When he was eight or nine, Carl's Dad remarried and quit drinking. He took Carl home, and for a while things were fine. The new wife was a good person, whom he trusted. Then, in the second year there, his Dad started drinking again, and the violence returned. On one occasion when his Dad struck him, the new wife came to protect him and his Dad turned on her. She was pregnant at the time and lost the baby as a result of that assault. Carl blamed himself for the loss of the baby. Not surprisingly, he began sniffing solvents more frequently.

Then, by his own admission, he started taking his anger out on people less powerful than himself. At age nine, he forced intercourse on a six-year-old girl who was his cousin. In his own words, he did so on "countless" occasions. At age ten, he forced intercourse on an eight-year-old girl, and did so some four or five times. At age ten, he forced anal intercourse on a five-year-old boy.

Then, when Carl was about ten or eleven, his Dad's new wife arranged for him to return to his grandparents, apparently afraid for him, but unaware of what had happened there before. He stayed with his grandparents until he was nearly thirteen. During that period, the male cousin who had sexually assaulted him resumed his abuse, supplying him with marijuana and hashish as rewards this time. He grew to use them almost daily. Another boy, who was about five or six years older, forced him into acts of oral and anal sex on four or five occasions, pretending to others that he was there to teach him martial arts. At the same time, Carl began to threaten his grandparents and to steal from them to buy drugs. He also continued to abuse others. He forced intercourse on a nine-year-old girl after watching a porno movie. He also forced intercourse on a girl his own age, a girl whom he says he liked. He also began to think about suicide, later telling the probation officer: "I remember feeling ashamed and wanting to kill myself. I'd tell myself that I was no good and that I should just kill myself."

In fact, he attempted suicide several times, later saying: "I was having bad memories of Dad slapping [the new wife] around, and being sexually victimized as well." Because of the suicide attempts and threats of violence to others, he was placed in a group home a couple of months before his thirteenth birthday. That, however, changed nothing. While there, he learned that his Dad's new wife had committed suicide. He had now lost the one person who had not abused him, the one person he trusted, and he blamed himself for her suicide.

Then, in the spring of 1991, at age thirteen, he went back to his Dad. He was using hash and marijuana on an almost daily basis, smoking with his brother, his uncles, his cousins—and even his Dad. He also resumed his own abusive behaviour. He again forced intercourse on his younger cousin, sometimes being assisted by one of his brothers. It was also at this time that he committed the offences that brought him to court—forcing anal and vaginal sex on the two girls aged four and six, keeping them imprisoned for several hours. In his words later, it was "as my father had done to us." He was charged with those offences.

In the words of the probation officer who prepared the evaluation report for court, Carl had learned a number of things growing up in such conditions: (1) "He learned as a young child to both lie and pretend, to protect himself from his father's violence." The primary lie was that his family life was good, while secondary lies involved such things as why he was staying away from home. (2) "He ... learned to become a sexual perpetrator. His victimization experiences [led] him to de-value himself and his very existence. It was only a matter of time before he started de-valuing the needs of others." In his own words: "I told myself that I was no good. I'm a nobody. I'll only end up in jail anyway, so I'll do what I want ... I victimized to regain the power I lost when I was being victimized."

In summary, this fifteen-year-old boy was sexually victimized by at least *four* people: his father, his mother, an older cousin and another older boy. At the time of his sentencing, he acknowledged victimizing at least the following *seven* people: a six-year-old girl cousin, repeatedly; an eight-year-old girl some four or five times; a five-year-old boy, once; a nine-year-old girl, once; a same-age girl-friend, several times; and two little girls, aged four and six. Since his sentencing into custody and treatment, he has now acknowledged sexually abusing at least another six people. This boy is only fifteen.

As this one painful story illustrates, the cancer of sexual abuse, as long as it remains hidden, spreads from generation to generation, multiplying as it goes. In many communities, health-care workers estimate that such sexual abuse spans three or four generations. It is considered an illness because it is passed from one person to another as victims try to compensate for their own degradation by degrading others. This was the situation facing the people of Hollow Water, although they didn't know its full horror at the time.

As Hollow Water has learned, however, it is impossible to deal with the Carls of this world simply by prosecuting their abusive fathers. Instead, it is necessary to ask how those abusive fathers got that way, how the illness that erupts as sexual abuse got started. Until that is done, until the factors that first spawned such disharmonies are identified and dealt with, the illness will continue to afflict one generation after another.

The most basic question, then, is: Where did it all begin?

At this early stage there is one thing I would like to make clear: all the evidence I have seen thus far sends me the unequivocal message that such widespread abuse was not a part of traditional life. In fact, it appears to have been a very rare occurrence, and the object of strong condemnation.

For instance, many early explorers, like David Thompson, were moved to comment on how much love and protection children were afforded and how much they were the healthy centre of a strong and caring society. At the same time, sophisticated measures designed to prevent such abuse were prominent in traditional society and these are still used in communities where such traditions have been maintained. In the Midewewin Lodge of the Ojibway, for instance, a place in the circle remains reserved for the Deer Clan, despite the fact that no members of the Deer Clan have existed for centuries. The disappearance of this most gentle, song-filled and poetic clan is traced in Ojibway storytelling to their refusal to heed the Creator's warning against incest, even when their continued misbehaviour sent them afflicted children. As a result, the Creator was left with no choice but to see to the disappearance of the entire clan. The vacant place that still remains within the Midewewin Lodge thus stands as a reminder from those ancient times that incest is abhorrent in the Creator's eyes.

There are a great many other practices and traditions that were clearly established to prevent sexual abuse—including the prohibition of direct communication in some groups between fathers and daughters during adolescence. I leave it to others to present them more completely than my knowledge permits. I only wish to indicate my present view that the plague of sexual (and other) abuse that afflicts so many Aboriginal communities is not a "natural" event within what the settler nations called a "pagan" society. On the contrary, I see it as an almost inevitable consequence of historically labelling *everything* Aboriginal as pagan, of declaring at every step and in every way that every aspect of traditional life was either worth less than its European equivalent— or just plain worthless.

Losing the Centre

One event in particular began to guide me towards this most uncomfortable conclusion. A few years ago, I heard an Ojibway woman tell her story at a workshop on sexual abuse. She told us that she had been born into a tiny community that survived on its trapping, hunting, fishing and rice harvesting. Then, at age six or seven, she was taken away to residential school, along with all the other school-age children. She stayed there until she was sixteen. Contrary to what I expected, her sexual abuse did not begin at that school. While there were unquestionably many schools where the physical abuse of children, sexual and otherwise, seems to have been commonplace, she was in one where "only" the children's language, spirituality, culture and worldview were abused—as the priests and nuns tried to train the "Indian" out of them. This woman was not sexually abused until, at the age of sixteen, she was released from school and went back to her tiny village. First it was an uncle, then older cousins—her own people.

She spoke to the workshop about how she handled the abuse of her "Indian-ness" by the nuns and priests and the abuse of her body by her relatives. She first went into the predictable downspin of alcohol and drugs, winding up on the streets of a city abusing herself in virtually every way. Then, to the surprise of many, she did what she calls a "complete flip." She got sober, went back to school, graduated from university, got married and had children. She thought everything was fine.

Then, she told us, a day came when one of her daughters returned from school with a straight-A report card. She asked her daughter why there were no A-plus marks on it. The daughter's tearful response was to ask why they had to be *better* than everyone else, and in everything they did. It was at that point that her mother understood that she was still hiding from her sexual abuse, that she had only traded alcohol and drugs for perfectionism. She began to understand that she still had not come to grips with the pain, the guilt and the "dirtiness" of being a victim of sexual abuse. Needless to say, the fact that she had been abused by her own people did not help.

In the years that followed, she returned to her tiny community and began to speak openly about what had happened to her, about the sexual abuse that had caught so many people in its web. Despite hostility and fear, she persisted. She sought guidance from the elders about how to face up to realities, how to put the pain behind her, how to embark on healing both for herself and for the community. It was, she told us, the elders who helped her understand the reason why it was her own people, her own family, who had abused her that way. "I began to learn," she said, "that the people I came back to at age sixteen were not the same people I had left at age six. The change began on the day we were taken from them."

I will never forget how powerfully her simple declaration affected the room. I could almost feel everyone being jolted into sharing her realization: her abusers, Aboriginal people all, did not abuse because they were Aboriginal people, but because they were

changed Aboriginal people. If that was so, then there was something they could do to reverse the downward spiral that had
everyone so firmly in its grip: they could look back to see when
the changes began, what they were, how they touched people—
and how they might be reversed. In other words, there was a
chance that they could rescue themselves.

As she spoke, it became clear that residential schools were not
the solitary cause of social breakdown amongst Aboriginal
people. Rather, they were the closing punctuation mark in a
loud, long declaration saying that nothing Aboriginal could
possibly be of value to anyone. That message had been delivered
in almost every way imaginable, and it touched every aspect of
traditional social organization. Nothing was exempt, whether it
was spiritual beliefs and practices, child-raising techniques,
pharmacology, psychology, dispute resolution, decision making,
clan organization or community governance. In time, even
economic independence was stripped away as governments built
community schools, which made it impossible for families to
tend traplines often a hundred kilometres back in the bush. Even
the law added its voice to the degradation, making it illegal to
possess medicine bundles, vote in Canadian elections, hold a
potlatch to honour the assistance of others or (difficult as this is
to believe) hire a lawyer to even *ask* a court to force governments
to honour their treaty obligations.

Taking the children away to residential school was, in a way, just
an exclamation mark ending the sentence that declared: All things
Aboriginal are inferior at best, and dangerous at worst. When the
children were gone, however, so was the centre of life for everyone
left behind. I find it impossible to imagine the feelings that must
have swamped all those mothers and fathers, aunts and uncles,
grandmothers and grandfathers. Some of them thought that such
a drastic step was necessary for future generations to gain the skills

needed to survive in the non-Native world. Some of them, however, still rage at the arrogance of such a move and lament the loss of social and personal health that followed for everyone concerned. No matter how much the outsider's education was desired, what was left behind for all the adults was a gargantuan hole, out of which many were unable to climb.

Those of us in the criminal justice field are familiar with studies of what happens in one-industry towns where the mine or mill closes. When those jobs suddenly vanish, the unemployed are robbed of one source of self-esteem: the ability to provide adequately for their families. Alcohol and drug use increase measurably, along with the rate of family violence. If the loss of that *one* source of self-esteem can have such a significant effect, what must have been the effect on all of Canada's Aboriginal people as our institutions attacked *every* aspect of their lives?

Try a short exercise in role reversal, imagining a non-Aboriginal mine worker whose job was taken away by all-powerful outsiders. Imagine that he knew he had no realistic chance of ever qualifying for another one. Imagine that he was unable to go for comfort and help to his own churches and his own psychiatrists and hospitals, because those same outsiders had made them illegal. Imagine that, whenever he went to their versions of such helping places, the professionals who staffed them could not speak his language, but demanded that he learn theirs. Imagine, as well, that all those powerful outsiders held him, his language and his culture in such low esteem that they forcibly removed his children, to raise them to be just like them. Imagine, at that point, waking up to silence throughout your entire community where only the week before there had been the raucous voices of new generations. What reason would there be to even get out of bed?

And what happens when you are told, from every direction and in every way, that you and all your people have no value to anyone, no purpose to your lives, no positive impact on the world around you? No one can stand believing those things of themselves. No one can bear considering themselves worthless, essentially invisible. At some point people brought to this position stand up and demand to be noticed, to be recognized as being alive, as having influence and *power*. And the easiest way to assert power, to prove that you exist, is to demonstrate power over people who are weaker still, primarily by making them do things they don't want to do. The more those things shame and diminish that weaker person, the more the abuser feels, within the twisted logic of victimization, that they have been empowered and restored themselves. Further, nothing is more attractive to those who need to feed off the denigration of others than the road of sexual abuse, and the safest and easiest sexual abuse is of children.

When Everything Goes to the Dogs

I read many years ago that sexual abuse was primarily a crime of power and degradation, not sexual fulfilment, but I didn't understand how seductive a crime it was until I began to understand the full extent of the degradation of Aboriginal people in Canada's history.

I have another story to share about how degradation gets passed along—a short one this time. It came from a Cree man, who spoke to me after I had made a presentation about coming to understand the origins of sexual abuse in Aboriginal communities. He started by saying that he agreed with the analysis I had given, then added that he could tell whether a community was healthy or not just by looking at the dogs. At first, I thought he was either joking or about to lead me into some "mystical" things I wasn't quite ready for. Instead, his explanation was direct and clear. If Dad came home with anger, he said, he would take it out on the next weakest, Mom. She would then seek out someone weaker still and take the anger out on one of the children. And so it would go, down the line from stronger to weaker, until the smallest child had only one place to turn—and the dog would have to take it all. Unless something comes along to break up that chain of abuse, it seems that few people are able to continually absorb the anger and degradation. They find someone weaker to pass it on to, or they take it out on themselves, in substance abuse and self-mutilation. Most do both.

If that is the reality, it becomes easier to understand why Western courts have had such little success in turning things around. Can the threat of jail possibly have greater power over someone like Carl than the demons that have driven him since infancy? Can our lectures about "right" and "wrong" carry more weight than his own needs for psychic and physical survival in a desperate world?

I acknowledge that when I first began to glimpse how desperate the world really was for so many Aboriginal people, I despaired of ever finding something powerful enough to change things for the better. I knew only that my own system was unlikely to penetrate more than the surface of that huge social cancer. However, two things happened. One of them was being told about Hollow Water, and having the chance to visit, listen, feel and learn. The other was coming upon certain groups of Aboriginal people who were willing to expose me to traditional teachings about Creation and about the dynamics that join the multitude of "things" together within Creation—including human beings. The determination to take a healing and teaching approach to justice flows out of those teachings and cannot be understood without referring to them.

And Remembering the Fool

Before turning to that philosophical context, however, I want to repeat a story from the Ojibway Creation teachings, for some aspects of the tone of this book are about to change. The story tells of Waynaboozhoo (the Original Man, or Spirit of the Anishnaabe people) and his travels over Mother Earth to gather the lessons that would be important to humanity in the future. At one point, crossing the prairie, he encounters a small whirlwind racing around in front of him. Since it was Edward Benton-Banai's wonderful work *The Mishomis Book: The Voice of the Ojibway* that gave me this story, I'll let his words take you through the rest of it:

> A small whirlwind raced away just in front of him. His feet gave way to a desire to run. He found himself racing across the prairie trying to catch the whirlwind. The whirlwind was actually laughing at him. No matter how hard he ran, the whirlwind could always stay in front of him. The whirlwind would dodge this way and that.
>
> As they were racing across the prairie, the whirlwind called out to Waynaboozhoo: "My name is Bay-be-mi-say-si, catch me if you can! I am brother to the Gee-zhee-ba-sun (tornado). I am brother to the waterspout of the oceans and seas. Their power is my power and my power is theirs. My brothers choose to destroy and, thus, demonstrate the awesome powers of the Creation. I love to tease instead. You can find me in all places and in all seasons. I think I love the swirling snow the best!"
>
> Waynaboozhoo was annoyed at Bay-be-mi-say-si, and he shouted as he ran: "Tell me, brother, what purpose does your foolish life of teasing contribute to the Creation?"
>
> Bay-be-mi-say-si replied in a laughing voice: "My life may be foolish, Waynaboozhoo, but I have a purpose in life as noble as yours. My purpose is to tease those who take them-selves too seriously. I tease the human beings, I tease the buffalo and all the four-leggeds, and I tease the spirits too.

There is a place for foolishness in the Creation. You better watch yourself, or you will see me often!"

From now on, I will try to observe this teaching of Bay-be-mi-say-si that serious things must be balanced with more light-hearted ones. For instance, I will start to use topic headings that indulge in the Aboriginal love for double meanings and word play—a topic in its own right, which I will discuss later. Further, I will start the next chapter by telling an embarrassing story about myself. It concerns a mistake I made in interpreting the behaviour of two old people, and it shows how easy it is to misread people who have a "different understanding" about the world we all share.

CHAPTER 3

DIGGING FOR THE ROOTS OF THE HEALING VISION

Twelve Paces/Two Faces

My own cultural eyes have often tricked me into seeing things that Aboriginal people did not—or completely missing things they thought too obvious to point out. One of the most significant came one day when I was having coffee with an Ojibway friend. I asked her about something I often saw in the North: older couples walking along with the man twelve paces out in front, his wife bringing up the rear. I asked her how that behaviour fit with what I was being taught about equality between men and women in traditional times. She laughed, then said something like "Rupert, Rupert, that's only your eyes again! You have to look at it the way we do!"

She began by asking me to remember where those old people had spent their lives, to imagine walking a narrow trail through the bush with my own family. She asked me to think about who I would prefer to have out in front, my wife or myself, to be the first to face whatever dangers the bush presented. In one way, she said, it could be compared to wartime. "Where," she asked, "do you put your generals? Are they out front or are they in the rear, where they have time to see and plan and react?"

Viewed in that way, things appeared to be the opposite of what I had first supposed. Instead of occupying an inferior position, the woman was seen as the organizer and director, while the man out front was counted on for his capacity to take action under her direction. Instead of remembering the bush context in which they had lived their lives, I had put them in my own urban context where such a formation might indicate the opposite. "So," I said, "she's really the general and her husband is just the footsoldier!"

There was a pause then, and she chuckled again, shaking her head. "Not really," she said. "The problem is ... you see everything in terms of hierarchies, don't you? Why do you do that?" I had never considered that possibility before. Did I really approach things asking who occupied the superior position and who the inferior? Did I *impose* hierarchical structures where none were to be found? By merely switching the status of the man and woman, had I remained trapped within my own hierarchical way of seeing them?

She tried to express her way then, the way she understood from the teachings of her people. In those teachings, all things have a purpose, and unless these are fulfilled, the strength of the whole is weakened. The jobs of the husband and of the wife were just that, their jobs, assumed on the basis of their having different skills and capacities—different *gifts*—none of which had to be compared with each other in terms of worth or importance. Comparison itself was seen as a strange thing to do.

As she spoke, I was flooded with recollections of other events that raised the issue of out Western dependence on hierarchies of worth and power.

I was reminded, for instance, of an Ojibway elder who told about how she understood some of the teachings of the forest. In the forest, she explained, there were so many different trees, bushes and grasses, insects, birds and animals. You would not compare the worth of the white pine tree with the worth of the blue jay. You would not compare the worth of the juniper bush with the worth of the frog. They were all necessary for that place to continue in health. They were all sacred.

I was also reminded of a time speaking with a Mi'kmaq friend at the Eskasoni First Nation on Cape Breton Island. He was telling me about many things in his life, and he took himself back to residential school, over thirty years earlier. As he spoke of those days, his voice kept halting and cracking, but he seemed to feel it was important that certain things be said. "One of the things I could never understand," he said quietly, "was about the priests and nuns. How they called people stupid. Why did they do that? In our Mi'kmaq language we don't even have a word for stupid." He paused and looked out through the rain to the trees beyond us. "We are taught that everyone comes with their own gifts. It is the job of teachers to find those gifts. To help the children grow."

I was also reminded of an Ojibway medicine man who passed on his people's teaching that all children are born with four gifts. They might be good runners or good hockey players. They might be good listeners who could take burdens from other people. Maybe they could make children feel comfortable and safe. It didn't matter. Everyone was to be respected for their gifts, and everyone had a duty to help children find and develop their special gifts, whatever they were. All the gifts were sacred.

As those teachings came flooding back, I thought again about the old man walking twelve paces in front of his wife. I tried to imagine how *they* saw their world, and the picture I got then was different from the one I had superimposed on them. The issue of who was making the "best" contribution or who had earned the "highest" status as a parent was not their issue at all. It was mine, and I had "seen" them through it. The issue that engaged them, that came from their teachings, was how each of them could use their own unique gifts to the fullest so that the partnership would achieve its fullest potential, and the family would be as strong as it could be.

Through a Hierarchy Darkly

As time went on, I was startled to see how frequently hierarchical thinking dictated first what I saw and then how I chose to respond to what I saw. One of the more startling instances took place at a series of justice workshops where Aboriginal women started speaking of the physical and sexual abuse in their communities. They were worried that self-government in justice might leave them and their children even more exposed to abusive behaviour, since the men already occupied all the powerful positions in the community. If they got power over justice as well, the women foresaw even greater cause for concern. The discussion then turned to what might protect them, and everyone's attention quickly focused on a "charter of rights," either general or Aboriginal. I had doubts about how much the present charter could provide that kind of safety, since it serves primarily as a shield for offenders against improper prosecutions by agents of the state—but I understood their desire and supported that kind of search. At that point, however, one of the Aboriginal women said something that threw me for a loop.

"In our community," she said, "we see the charter as just one more step down the whiteman's road. We don't want to take that step. We want to try a different path instead." She went on to tell us that, as they saw things, the problem was not so much the *abuse* of power by those who held it. Instead, it was the *giving* of such power to individuals or small groups in the first place. She told us that her people wanted to get away from "the hierarchies of the whiteman," hierarchies imposed on her people in every way. She specifically mentioned the governing system imposed by the *Indian Act,* with its elected chiefs having the power to tell other people what they could and could not do in so many spheres of life. As long as you had such a system, she said, then you would need things like a charter of rights to keep them under control. But that was not the traditional way. They wanted to restore the situation where no one received such power over others, where such decisions came out of the clans and families from the bottom up, not the top down.

And there it was—another example of thinking in terms of hierarchies. I don't pretend to understand what nonhierarchical organizations might look like, how they were or will be structured or how well they can handle the late twentieth century's need for fast decision making (or is that too a restraint we have imposed on ourselves?). I do know, however, that I am hearing Aboriginal people tell me that the Western insistence on creating hierarchies for everything is a major part of the problem they face. As they see it, the challenge does not involve creating checks and balances *within* those hierarchies, but recognizing that they are problems in and of themselves, then getting rid of them altogether.

To illustrate how common this complaint is and how it arises within the context of justice, Philmer Bluehouse and James Zion included the following comments in their article on the Navajo Justice and Harmony Ceremony I referred to earlier:

> The dynamics of mediation and adjudication are different. Adjudication uses power and authority in a hierarchical system. A powerful figure [the judge] makes decisions for others on the basis of "facts" which are developed through disputed evidence, and by means of rules of "law" which are also contested by the parties.... In sum, adjudication is a vertical system of justice which is based on hierarchies of power, and it uses force to implement decisions.

In contrast, mediation is based on an essential equality of the disputants. If parties are not exactly equal or do not have equal bargaining power, mediation attempts to promote equality and balance as part of its process. It is a horizontal system which relies on equality, the preservation of continuing relationships, or the adjustment of disparate bargaining power between the parties.

When we look back to the Family Group Conference processes in Australia and New Zealand and the healing program in Hollow Water, we can see a similar attempt to return responsibility for problem solving to those directly involved with the problem, rather than keeping it in the hands of powerful strangers. Justice processes are structured to restore that authority while at the same time remedying any power imbalances that either the crime or the relationships themselves have created.

One of the most striking illustrations of the Aboriginal preference for avoiding hierarchies can be seen in the traditional Ojibway concept of leadership. Basil Johnston, an Ojibway scholar, first introduced me to it in his wonderful book *Ojibway Heritage*. As he explained it, leadership was understood to be one of five essential needs for society along with defence, sustenance, learning and medicine. A healthy society thus had to have its chiefs, its warriors, its hunters, its teachers and its healers. By tradition, each was represented by its own emblem, or *dodaem,* which gave rise to the English word "totem." A person's *dodaem* meant so much that when they introduced themselves they did so by indicating their clan. That would automatically tell others a great deal about how they had been raised and what responsibilities they had assumed.

Of the leadership *dodaem,* represented by birds, there grew to be many clans, including the Crane, Goose, Loon, Hawk, White-headed Eagle, Black-headed Eagle, Seagull, Brant and

Sparrow Hawk clans. Mr. Johnston explained why the Ojibway chose the crane as the pre-eminent symbol of leadership and direction:

> The call that he uttered was as infrequent as it was unique. So unusual was the tone and pitch of the voice that all other creatures suspended their own utterances to harken to the crane. When the crane calls, all listen.
>
> As the crane calls infrequently and commands attention, so ought a leader exercise his prerogative rarely.... A leader, having no other source of authority except for his force of character and persuasion, did not jeopardize his tenuous authority. Moreover, a leader was first in action, not merely commander; *as a speaker, he did not utter his own sentiments, but those of his people.*

It was for that reason, as Mr. Johnston explains, that the birds were known as "echo-makers."

Basil Johnston mentions another aspect of the traditional view of leadership which seems unique: its temporary nature, depending on the particular needs of the day. "Leadership was predicated upon persuasion; its exercise upon circumstances and need. It was neither permanent nor constant for a chief—just as the need for leadership among birds arises only twice a year, at the times of the migrations." So there is no such thing as a leader who has authority over all things. Instead, it is a question of exercising leadership *skills* as the occasion demands, rather than having authority over others given to you for a set period of time.

Finally, leadership is exercised in a way that does not involve chains of hierarchical command and obedience: "Even when circumstances demand leadership, *the act of leading is without compulsion.* The followers follow freely and are at liberty to withdraw. When the flock arrives at its destination, the members disband and terminate the conduct of leadership...."

A leader who only uttered the sentiments of his people? Who had no authority to require others to do his bidding? Who had to rely on persuasion and moral stature instead of force? How different is that concept of leadership from the one that has prevailed in European societies for many hundreds of years and the one that has now crept into so many Aboriginal communities as well?

When I first came across those descriptions of traditional leadership, I couldn't help but imagine an English fur trader standing on the riverbank at a Native encampment two hundred years ago, insisting that a *man* come to talk with him, a *leader* able and willing to make, on the spot, decisions that would bind his people for years or forever. Did he grow impatient and start pushing for answers when he encountered their reluctance to behave in that way? When I consider the hierarchies that prevail in many Aboriginal communities today, I wonder how much their emergence is traceable to those early contacts. Were the fur traders even aware of the fact that while Aboriginal men were often the "echo makers" for their groups, they seldom possessed an overriding power to make general decisions binding on anyone else?

The same potential misunderstandings occurred when Aboriginal people encountered representatives of *every* Western institution, whether it was our churches, our armies, our governments or our corporations. It was men who held the power in those institutions, men who were likely unaware of the traditional respect for the capacity of women to add a careful, long-distance view to the discussion. The more I picture those first meetings between the two cultures, the more I can see European men showing impatience with what looked like "indecisiveness" to them—and making insistent demands, no matter how politely expressed, that those Aboriginal men "act like leaders" and make decisions on the spot—and on their own.

Even in those "small" ways, then, the ancient balance of respect and contribution between men and women may have been undermined in favour of male-dominated hierarchies based on power and force. Whatever life was like in precontact days, however, power hierarchies are deeply entrenched in many Aboriginal communities today. In some, the men at the top of those hierarchies show no sense of responsibility whatever to the people whom they were elected to serve.

I mention these issues of leadership and hierarchy because they are down-to-earth illustrations of something that the larger society has difficulty either understanding or accepting: the Aboriginal declaration, "We see the world differently than you."

It has been said for so long. In his introduction to *Dancing with a Ghost*, Basil Johnston reported what Red Jacket, a noted Seneca orator, said in 1805, when he explained to the missionaries why his people would not "forsake their manitous and their uncivilized ways, and espouse the Bible and civilization." What Red Jacket told them was this: "Kitchi-Manitou has given us a different understanding." Rather than ask about that different understanding, it appears that the settler nations were content to assume that anything different was inferior, and to treat Aboriginal culture as exactly that.

Later in this chapter I will write about a man who developed an opposite suspicion. He was a physicist who worked with Albert Einstein, and before his recent death he was acknowledging (with some excitement!) that many North American Aboriginal languages contain, in their structure as well as in their expressive capabilities, a sophisticated *post-Einsteinian* understanding of the universe that English is often unable to capture. One of the central questions in his final years was how such a "primitive" people had clearly been living within a vision that Western physicists, with their astounding technology, were only recently beginning to grasp.

It is this different vision, and the teachings that contained and expressed it, which will now be explored. As I go along, I will point out the connections I am starting to see between traditional teachings and the kinds of "justice-as-healing" processes that are being developed by Aboriginal people as their alternative to Western justice. It must be understood at all times that the teachings are not just seen as a means of restoring social and individual health in Aboriginal communities. They go much deeper than that. They are understood to be the source of meaning, identity, purpose and fulfilment in life. Further, they are not seen as being in any way out of date, or useful only to those who live in the bush. Instead, they are considered to be more important at this time in history than ever before, and for people living urban as well as rural lives.

In the Beginning Was ...

Given that I have spent so much time talking about the absence of hierarchical thinking in traditional times, the whirlwind Bay-be-mi-say-si would probably approve of my starting this section by saying that there apparently was a fundamental hierarchy in traditional thought. I am speaking here of the hierarchy that exists within the Four Orders of Creation: Mother Earth, the plant realm, the animal realm and the human realm.

In 1993, Associate Chief Judge Murray Sinclair of the Provincial Court of Manitoba, himself Ojibway, spoke of it in an address to an Aboriginal justice conference in Saskatoon:

I am not a biblical scholar, but as I have come to understand it, in the Judaeo-Christian tradition, man occupies a position just below God and the angels, but above all other earthly creation.... According to the Genesis account of creation ... "God said, 'Let us make man in our image and likeness to rule the fish in the sea, the birds of heaven, the cattle, all wild animals on earth, and all reptiles that crawl upon the earth....'"

In sharp contrast, the aboriginal world-view holds that mankind is the least powerful and least important factor in creation.... Mankind's interests are not to be placed above those of any other part of creation.

In the matter of the hierarchy, or relative importance of beings within creation, Aboriginal and Western intellectual traditions are almost diametrically opposed. It goes without saying that *our world-view provides the basis for those customs, thoughts and behaviours we consider appropriate.* (emphasis added)

Basil Johnston also speaks of the Ojibway hierarchy of Creation in *Ojibway Heritage.* It is not based on intelligence or beauty or strength or numbers. Instead, it is based on dependencies. It places the Mother Earth (and her lifeblood, the waters) in first place, for without them there would be no plant, animal or human life. The plant world stands second, for without it there would be no animal or human life. The animal world is third. Last, and clearly least important within this unique hierarchy, come humans. Nothing whatever depends on our survival.

So much seems to flow from that focus on dependencies. Because human beings are the most dependent of all, it is we who owe the greatest duty of respect and care for the other three orders. Without them, we perish. Our role is therefore not to subdue individual parts of them to meet our own short-term goals, for that may disturb the balances between them. Instead, our role is to learn how they all interact with each other so we can try our best to accommodate ourselves to their existing relationships. Any other approach, in the long run, can only disrupt the healthy equilibria that have existed for millions of years and which, obviously enough, created the conditions for our own evolution.

Learning how those three orders interact thus becomes the central focus of Aboriginal science. It appears to be a somewhat different emphasis from the one Western science makes, at least in its most recent past. Milton M.R. Freeman, professor of Anthropology at the University of Alberta, explored that difference in an article about traditional ecological knowledge:

> [T]he methods of [Western] science are essentially reduction-ist, that is to say, they seek to understand organisms or nature by studying the smallest or simplest manageable part or sub-system in essential isolation.
>
> The non-Western forager lives in a world not of linear causal events but of constantly reforming, multidimensional, interacting cycles, where nothing is simply a cause or an effect, but all factors are influences impacting other elements of the system-as-a-whole ...

That passage struck a chord with me. I recalled, for instance, studying plants in high school. We learned about their cell struc-ture, photosynthetic processes, root systems, reproductive systems and so forth. We did not, however, learn much about how they contributed to the other plants, birds, insects, soils and animals that shared their meadow, or vice versa. It was, as Freeman suggests, a reductionist approach, focused not so much on the relationships *between* things as it was on the characteristics *of* things.

By its relative silence on the connections between things, it worked to create the opposite impression. Nothing seemed to be an essential part of anything else. Rather, all "things-out-there" became separable resources to be extracted (or ignored, poisoned, paved over, etc.) at our whim. In that frame of mind, it would never have occurred to me to consider accommodating myself to the realities of *their* equilibria. Instead, they were there to accommodate mine. It was clearly a human-centred, human-dominated universe that I was being taught to see, even though no one ever said it.

I do not suggest for a moment that Western and Aboriginal science took mutually exclusive directions, for that is clearly not the case. Aboriginal people indeed studied the characteristics of individual things: over 70 percent of all Western drugs, for instance, have come from isolating the active ingredients in plants and animals that the world's indigenous peoples had already been using for medicinal purposes for centuries. And on the other side of the coin, Western scientists have indeed paid attention to the workings of "things-put-together"—whether in agriculture, chemistry, meteorology, geology or physics.

It does seem, however, that there has been a difference in *emphasis* between the two groups. The result appears to be that Western science has achieved special excellence in its understanding of things and their properties, while Aboriginal science has achieved a special excellence, only now being recognized, in how things work together within systems-as-a-whole. In fact, as Freeman points out in his article, Western scientists have recently "granted" Aboriginal science its own acronym, TEK, which stands for Traditional Ecological Knowledge.

This determination to place the primary emphasis on studying the relationships between things—and to try to accommodate those relationships instead of dominating the things within them—seems to lie at the heart of a great many Aboriginal approaches to life. For instance, an Ojibway friend of mine gave me a sheet of paper entitled "Twelve Principles of Indian Philosophy." The very first principle on that sheet read as follows:

WHOLENESS. All things are interrelated. Everything in the universe is part of a single whole. Everything is connected in *some way* to everything else. It is only possible to understand something if we understand how it is *connected* to everything else. (emphasis added)

I must mention that I showed that sheet of principles to a Mi'kmaq elder who teaches traditional spirituality on Cape Breton Island. I asked whether it reflected the understandings of her people as well. She answered that while her people might phrase things differently, the concepts were substantially the same. She then had it photocopied for immediate distribution to her class, and we spent the next hour or so discussing how similar the Mi'kmaq and Ojibway spiritualities are.

I later came to discover that the wording of these principles came from a very special book, *The Sacred Tree,* produced by over thirty elders, spiritual teachers and professionals from Aboriginal communities across North America. They had come together to look for understandings that might be common to them and to search as well for ways to express them in English. (All twelve principles are listed in the appendix.)

Traditional teaching suggests that the principle—or law—of wholeness applies not only to the nonhuman realms, but to the human one as well. When people cause problems, for instance, this law of interconnectedness requires that a justice system investigate all the factors that might have contributed to the misbehaviour. That investigation must go back much further in time than is the custom in Western courts and it must encompass a greatly expanded circle of friends, family, employers and other influences. Further, any plan of action must involve not only the individual doing what he or she can with *his or her* problem, but the whole, larger group doing what they can about *their* problem. Disharmony within one individual is seen as everyone's disharmony, for it "infects" all relationships which involve that person. The principle of wholeness thus requires looking for, and responding to, complex interconnections, not single acts of separate individuals. Anything short of that is seen as a naïve response destined to ultimate failure.

I don't think I really understood how central this theme of connectedness really was, however, until the autumn of 1993.

New Eyes, New Knows: Who's Crazy Now?

It happened one day when I was visiting an Ojibway friend at a substance abuse treatment centre for Aboriginal people. She gave me a tour of the facility and showed me into the ceremonial room where about twenty chairs were arranged in a circle around a large ceremonial drum. While standing at the doorway, she made this comment: "In our teachings," she said, "people heal best when they heal *with* each other."

I HAD HEARD WORDS like these many times before. I had heard that people cannot heal in isolation, because isolation and alienation are seen as the disease. I had heard that, in the circle, it is the hope that people will come to understand they are not alone— neither in their fears, their joys, their guilts nor their sorrows. Their time together in the circle presents them with an opportunity to take their first, frightened steps towards creating healthy connections, as the circle becomes a safer and safer place to honestly share with others. Until then, I felt I had understood all those things. I know now that I had been operating only on an intellectual level.

At that moment, looking into that circle of chairs surrounding the drum, another level suddenly appeared. In a way I can't quite describe, I felt a circle of lonely, ill and frightened people being brought gently into new feelings of connection and communion with each other by the power of the drum and the teachings of the songs. I felt them gaining the confidence, perhaps for the first time in their lives, to start sharing the secrets of abuse that had been haunting them. I felt them *coming out of themselves,* and that seemed to change everything.

The word "connecting" leapt at me. It captured not only the dynamics I imagined in that room, but also the key feature of all the traditional teachings I had been exposed to thus far. Until then, I had somehow missed it. It involved a double obligation, requiring first that you learn to *see* all things as interconnected and second that you dedicate yourself to *connecting yourself,* in respectful and caring ways, to everything around you, at every instant, in every activity.

I was also struck by another thought: the possibility that my own culture regularly seemed to have taught me to see myself as *disconnected* from other aspects of creation. Without doubt I had learned to see myself as somehow separate from and superior to the animal, mineral and plant worlds. Was I also being taught to see myself as fundamentally disconnected from my fellow human beings? As I stood in the doorway, those two words, *connecting* and *disconnecting,* began to form into lenses through which I found myself re-examining everything I had seen and heard in my travels with Aboriginal people. I remembered a number of things instantly.

I remembered what I had learned about the traditional perspectives that must be passed on to children. Children had to be shown that they were involved in ongoing relationships, not just with each other but also with all other things around them. They had to learn to see themselves not as separate, individual beings but as active participants in webs of complex interdependencies with the animals, the plants, the earth and the waters. Their first obligation, then, was to look for all the connections and relationships that surrounded them, to understand "things" in that dynamic way. The second was to learn, as best they could, over a lifetime of study, how they all worked together. Third, they had to forever look for ways to accommodate themselves to those dynamics, rather than trying to dominate them. At its most basic, life was taught to be a process of *connecting* yourself, in accommodating ways, to everything and everyone around you.

I remembered as well that in Navajo one of the greatest compliments is to say of another that "he takes care of his relatives," where "relatives" means not just other people but all aspects of creation. Similarly, each round of an Ojibway sweat-lodge is closed by saying "All My Relations," again referring to all of Creation and underlining our connections to it. In fact, as each of the glowing rocks is brought inside the sweat-lodge, it is greeted out loud as "Grandfather" or "Grandmother." I have also been told that the Lakotah people of the Northern Plains states call the sweat-lodge by a phrase translatable into English as "The Stone People's Lodge," recognizing (among many other things) the need to maintain respectful relationships with those rocks, and with all other aspects of Creation as well.

I have struggled since that moment to find a short and snappy way to express the change in perception that occurred as I stood at that door, looking into that room, seeing not empty chairs but a circle of people experiencing together the strength of interconnecting Creation through the drum, the circle and the songs. It is not easy. The best expression I have come up with so far is this: Until that moment I would have said, "I, Rupert Ross, *have* relationships," whereas the new perspective would require me to say, "I, Rupert Ross, *am* relationships."

Since that moment at the doorway, everything I have come across seems to shout out the distinction between a connecting and a disconnecting approach to existence. I offer, for instance, another part of the Bluehouse-Zion article, where they write about someone who has denied their "Navajo-ness" by acting against

Navajo teachings: "[This denial] is expressed in the maxim 'He acts as if he had no relatives.' A person who acts that way betrays solidarity and kinship; he or she is not behaving as a Navajo, and may behave in a 'crazy' way." There are two different worlds emerging here. There is the world I am learning about, where people will consider someone crazy if, for instance, he *denies* his relationship with rocks, and there is my own world, where we will call him crazy as soon as he *does* start talking to them!

This emphasis on interconnection, on seeing life in terms of the relationships *between* things instead of the characteristics *of* them, has clear application to the design of justice processes. It stands behind the insistence we have already noted that offenders not be dealt with alone, separated out from their victims and all the other people touched by their behaviour. Instead, it requires examining and dealing with the relationships between all of them. Further, it stands behind the insistence that justice processes be designed so they contribute to the restoration of health to those relationships and not to their further deterioration. Adversarial processes of attack, blame and denial are seen as moving those relationships even further out of health. Diane LeResche emphasized this special focus in her contribution to the special issue of *The Mediation Quarterly* I referred to earlier: "Peacemaking is more conciliation than it is mediation. *It is relationship-centred, not agreement-centred....* Native American Peacemaking is inherently spiritual; it speaks to the *connectedness* of all things...." (emphasis added).

This constant emphasis on relationships has consequences far larger than I first supposed. Relationships, by definition, are never static. Instead, they are always in the process of changing. Where the focus shifts away from static "things" to the relationships that flow between them, the world itself becomes a much more fluid place, and we have to adapt accordingly.

Raptors, Coyote and Humbleberry Pie

The second of the "Twelve Principles" taken from *The Sacred Tree* reads as follows:

> CHANGE. Everything is in a state of constant change. One season falls upon the other. People are born, live and die. All things change. There are two kinds of change: the coming together of things and the coming apart of things. Both kinds of changes are necessary and are always connected to each other.

And the third principle adds a further element:

> CHANGE OCCURS IN CYCLES OR PATTERNS. They are not random or accidental. If we cannot see how a particular change is connected, it usually means that our standpoint is affecting our perception.

When I first read those two principles, I saw nothing foreign about them. They seemed to express something very familiar to me: the belief that if we refine out standpoint far enough, we will at some point in the distant future be able to map out how each change connects with every other one. After that, we should be able to design tools of such sophistication that we will be able to orchestrate all those changes so we get only the ones we want. That, it has always seemed to me, was the fundamental assumption of Western science.

But that is almost exactly the opposite of the assumptions that lie behind the Twelve Principles. Instead, there appears to be the belief that we will *never* be able to understand everything well enough to fully appreciate, predict, control or rearrange all those changes with any degree of certainty. It says that the web of ever-changing inter-dependencies is so complex and so dynamic that only an arrogant fool would presume to understand it, much less pretend to be able to express it in words comprehensible to others. It says that while some patterns *can* be perceived over time—and people should always try to perceive them—there can be no certainty that they will repeat themselves in an identical fashion each time.

In short, accurate prediction and effective control are seen as illusions, and dangerous illusions at that. The better stance is to humbly acknowledge how powerless you really are against such large and incomprehensible forces, and to be constantly ready to accommodate yourself to whatever new dynamics they send your way. This opposite assumption about the ultimate unknowability and uncontrollability of the universe leads, unsurprisingly, to some opposite ideas about "proper" behaviour. For one thing, it leads to a conviction that we must all approach the universe from within a posture of profound humility, acknowledging not our power over it but our dependency upon it. This philosophical humility exhibits itself in almost every aspect of traditional teachings.

There is, for instance, the very use of those English words "teachings" and "understandings" when Aboriginal people talk about how they see things. As we have noted, there is no claim to truth or to universal validity. As Basil Johnston expressed it in his introduction to *Dancing with a Ghost,*

> The highest compliment or tribute they could pay a speaker was to say of him or her 'w'daeb-wae,' taken to mean 'he/she is right, correct, accurate, truthful.' It is an expression *approximating* the word for 'truth' in the English language, except that it means one casts one's knowledge as far as one has perceived it and as accurately as one can describe it, given one's command of language. Beyond this one cannot go. *According to this understanding, there can be no such thing as absolute truth.* (emphasis added)

And, when Mr. Johnston described Red Jacket's rejection of the missionaries' invitation to conversion, he noted that this essential humility was present in how that rejection was expressed: "In ... preferring to abide by traditional understandings, Red Jacket did not imply that his people's understandings were better than those of the newcomers."

In the same vein, Aboriginal people regularly choose the more humble English word *gifts* over the more boastful word *talents*. They are not seen as either the creation or the property of an individual. Further, because they are "gifts," people are not free to use or abuse them as they see fit, nor to brag about them, nor to claim status from them. Rather, they have a responsibility to honour them by exercising them for the benefit of others, and by doing so in a grateful, not boastful, state of mind. Such gifts also have to be nourished and respected, or they can be taken away. Some gifts are seen as so powerful that they are frightening; clear choices about accepting or refusing them have to be made. In all respects, the teaching concerning gifts reflects the underlying attitude of humility.

This central commandment towards humility has many other direct practical consequences. In my region, for instance, it is common knowledge among lawyers that many Aboriginal witnesses can be easily "led" on cross-examination. If we ask, "Isn't it possible that X happened?" they are much more likely than non-Aboriginal witnesses to agree—even if they have just said the exact opposite to the other lawyer! What we regard as their "uncertainty" lessens their credibility and destroys the impact of their evidence. Within Basil Johnston's expression of traditional thought, however, it is clear that they feel no more personal uncertainty about what they have seen or heard than any other witness. Instead, thousands of years of teaching have instructed them to acknowledge the *philosophical* possibility that things might have taken place differently than the way they had perceived them. To insist that the other person's suggestion is wrong (especially if that other person happens to be a lawyer in a court of law) is seen as an insult not only to them, but to the teaching as well.

This traditional understanding that it is impossible to fully know or control things because of the complexities of their inter-relationships is now getting support from Western science. I have attended three of four sessions sponsored by the Fetzer Institute of Kalamazoo, Michigan, entitled "Dialogues between Indigenous and Western Scientists." The purpose of those Dialogues was to compare traditional Aboriginal perspectives and those of post-Newtonian and post-Einsteinian physicists.

The physicists spent some time explaining something new to their science, something known popularly as Chaos Theory. As they described it, Chaos Theory argues that in any *open* system (i.e., out of the laboratory), the variables are so great that accurate prediction—much less full human control—is a myth. In *Jurassic Park,* to use an example they cited, the owner of the island had the illusion that his scientists could indeed both predict and control the behaviour of his resurrected dinosaurs. As we know, that illusion led to disaster for his enterprise—and a highly entertaining movie for the rest of us!

After the physicists gave us some understanding of Chaos Theory, the Aboriginal people at the Dialogues went on to discuss a prominent figure common in many Aboriginal traditions. Often known in English as Trickster, one of his many jobs involves teaching humility, primarily by luring people into feeling certain about something, then turning everything upside down at the last moment. If you are the one who ends up face down in a mud puddle just when you thought you were about to touch down on the Road to Oz, the teaching holds that you should laugh at your-self for thinking you could control or predict things in the first place. Within the teaching, it is foolish to see yourself as powerful enough to *determine* the full course of your own existence.

Two verses from *The Elderberry Flute Song* by Peter Blue Cloud show how Trickster (in this case, named Coyote) loves to poke fun at the conceit that anyone, human *or* superhuman, has anything close to a profound understanding of Creation. In the first verse, Coyote sets you up to expect nothing but cosmic wisdom, and in the second, he crashes you back to earth again:

> Coyote, Coyote, please tell me,
> What is Magic?
> Magic is the first taste of ripe strawberries, and
> Magic is a child dancing in a summer's rain ...

> Coyote, Coyote, please tell me,
> What is Power?
> It is said that power is the ability to start your
> chainsaw with one pull ...

The need to acknowledge uncertainty and uncontrollability even shows itself in the courtroom. I have frequently heard a judge ask someone if they will return to court on a particular day, only to hear the person answer, "Maybe." Without question, some people said it as an expression of indifference or contempt. I recall, however, the same answer coming from some very proper and respectful people. From their lips, it seemed to reflect a belief that because no one can control what will happen, no one can predict with certainty either. To promise the judge otherwise would not only be an act of arrogance, but an insult to his or her intelligence. Once again, what is uttered as a signal of respect in one culture can easily be spoken as a signal of exactly the opposite in another.

This notion of not being able to influence events does not mean, however, that there's no point in trying. Nor does it mean that we have no responsibility to work towards the best future we can imagine. On the contrary, there are substantial roles for individual contribution and wide spheres of human responsibility. They must, however, be undertaken within certain clear limits.

The Teaching of the Five Waves

I remember, in this connection, speaking with an Inuit woman in Yellowknife. I had been talking about the insistence of Aboriginal people that the justice system look beyond the particular crime and try to examine all the events and forces that lead up to it. She immediately told me about something her father told her when he took her down to the shores of Hudson Bay as a youngster. It took me a while to understand that she was talking about the same thing I was!

Her grandfather told her that before she ventured out she had to learn how to look for and understand how "the five waves" were coming together on any particular day. I'm not sure I recall each of those fives waves accurately, because at the time I was trying to figure out what waves on Hudson Bay had to do with a justice system, but I'll give it my best shot. The first waves were those of the winds that were building but not yet fully arrived, the waves that would grow strong as a new weather system came in. The second waves were the ones left over from the weather system that was now fading, for they would still continue to affect the water even after the winds had gone. The third were the waves caused by all the ocean currents that came winding around the points and over the shoals, for they would present their own forces against the waves from the winds. Fourth were the waves caused by what Westerners call the Gulf Stream, and fifth were the waves caused by the rotation of the earth. Until you looked out and saw how all those forces were coming together, then developed some idea of how they would interact as the day progressed, it was not safe to go out and mingle with them.

As I have slowly come to appreciate, the teaching of the five waves has direct application to the ways in which a justice system ought to approach offenders. It suggests, for instance, that we cannot come to understand their behaviour until we gain some understanding of all the waves, old and new, that have converged on them during their lives. It suggests that they will continue to face the same waves tomorrow and the day after that, and that many of them cannot be changed. It suggests that what is necessary in the face of that reality is a process that helps them develop the skills they will need to ride all those waves more successfully in the future. Further, it suggests that the very *last* thing any justice processes should do is cause a reduction in whatever riding skills offenders already possess.

In that regard, I remember an Aboriginal woman at a justice conference complaining about the use of jail. She felt that jail was a place where offenders only learned to be more defiant of others, more self-centred, short-sighted and untrusting. Further, because they had so many daily decisions taken away from them, she felt that their capacity for responsible decision making was actually diminished, not strengthened. "We know that you put him in jail for our protection," she said, "but to give us protection in that way, you'd have to keep him there forever!" Since that was not the case, she wondered why we couldn't support her "healing way" instead. If jail actually causes people to lose some of the coping, balancing, riding and steering skills they originally had, or to develop habits that make improving those skills harder still, then it only adds to their disabilities and to the misery of all.

Whenever I want to achieve a gut-level understanding of the teaching of the five waves, I only have to think of that fifteen-year-old boy I called Carl. I think of all the waves of abuse in his early years that propelled him, almost unavoidably, into such horrible abuse of others. And then I have to go back further, to the waves that must have propelled his brutal father. And then I go back, as my Aboriginal teachers regularly insist I do, past the residential schools, past the centuries of open slander and prosecution of everything Aboriginal, right back to the little waves that first appeared when fur traders paddled up to an encampment, called for a man to speak to, and asked him to "act like a leader." Going back in that way is not for the purposes of assessing fault or apportioning blame. Instead, it is done to gain an understanding of all the currents that swirl about Aboriginal people at this exact point in time. Only then, with an accurate reading of what must be accommodated and responded too, is successful manoeuvring possible.

Further, the passage of time is not seen as an important factor when it comes to waves like this, where movement is towards disharmony and every force being added to the mix seems headed in the same direction. In such cases, time just permits such waves to gain depth and power, and requires that even greater attention be paid to them. Ojibway teachings live within this notion of longer spans of time. There is, for instance, the duty expressed by Ojibway people to look seven generations into the future whenever substantial change is being contemplated. If you cannot be fairly confident that the changes will still be exerting a positive influence at that time, then those changes should not be made.

The story of the five waves gave me something else as well, though it took a while for me to understand it: a way to think about how you can be at the mercy of forces beyond your control and yet still be significantly responsible for the course of your own life. Since my university days I have struggled with the philosophical battle between free will and determinism, and teachings like the five waves finally gave me a way of resolving what appeared to be an unbreakable tension between them.

CHAPTER 4

TOWARDS A FLUID REALITY

C learly, you cannot control the waves that constantly form beneath and around you. They will come, driven by forces far outside your control, many of them unleashed long before you were born. You can, however, like an ocean surfer, learn to ride them.

Both surfing and responding to the forces that shape your life require skills of observation and anticipation. They require that you focus on whatever is on the verge of emerging from your surroundings, as well as constantly repositioning yourself as everything shifts beneath you. If you succeed in developing those skills to a moderate degree, you can ride the waves without being thrown head over heels and without causing harm to others riding alongside. If you manage to develop superior skills, then something quite different may be possible: you may be able, like the expert surfer, to participate in the exhilaration that comes from hitting the intersection where all the forces come most powerfully together and riding faster than you ever have before. While you cannot control the waves, you can control how you meet them and attune yourself to their energies. So too each person can do little to change the major (and many of the minor) events that shape their lives— but each bears a responsibility for developing and using all the skills that can keep them afloat. So while there is strong determinism with respect to the forces that come bearing down on you from way back in time and from all the people and events that presently surround you, there is a complementary belief that we have the innate capacity to ride the vast majority of them successfully. To do so, however, we must honour, nourish and use the teachings that can release that capacity in all of us.

I mentioned the story of the five waves not only to highlight certain approaches to understanding and to dealing with problem behaviour. I also used it to introduce another aspect of traditional thought that has long perplexed me. Basil Johnston said it this way in *Ojibway Heritage,* in his discussion about the Four Orders of Creation: "From the last to the first, each order must abide by laws that govern the universe and the world. Man is constrained by this law to live by, and learn from, the animals and the plants...." When I applied that kind of thinking to the story of the five waves, I could see how some things in the nonhuman world might give us clues about how to approach problems in the human one, or at least valuable metaphors to help us keep a certain focus. But *laws?* How can we possibly think of ourselves as "constrained" to live under the laws that govern plants and animals? How can we possibly learn from them?

As I am starting to appreciate, humans have *always* been preoccupied with "natural law" and have, on many occasions, used it to justify the structure of their own institutions. Euro-American humans appear to be no exception. It's just that our definition of that "natural law" seems to be almost exactly opposite to the definition contained within many Aboriginal teachings. It all depends, much like the issue of hierarchies, on what lens you wear when you examine that nonhuman world.

Es-chewing a Dog-Eat-Dog Vision of the Universe

When I think about Western science, one phrase from Charles Darwin keeps coming back: "The survival of the fittest." It has always stood as a "natural law" to me, telling me that fierce competition in every aspect of existence is both the way of the world and the best guarantee of progress for man. We seem to reward victors almost regardless of *how* they won, and at times life seems defined as a series of activities specifically created just to separate winners from losers. An advertising campaign for outboard motors in the summer of 1994 summed up the attitude: "Life Is a Race—Don't Come in Second."

This law of fierce competition, however, does not appear to be the law that many Aboriginal peoples derive from their study of the nonhuman world. Instead, they have drawn an opposite conclusion: that Creation demonstrates, at its most fundamental levels, principles of mutualism, interdependence and symbiosis. At those levels, all aspects of the created order are essential to the continued survival of Creation as a whole. According to that perspective, the obligation of humans is not to attack, insult or diminish them or each other, but to demonstrate respect, to offer support, to work towards cooperation.

In this view, even verbal insult is arrogant and wrong, whether the target is other humans, animals, plants or earth. As the opening paragraph of Ruth Beebe Hill's startling book *Hanta Yo* establishes, the Lakotah had no *language* for insulting those other orders of existence: "… pest … waste … weed …—neither these words nor the conceptions for which they stand appear in this book; they are the whiteman's import to the New World, the newcomer's contribution to the vocabulary of the man he called an Indian. Truly, the parent Indian families possessed neither these terms nor their equivalents." While this nature-derived law of mutual respect did permit each species to use others for food, that was the only justification for interference. For humans, certain ceremonial observances were required to demonstrate both respect and gratitude whenever some other aspect of Creation was used for their benefit.

That was so, whether the task involved slaying an animal or cutting saplings to construct a sweat-lodge. In the latter case, for instance, Ojibway law required placing tobacco in the ground to acknowledge that one creature, the sapling, had permitted its energies—its spirit—to be converted into the service of another. All such observances helped to maintain the core teaching that all aspects of Creation were essential, none were superior and each must be respected if all are to survive.

It is interesting to note that some Western scientists are now beginning to question the survival-of-the-fittest lens through which they were trained to look at the world. For instance, in an article entitled "Is Nature Really Red in Tooth and Claw?" medical scientist Anne Fausto-Sterling wrote: "Modern textbooks still like to talk of cutthroat competition, of the survival of the fittest, as the overriding force that drives evolution and determines the ways species interact. Yet research in the past two decades shows that cooperation among species plays at least as big a role as violent struggle.... And suddenly, it seems, you can find cooperation in plants and animals wherever you look—suggesting a whole new view of evolution and interdependence among all forms of life."

Sadly, after this statement, Fausto-Sterling falls prey to the same Eurocentrism that has led the settlers and their descendants to ignore the sophistication of Aboriginal thought ever since contact: "Strikingly, those who did appreciate the degree of cooperation going on in the natural world were often those who espoused a vision of cooperation in human society—notably the gentle nine-teenth-century Russian revolutionary Pyotr Kropotkin, the German socialist Friedrich Engels, and, in the 1940s, the American Quaker Warder C. Allee." Why is it that a Russian, a German and a Quaker are listed as having such a vision, when the more numerous first inhabitants of this land are not? Can we understand a little better from this one small passage (and its very large omission) why

Aboriginal people are asking for greater control over the education of their own children?

Fausto-Sterling's comments caused me to remember a certain passage I read many years ago in Robert Ardrey's *Territorial Imperative*. It was about two fish with neighbouring nests on the ocean floor. When one intruded into the other's territory, the second left its nest to drive the first one back, chasing it until it too became an intruder. Then the first fish, feeling bolder because it was closer to home, would turn and drive the second one back again into its territory, though not as far. The two fish would continue to chase back and forth until, at the end, they were motionless, staring at each other across what had been established as the boundary between their two territories. Then they'd go home to their nests again.

When I first read that, I saw it as another survival-of-the-fittest story about two creatures fighting over territory. It was only recently that I realized they *didn't* fight! The stronger one did not demolish the weaker, then take over its territory. Instead, there seemed to be a clear acknowledgment that, as far as territory was concerned, they each had a *right* to their own space. By going back and forth without bloodshed, they established the boundary, after which they both went home. When I first read the story, I didn't "see" their agreement to coexist. I saw only what I was trained to see: competition and struggle.

A prayer attributed to the Sioux Chief Yellow Hawk touches on all these issues: "Make my hands respect the things you have made, my ears sharp to hear your voice. Make me wise, so that I may know the things you have taught my people, the lessons you have hidden in every leaf and rock. I seek strength not to be superior to my brothers, but to fight my greatest enemy, myself."

Since I was given the image of the five waves and its clear application to justice, I have had a much easier time understanding such declarations. In that case, the "natural laws" governing the waters of Hudson Bay teach that although the waves that have an impact on each of us in the human world cannot be fundamentally changed, we can develop the skills to anticipate their interaction, as well as the skills to ride them. As the elders stress, these are more than lessons that we are free to employ or ignore. Instead, they have the force of law, for in the long run the laws that provide peace and harmony in the nonhuman world are seen as the only laws capable of producing peace and harmony in ours.

I remember an old Ojibway man talking to me one day, explaining some of the teachings about his drum. At one point he looked out the window to the forest and the lake and said, "Look out there. That is where the law is. It is not in books. Law does not come from man. It comes from out there, from the Creator. That's the place you go to find out about the law." At the time, I had no idea what he meant, only that I was hearing the same thing wherever I went in Aboriginal Canada. Now, finally, I think I'm starting to gain some small understanding of what they were saying.

Having understood what they meant, however, did not mean that I found it possible to agree with them. For instance, could this Aboriginal "law" of mutual support and recognition within the nonhuman world have any application to human affairs as well? At first glance, especially at the daily newspapers and nightly newscasts, that seemed a ridiculous thought. Everything I saw, heard and read seemed to tell me the opposite, that we are not our brother's keepers, but our brother's oppressors.

At that point, however, another question emerged, and it was not a very comfortable one, especially for a member of the justice profession: what if the violence we so frequently do to each other is not the result of a "natural" dog-eat-dog predisposition towards life, but the result of being *taught* to behave in competitive and often antagonistic ways? Has the competitive model of nature polluted our thinking so much that the thought of helping others is a "foreign" concept to us? To what extent have we been trained into adversarial stances and away from mutual support? To what extent do all our adversarial and competitive institutions *require* us to act in that way and so quash whatever generous impulses may lie within us? Why, in blizzards and earthquakes and epidemics, do so many people shed their selfishness so quickly and come to the aid of others? Can our institutions be forcing us to deny who we really are? No matter whether our "born" inclination is towards competition or cooperation, there can be little doubt that we will be moved towards one extreme or another depending on what we understand to be "natural law." Once we confer the status of law on any world-view, we immediately start building it into all the institutions that surround us, and every time they touch us, they teach us as well.

Within the justice system, is it because we have declared "survival of the fittest" to be the primary law of nature that we have elevated legal combat to such high status? And why is it that Aboriginal approaches to justice, whether in New Zealand, Navajo country or Hollow Water, seem so determined to go in the other direction? Why do they all insist on removing the legal warriors from the picture in order to allow the parties to speak for themselves?

But this dog-eat-dog perspective is only one of the lenses that Euro-Canadians wear when looking at the world around them and then creating governing institutions. There is another lens as well—one that is much harder to perceive. For that very reason, it may be more powerful still.

Navajo Pots and the River Thames

I was told an interesting story about a renowned Navajo pot-maker. Two film crews, one of them Navajo, decided to capture her for posterity. When their work was over, it was discovered that they had made two entirely different films. The Western crew had focused primarily on the products of her work, including the fame and fortune her pieces had brought her. The Navajo crew, by contrast, focused primarily on how she had collected her materials, the ceremonial steps she had observed and the way she had crafted them to express certain teachings of her people. For the Navajo, it was the processes within her art that counted most, particularly the state of mind and spirit she had adopted and portrayed through her works. For the Western crew, the way she had produced her art, her state of mind, and especially her state of spirit, seemed almost irrelevant. In short, the two crews "saw" her work through very different lenses of significance.

When I heard that story, it reminded me of a time I had watched two Tibetan monks creating a sand mandala at an art gallery in England. The project, we were told, would take several months, for it involved blowing grains of different-coloured sand through a straw-like affair into an intricate pattern of shapes and fine lines, thus gradually filling in a circle some five feet in diameter. We were then shocked to learn that after it was completed they would dump it in the River Thames! That dumping, we were told, was meant to underline the central teaching: life was not about products, things or even fine works of art. It was about process, about *how* you lived it. Your central duty was to undertake each aspect of every process with the same virtues of care, patience, respect and humility that the monks demonstrated as they created that mandala.

The more I thought about it, the more I saw how much I lived in a world of things, of products, where indeed most "ends" justified most "means," no matter how mean they really were to the people whose dignities were trampled in the process.

By way of illustration, my product-seeing eyes caused me to miss something very significant about traditional child rearing when I wrote *Dancing with a Ghost*. I wrote about the noninterference approach to raising children that I saw as existing in many communities today, with its understanding that it is improper to tell children what to say, do, watch, build, read, listen to and so forth. To me, that seemed like a recipe for chaos in today's world. I acknowledge believing that it was one practice from traditional times that clearly had to be swept away in favour of methods based on a greater degree of interference. I now know, however, that I was missing something, for traditional Aboriginal child rearing was not the "leave-them-alone" thing I thought it was.

What I missed was the fact that in traditional times, before the residential schools, children were indeed being taught things at almost every instant and in a wide variety of ways—through the stories and the ceremonies, through the naming practices and through the clan system itself. That teaching, however, was not the kind I was used to, for it did not focus on teaching each person exactly what to say, think or do—a product-based teaching, if you will. Instead, it focused on two other elements of life.

It taught first that life was a matter of responsibilities that all people had to bear at all times. Second, it taught children how to develop the personal qualities they would need to be able to carry out those responsibilities. What people actually did in fulfilment of their duties, however, was largely a matter of free choice.

For example, there are the clan system teachings that Basil Johnston has described in *Ojibway Heritage*. According to that system, members of each clan were born to carry certain responsibilities throughout their lives and were constantly guided into developing certain capacities. (People with special gifts, however, were never denied the chance to develop and use them, even if those gifts were associated with the responsibilities of other clans.) Children born to the bird clans, for example, were expected to put special effort into developing their leadership skills by concentrating on such things as speaking, grammar, history and tradition, given that leaders, as we have seen, had "no other authority except the force of ... character and persuasion." Children of the provider clans (represented by the Marten, Beaver, Moose, Caribou, Deer and Muskrat) were obliged to develop such personal qualities as patience, endurance, strength and resourcefulness to fulfil their provider responsibilities. In all cases, the emphasis was not on the particulars of what each person should do, but on how they should equip themselves for *whatever* responsibilities their clan membership specified.

Since writing *Dancing,* I have come to see traditional child rearing as a three-legged stool, where two of the legs (teaching children responsibilities and developing their personal attributes and skills) made it possible to allow for a third leg of almost complete freedom to make particular choices. The first two legs, however, were cut away when the ceremonies were outlawed, the clan system was derided as pagan and residential schools took over with their long, product-based lists of things that should and should not be done, backed up by punishment. The only leg remaining was the *habit* of noninterference.

All by itself, that habit does indeed promise chaos. That does not mean, however, that the approach has to be discarded, as I once thought. Instead, the other two legs need to be reattached to the stool—and in Aboriginal Canada strong efforts are being made to do just this.

This different approach to education is illustrated by a one-page document someone sent me entitled "A Letter Written by an Indian Parent" and addressed "To a Teacher." It was distributed by the "North American Indian Travelling College," and included the following passage: "Will you help [my child] develop problem-solving skills, or will you teach him that school is where you try to guess the answer the teacher wants? ... Respect my child. He is a person. He has a right to be himself."

These process-oriented aspects of traditional teaching I failed to see, so strong was my Western focus on teaching children by specific instruction. The problem in many Aboriginal communities, I now suspect, lies not in noninterference but in the fact that this approach is no longer accompanied by teaching about responsibilities or by any guidance in developing essential personal capacities.

It took me an embarrassingly long time to understand the difference and to see that I had missed it completely when I wrote *Dancing with a Ghost*. A small story shows just how slow I was—and just how patient my Aboriginal teachers have been! I was travelling across southern Alberta by car with a Blackfoot friend, Leroy Little Bear, heading for Lethbridge University, where Leroy had asked me to make a presentation to his Native Studies Class. We were telling stories about our experiences in law school, and I told him about a lesson I had learned in my first year at the University of Toronto. In February of that year I realized that we had covered only a small part of the material in one of my courses. It was clear that we would never get to certain statutes or case studies if we did not increase our pace. I raised that issue in class, mentioning that while I really enjoyed the free-for-all discussions we were having, I was worried that I wouldn't know what to do in certain areas once I began the real-life practice of law.

My professor at the time, Rob Prichard (now president of the University of Toronto) immediately called a halt and asked us to discuss his approach to things. As it came out, he didn't particularly care if we studied every piece of legislation or all the cases that dealt with it. As he reminded us, the government would always be passing *new* pieces of legislation, just as "real-life" people would always bring us problems the courts had not yet considered. As I recall, he said something like this: "As your professor, I want to know that when you leave here you know how to *think*, to analyse whatever problems and laws come along, to be able to decide what is relevant and what is not, what factors are most important and how to make the best case you can for whatever direction you choose to go. Anyone can memorize what others have thought. I want you to learn how to think on your own."

When I told Leroy that story, he seemed quite animated, asking that I repeat it when the time came to make my scheduled presentation to his class. I agreed, but I was puzzled. I still had not seen the similarities between Rob Prichard's attitude and traditional Aboriginal approaches. When Leroy and I got to Lethbridge, I repeated the story to his class but still didn't make the connection!

It wasn't until some months later, after continually wondering why Leroy had found that story important, that it came to me. I was rereading a section of *Ojibway Heritage* where Basil Johnston discusses the traditional way of raising children into responsible adults by providing them with (among other things) an endless supply of stories, rather than endless lists of particular do's and don'ts. As he expressed it: "To foster individuality and self-growth, children and youth were encouraged to draw their own inferences from the stories. *No attempt was made to impose upon them views*" (emphasis added). While such stories might be repeated many times to permit lessons to be developed and refined, they still focused primarily on teaching children *how*, rather than specifically *what*, to think.

I include this story in particular because it demonstrates how much Leroy himself insists on being a teacher within that traditional model. He never once made the connection *for* me, which he could have done by saying, "That law school story of yours is just like the way we once educated our children." Instead, by emphasizing it, he prompted me to keep it in my mind and wrestle with it long enough to finally make the connection on my own. It is a different way of teaching and a different way of learning. It requires

careful notice of the various things people present to your attention—and equally careful notice of things they do *not* put before
you! In all cases, however, it is up to the learner to find significance,
not the teacher to present it. In that way, it is an intensely respectful process, for it seldom presupposes what is right and what is
wrong, or suggests that only the teacher knows which is which.

Respectfully Yours ...

A similar care not to impose conclusions on others is apparent in
decision making as well. Every effort is made to create a process
that supports individual dignity and self-esteem. In *Dancing with
a Ghost,* I wrote about decision-making techniques whereby people
are *not* asked to state their recommendations, then fight for
them—because in such processes, there will inevitably be those
who come away feeling like winners, while others may feel either
left out or put down. To traditional eyes, few decisions are worth
such kinds of unhealthy developments in the relationships between
people.

Instead, everyone is given an equal, often formal, chance to
participate, and people commonly speak only about the kinds of
factors they are considering as they struggle towards a conclusion.
Politeness and humility often prompt people to begin by saying
something like "These are only the things I have considered so far,"
acknowledging that other information may be important as well. If
no substantially common approach appears to be emerging, the
decision may well be put off to another day. Because everyone
seems equally committed to finding solutions that respect the
contributions of all, compromises are common and stalemates are
not as frequent as I expected. It is the *process* that must be the
winner, not simply one of the participants, and egos are asserted
less frequently because they are less at stake.

This need to constantly demonstrate respect for the positions of others is often misinterpreted by non-Aboriginal people. I recall, for instance, a film made in 1993 for the Ontario government. In it, an Aboriginal woman spoke about the main difficulty she faced during meetings with her non-Aboriginal coworkers in the civil service. Within her teachings, she explained, it was necessary to wait until the other person had fully completed speaking before offering your own words. In fact, it was better still if you left a period of silence before you responded, to show that you were giving serious thought to what the other person said. In the bureaucracy, however, she felt that the rule seemed to be exactly the opposite. Everyone waited with their mouth half open, ready to jump in as soon as it looked as if the present speaker was coming close to the end of a sentence. People often interrupted speakers long before they were finished—an unconscionably rude behaviour according to her teachings. When she couldn't bring herself to do those same things, she seldom got a "chance" to speak. As a result, she had little input into decisions. Just as importantly, she was certain that her relative silence caused her coworkers to think of her as uninterested in her work, too stupid to contribute or both.

While this may seem a minor instance of cross-cultural misunderstanding, the complaint is nearly universal among Aboriginal people working in non-Aboriginal settings. In fact, such problems of communication are often cited as a major reason for quitting and returning to Aboriginal organizations.

I should add in passing that I suspect something else is going on in those silences, especially with elders. I suspect that elders use them not only to consider what you have said but to consider two other things as well: how much they can tell you (in the sense of how much you are capable of absorbing at your level of wisdom and maturity) and how to tell you those things in ways that will not leave you feeling stupid for having missed them in the first place!

Leroy Little Bear, for instance, waited almost two years from the publication of *Dancing* to find a way to draw my attention to the possibility that I had missed two legs of the three-legged stool, and he did so in such a way that it was still up to me to "discover" the missing pieces on my own. When I first came across people who surrounded themselves with such restraint and silences, I confess that I wondered if they were just bored by the conversation and reluctant to participate in it, or if they were a little on the "slow" side and needed extra time to ponder what I had said. Once again, I was wrong. Once again it was their determination to promote healthy relationships, mutual respect and continuing contribution that was behind it all. To them, those kinds of concerns were much more important than arriving at a speedy decision—or even coming to the end of the discussion itself!

I saw a concrete illustration of this long-term, relationship-based perspective during a cross-cultural workshop in Kenora. Inspector Jim Potts, then of the RCMP, opened with a moving account of how he was working to incorporate traditional teachings into modern-day policing. The second presentation was mine. Extending through lunch and into the afternoon, it focused on the powerful impact of traditional healing approaches in the areas of family violence and sexual abuse. Needless to say, it was a "heavy" presentation. The final speaker was Charlie Fisher, the elder from the Wabaseemoong First Nation whom I had written about in *Dancing with a Ghost*. Charlie, now retired, was Ontario's first full-time Native Justice of the Peace and remains a friend and teacher to me. I had heard Charlie make many presentations over the years. He always uses a great deal of humour, often at his own expense, but he always covers a great deal of serious material as well. This time, however, the serious material was largely absent. Instead, Charlie told four long jokes, then sat down. His listeners howled with laughter, then adjourned for the day, but I was perplexed.

Several months later, I asked him why he had taken such a light-hearted approach with the audience. He said that by the time it was his turn to speak, "their pack-sacks were already pretty heavy." What the audience needed more than further information—more product—was to walk out of that room carrying forward a good *relationship* with each other. According to traditional teaching, humour (especially of the self-deprecating sort) is one of the most powerful tools for bringing people together. That was how Charlie saw the purpose of the day, so that is what he did.

The elders who have maintained (or regained) their health, teachings and spirituality seem to live within such larger, relationship-based analyses almost every moment of every day, seeing broader options in everything, making choices based on long-term health at every step. I often feel that I live a "blunt" existence by comparison, playing around on the surface of human interaction, preoccupied with the trivial business of particular issues (or "products"), neglecting entirely the larger ones connected with the mental, emotional and spiritual health of the group as a whole.

I caution that this focus on relationship, on process, does not mean that product is unimportant. On the contrary, it suggests that an exclusive focus on drawing up lists of specific do's and don'ts is not the best way to achieve many of the products we all want *in the longer term*. I frequently watch Aboriginal people shake their heads in disbelief at how often Western countries fall back on imposed "Codes of Minimum Behaviour" backed up by the threat of punishment. The belief seems to be that unless the spirit of the individual is changed, such codes will only anger them by forcing them to do what they don't want to do in the first place. Then, once angered, they will try to beat the codes any way they can. Further, they will never go *beyond* the bare, legislated minimums. Most importantly, they are likely to take their anger out on precisely the people whom the codes were meant to protect, using ways that have not yet been legislated. Reliance on codes is therefore seen as never-ending, self-strangling, counterproductive and a great waste of time. The important issue is frame of mind—or spirit—as well as a focus on creating good relationships.

This emphasis on process and relationships has an impact that extends well beyond how children should be taught or how decisions should be made at work. Once it starts to take hold, a great many things start to change. Certain new issues start to emerge as critical, while others slip into insignificance.

It Ain't What You Do, It's Understanding Why You Did It

Western law makes a critical distinction between "serious" and "minor" offences. Over the course of seven years of prosecuting in Aboriginal communities, I have observed something that has puzzled me: that distinction did not seem to mean too much at the end of the justice day. In fact, neither the severity *nor even the exact details* of the criminal act seemed to be important to the people who were involved in the offence—or in the sentencing. Their focus seemed to be elsewhere.

I recall, for instance, watching the elders in one remote community in northwestern Ontario as they considered what recommendations to make to the judge in two particular cases. In the first, a man had been stabbed in the chest by a very drunken assailant, and he had come close to dying. To us, it was a very serious crime which naturally called for a lengthy sentencing hearing, followed in all likelihood by severe interference in the offender's freedoms. In the other case, a young man had been found drunk, sitting outside by himself at midnight, breaking the band by-law against consuming intoxicants. In the Western system, you can plead guilty to such public intoxication offences—and pay your fine—entirely through the mails. No one would ever dream of having a lengthy sentencing hearing for such a minor offence, nor would we feel justified in discussing substantial measures to respond to his "problem."

What surprised me in that Oji-Cree community was that the elders did not seem to pay much attention to our distinction between the "serious" and "minor" natures of the two offences. Instead, they brought a very similar kind of analysis to each of the cases, spent approximately the same amount of time on each and, most perplexing of all, made almost identical suggestions to the court about what the sentences ought to be. In both cases, they wanted to know what was going on in the offender's life that was causing the abuse of alcohol.

In short, the severity of the offence did not seem to dictate either how the elders approached their task or the kind of resolution they proposed. In fact, the offences weren't discussed much at all!

At the time, I was puzzled by this strange way of approaching the issues. In the Western system, where different criminal acts carry different degrees of punishment, the entire court process centres on a search for the clearest possible picture of exactly what took place. It is only after a court finds someone guilty of a very particular act that it can take further action. Further, the severity of the crime substantially controls what the court can then do. As it is often expressed, "the punishment must fit the crime."

Was it just the absence of punishment as a goal that permitted the elders to shift their attention away from the act and to look instead at all the other issues? Or was something else going on as well? Did it have to do with the fact that things-in-themselves were traditionally less important than the relationships-between-things? A couple of illustrations will help me express this point more clearly and shed a little light on preferred traditional approaches as well.

The chief of an Ojibway First Nation in northwestern Ontario recently told me about one practice he had just heard of from the elders. If someone consistently refused to follow the teachings and was contributing negatively to the community, he might be placed on a blanket held by a number of men, then repeatedly tossed high in the air. At some point, they would all let go of the blanket and he would fall, unprotected, to the ground.

When I first heard about that response, I thought of it in terms of punishment, for the pain of landing would no doubt be severe. I have since learned to look at it in a different way. If you imagine being tossed higher and higher into the air, each time being caught by a group of your fellows, imagine as well how much you would silently (or even loudly!) begin to plead with them not to let that blanket drop from their grasp. In a very dramatic way, it would become crystal clear how much you needed the assistance of others to keep from coming to harm.

The blanket toss, then, is much more than an instrument of punishment. Instead, it stands as a metaphor for an Aboriginal understanding of life itself, where the only way to survive its inevitable ups and downs (I couldn't resist it!) is to develop and maintain respectful and mutually supportive relationships with others. Your time in the air and the pain of your lonely landing would stand as forceful reminders about the interdependencies that shape and give meaning to our lives and about the need to maintain respectful relationships at all times. You can be sure that care was taken to avoid serious injury, for the entire purpose of the exercise was to help the person start making the greatest possible contribution to the community.

As that story illustrates, we must be cautious when we examine traditional justice responses. What may appear to a Western eye to be a punishment-based approach may instead be employed as a way of teaching, even if painfully, some fundamental understandings about what creates a healthy and enduring society.

A second illustration makes the point more forcefully still. We are now seeing requests from Aboriginal communities that people be sentenced not to jail, but to long periods of time alone in remote locations, with only minimal visits and support. Once again we think of such schemes as primarily oriented towards punishment, and once again we may be wrong.

One of the best-known examples of such a "temporary banishment" dates back to 1979, long before most judges even listened to community proposals for alternative sentencing, much less invited and accommodated them. A young man named Frank Brown of the Heiltsuk peoples of British Columbia was before the court on a robbery that had included a serious beating. Only fifteen years old, Frank had already been much involved with the law, and this offence had taken place not long after his release from custody for an earlier crime. In those circumstances, it appeared that there was no choice but to put him back in jail for a much longer period. Certain people, however, proposed to the court that he be "banished" to a small island instead, with only occasional visits by others to provide guidance and food. A pioneering judge, Cunliffe Barnett of the British Columbia Provincial Court, accepted their suggestion, and Frank Brown spent eight months essentially alone in the bush.

As events have proven, it was a wise choice, fot Frank Brown emerged a changed young man. He completed high school and a two-year community college program. He then spent three years organizing the now-famous Glwa Expedition to Expo '86—which involved carving a thirty-foot oceangoing canoe and, with thirteen others, paddling over three hundred miles down the Pacific coast to Vancouver. He credits that change to his period of banishment, to the support he received and to the guidance he was given by his people and their traditional teachings. In 1990, he re-enacted the entire process at a community potlatch, where he honoured all those who helped him turn his life around, including Judge Barnett.

Frank Brown also worked to incorporate his own experience into a formal program to deal with troubled young people in his

Bella Bella region of British Columbia. In 1987 he prepared a proposal to establish what he called the Heiltsuk Rediscovery Project, which has since been put into operation. In that proposal he described his understanding of what had happened to him and what other youngsters needed, in the following words:

> Today for the majority of our Heiltsuk youth in the community, the social, spiritual and cultural diet is composed of TV and basketball.... This results in a stagnated environment with little room to grow. However, through removing our young people from this stagnant environment with its many external distractions, these individuals will have no choice but to reflect inward and begin to deal with themselves. This shall be achieved through *separation, transition and incorporation.*

The pain of being separated, of having to endure the loneliness, the fear and the anguish of self-confrontation, was not inflicted simply to achieve punishment for its own sake, as we might first assume. Instead, such pain is incidental to a process of "reflecting inward"— coming to realize how essentially small and helpless we are on our own. The assumption is that this is the most effective way to teach "lost" people that everything in Creation, including them, survives primarily because of mutually supportive relationships with everything else. Once that is understood, it is a short step to understanding that each being has a responsibility to contribute to the health of all those relationships, rather than just taking away as they please.

Common sense tells us that a wide variety of antisocial acts may demonstrate that people are drifting out of healthy and supportive relationships with family, friends and community. While the man who stabbed the other and the young man found drunk at midnight may not have committed the same "crime" within an act-centred legal order, in the eyes of the elders, those dissimilar acts seem to have demonstrated a very similar need for both teaching and healing. Even a relatively insignificant act may signal the need for a detailed investigation into a person's life, as well as a significant "intrusion" into the ways they are approaching the challenges ahead of them.

Shifting the Spotlight

Once I started to gain some understanding of those different kinds of justice goals, it became easier to understand why disruptive acts themselves might no longer occupy centre stage within a peacemaking process. While they can serve as clues to the degree of disharmony and alienation afflicting the life of the offender, that's essentially all they are. The real issue is how such states of disharmony have come into existence and what can be done to turn them around. That issue involves a more detailed and wider-ranging inquiry, as well as a different set of judicial responses at the end of the justice day.

In a related vein, I have reviewed a number of studies of traditional justice amongst Aboriginal peoples over the last three years, many of them conducted and written by Aboriginal researchers. One thing that puzzled me was that they seldom made any reference to trials or to any other processes for disputed fact finding. It was an unexplained "omission." How could it be that traditional processes seemed to avoid our reliance on formal ways to prove things that people denied?

Initially, I supposed that part of the explanation lay in the fact that punishment did not appear to be a major goal in traditional times. If there was little or no punishment, it seemed reasonable to suspect that fewer offenders would deny responsibility for their actions. There was also the fact that traditional teaching apparently encouraged people to acknowledge their wrongdoing and ask for assistance as quickly as possible if they wished to maintain their welcome in the group.

More recently, however, I find myself attracted to the thought that it is the focus on relationships that once again lies at the heart of it all. Put simply, since acts are not as important as the relationships that spawn them, trials *about* acts no longer occupy centre stage. This change in focus may even mean that, if the parties have been guided through an effective peacemaking process, it might be totally *unnecessary* to come to a conclusion about who did exactly what to whom!

Contrary to my first impression, it's not such a startling notion. Any parent who has had to intervene in disputes between their young children soon comes to realize that it is often both impossible and unnecessary to trace the long train of angry acts back to the first little insult that started it rolling. Instead, the issue becomes one of somehow discharging the existing anger, helping each child remember that they are all important to each other and that their behaviour is disrupting the lives of everyone around them, then perhaps joining with them in a search for ways to avoid such problems in the future.

In short, a true peacemaking system may on occasion see the particular details of past acts almost fade from view as the participants are directed to concentrate their efforts on coming to understand and acknowledge three things: (1) that they cannot continue in this fashion without life becoming increasingly worse; (2) that the antagonism between them is not a private matter, but is directly affecting others within their wider circles of families and friends; and (3) that for the sake of all concerned they have a responsibility to find ways to put their disputes behind them and to agree to a new way to deal with each other in the future. In some cases that will be enough all by itself, *whether or not the parties agree on who started what and exactly what took place.*

This shift in focus from an examination of acts to an examination of relationships has other dimensions as well, and challenges much more than our reliance on formal, complex and adversarial trial processes.

For one thing, it results in a reduced need to make precise definitions of crimes in advance, simply because much less will hinge on establishing exactly what took place. In fact, I recall one traditional Ojibway chief saying that there are really only about ten "laws" altogether and that even those ten are just offshoots of a single one. He didn't go on to express his understanding of what they were, but my experience so far suggests that they would all centre on traditional understandings of the concept of respect. As we have seen, respect stands as a central requirement once you think of yourself as living within, and completely dependent upon, a magnificently interdependent order of Creation. Paradoxically, this focus on relationships also suggests a much wider and more detailed examination of the "lead-up" or surrounding acts than is the case in an act-centred justice system. This is especially important in the cases involving family, neighbours, coworkers or friends involved in a pattern of escalating disturbance, with each party feeling increasingly wronged over a lengthy period of time. Concentrating simply on the latest event, or the one that just happens to break a particular law, does little to change the nature of the relationship between them.

There may also be something else at work whenever Aboriginal people dispute our determination to use adversarial trials to "get at the truth." Traditional teachings seem to carry a suggestion that people will *always* have different perceptions of what has taken place between them. The issue, then, is not so much the search for "truth" but the search for—and the honouring of—the different perspectives we all maintain. Truth, within this understanding, has to do with the truth about each person's *reaction to and sense of involvement with* the events in question, for that is what is truly real to them. And if that is so, then justice processes must somehow deal with and validate their reality while also giving them the chance to understand how others see things.

This notion of "individual reality" is especially important when we come to look at healing and at the concept of individuals "taking responsibility" for their acts within the healing process. Far from denying or insulting individual perceptions of reality, the healing process requires everyone to honour the others' visions of, and reactions to, what took place between them. It is seen as fundamentally important that we learn from others how they have come to see the events that join us. Only then can we anticipate the real consequences of our actions and make informed decisions about what we should and should not do.

The Western-based trial process denies many of those understandings. As long as it is believed that there is a single, objective reality out there, that it is discoverable, that it should occupy the primary justice spotlight and that the trial is a process that can uncover that single reality, learning will be impeded. I can imagine many of my Aboriginal teachers saying something like "Who cares if there is an objective reality out there? Who cares if your trial process is capable of finding it? Isn't the real issue not the act that has already happened, but the impact of that act on all those who were touched? Isn't that what is still with us, still touching us, still affecting all our lives and all our relationships? Aren't those the issues that a justice system should investigate and come to some understanding of, so all are able to move in healthier directions?"

Aboriginal people from coast to coast tell me something else as well—that those understandings are contained within the very structure of their languages. The old people, for instance, constantly say things like "Our language is our law." Until recently, I had no idea what they meant. How could a language not only "say" things, but also "stand for" things? What did people mean when they said I would never gain an understanding of Aboriginal approaches to justice (or any other aspect of their life) until I gained some understanding of how different languages can lead us to different understandings about what life is and how it should be lived?

That is the topic of the next chapter. I acknowledge at the outset that I speak no Aboriginal languages. I have had the privilege, however, of being invited to listen in on prolonged discussions between Aboriginal people from different language groups as they discussed the differences between their languages and English. As it turned out, what they were exploring was the possibility that English (and other European languages) focus on trying to capture and express one aspect of reality, while Aboriginal languages commonly try to capture and express a very different aspect instead. I will do my best to honour those who invited me to join them by passing along what I *think* they were saying to each other.

I don't embark on this topic just because it is philosophically interesting. Instead, I have been satisfied that traditional perspectives on justice flow out of traditional understandings *that the languages themselves contain.* For that reason, they cannot be pushed off to one side in favour of other perspectives showing opposite understandings. As someone put it, if you can only "speak of" justice in one way, you cannot be expected to "do" justice in any other way.

CHAPTER 5

WATCH YOUR LANGUAGE

Sorry, Just Nouning Around …

In *Dancing with a Ghost,* I wrote about an Ojibway woman who made a presentation at a workshop on sexual abuse. She explained that she would tell her own story of abuse in Ojibway, rather than English, because it was a "softer" language, one that tried to stay away from labels like "the accused" and "the offender." Those kinds of words, she said, had a tendency to stigmatize people, to "freeze" them within a particular classification, making it more difficult for healing to occur.

At the time, I made the guess that this choice of staying away from labels was connected to an understanding that all of life is a process, that every person is seen as a "thing-which-is-becoming," as opposed to a "thing-which-is." Whenever we use labels like "the offender," we tend to deny that understanding of constant change.

I confess that I had no idea how big an issue I was flirting with at that time. In fact, many Aboriginal people seem to have thought that I knew much more than I did! Fortunately, there were many others who understood that I was just gnawing at the edges and needed a great deal of help. As a result, they have put a lot of effort into explaining how significant the language differences really are and how they can cause us to respond very differently to events that are common in our lives.

If I had to summarize all the twists and turns I've been guided through with respect to language over the last four years, they would fit into two short sentences, both of which feel a little "radical" as I write them. First, I never realized how "harsh" the English language is, or how judgmental and argumentative we become as we speak it. Second, I had no idea that people could—and do—live otherwise, without having to respond to everything around them in such combative and judgmental ways.

AS I LISTENED to Aboriginal people discussing their discomfort using English, I began to notice a number of things. For one thing, English has an extraordinary number of adjectives that are not so much descriptions *of* things, as they are conclusions *about* things. Think, for instance, of adjectives like "horrible," "uplifting," "disgusting," "inspiring," "delightful," "tedious" and so on. When you really look at them, you discover that they don't tell us much about things-in-themselves, but only about the judgments speakers have made about them—and want the rest of us to accept. The closer I looked, the more I saw that there was an important difference between these judgmental kinds of adjectives and the more neutral ones like "green," "fast," "painful," "thick" and so forth that try to describe, in value-free terms, what each of our five senses has perceived about aspects of the Creation.

But we don't just use judgmental adjectives. We have also created an almost endless supply of negative nouns and we regularly use them to describe each other: nouns like "thief," "coward," "offender," "weirdo," "deviant," "phoney," "malingerer," "pervert," "fat-head" and "moron," to name only a few. We also have a large number of positive nouns as well, like "saint," "hero," "saviour," "mentor" and "friend." We have, it seems, created a noun for all judgments. Few of them, however, tell us much about why they might (or might not) be deserved by the people we apply them to. Instead, all they really give us is the speaker's personal conclusion.

When I started to notice such things in speech, I became aware of something else as well: how seldom Aboriginal people expressed such judgments in their everyday conversations—even when speaking English. In fact, the expression of judgments seemed to be avoided, rather than expected. At the same time, there did not seem to be any loss of communication. Let me try to illustrate what I mean.

Imagine, if you will, two English-speaking people coming out of a movie. The first says "Boy, that was a *depressing* movie!" The second, says "Boy, was that an *inspiring* movie!" It is almost as if they believe the movie "is" something all by itself. As a result, it seems perfectly reasonable to argue about who has characterized it "correctly" and who has missed the mark. Sometimes they are more careful, as when one of them says "Boy, that movie was depressing *to me*," following which the other can say "That movie was inspiring to *me*." While they appear to acknowledge that they might have different opinions and that it is okay to "agree to disagree," there still seems to be some notion that the opinion of one must be more accurate than the opinion of the other

When I am with Aboriginal people, however, I keep hearing a different way of exchanging information. The first might say "Boy, I feel depressed after seeing that movie," following which the other laughs and says, "No kidding, I feel really *inspired* after seeing that movie!" After that they both chuckle about how differently they were touched. There is no suggestion of arguing over whose judgment is correct, for no judgments have been expressed. Instead, the reaction is couched in each person's emotional reaction, and the *expectation* is that they are *likely* to be very different from each other. It is a difference that becomes all-important when we come to look at healing, especially in cases of extreme victimization.

Speaking in that way, it seems to me, constantly declares an understanding that part of the richness of life rests in the fact that all human beings are likely to respond in unique and interesting ways to the same events, things and people. In fact, the greater the difference between our responses to something, the greater the *amusement* we should feel at being shown once again how unique we all are.

Once I started listening for that nonjudgmental and nonargumentative way of talking about things in the Aboriginal community, it seemed to be everywhere. People said, for instance: "Oh, I laughed so hard I hurt!" They did not say, "Oh, *he* was so funny!" which would invite someone else to say, "No, he wasn't!" They said, "I was so interested to hear those things," not "Oh, those *things* were so interesting!" I also often hear victims in healing circles say things like, "When he did those things, I felt so disgusted," instead of saying, "What he did to me *was* disgusting" or, worse still, "*He* is disgusting."

In other words, as we have seen in other contexts, great care seems to be taken not to label things, people or events in terms of personal responses to them or to argue against anyone else's views about them. Instead, the emphasis is on continually stating the opposite, that your reaction is nothing more than a *personal* reaction, one which may or may not be shared by others.

Looking back, I should have been quicker to see how widespread this careful way of everyday speaking really is. As I mentioned, even when people are at meetings where their opinions are invited, it is commonplace for speakers to say something like "These are only the thoughts that have come to me so far" or "I can only speak of my own way of seeing this." If people guard so carefully against suggesting that their opinion, even when it is sought, might contain more "truth" or "validity" than someone else's, why should I have expected any less care in everyday speech, where they are not directly invited at all!

To Noun, Noun, Noun Me ... Is to No, No, No Me ...

In my experience thus far, it seems that traditional people see our reliance on judgmental words as a very *limiting* way to know the world around us, and to deal with the people in it. On an intellectual level, we all know that someone who has justly been called a "thief" in one context of his life might justly deserve to be called a "philanthropist" in another. Similarly, a man who is properly called "brave and open" in one context can deserve to be called "secretive and cowardly" in another. Whether we are using judgmental adjectives ("foolhardy," "reckless," "methodical," "cautious," etc.) or judgmental nouns ("goon," "liar," "deadbeat," "coward" and so on), they are usually only accurate if they are applied to a few narrow *events* taken from a few select *moments* in an individual's total life. When we apply such labels to real people, however, they tend to stick. And when they stick, they cause us to start denying the complexity and wholeness of the human beings we are speaking of. At the same time, they cause us to minimize the possibility of change. I remember an Inuit man who complained that the worst thing the judge and Crown did when they came into his community was to call someone "bad." "You can't do that," he told us, "and expect them to be good!"

This limiting impact of judgmental words leapt out at me when I first read about the Family Group Conference involving the fourteen-year-old girl. When she came into that conference, she came as an "offender" in the eyes of everyone, especially the parents of the victim. Because of that simplistic, one-dimensional label, they approached her with only one feeling, anger. As the conference progressed, however, the barriers broke down between them, as did the usefulness and accuracy of that noun-label. By the end, as the article described it, she had become "a whole person" again, someone for whom anger was too simple a response. When they saw some of the other "sides" of her, their anger was joined by a wider range of feelings, including concern and care. I don't mean that the anger evaporated, just that it ceased to be the only response to complex issues surrounding a complex human being.

That FGC story really touched a nerve with me, as I suspect it will with most people involved in the criminal justice system on a daily basis. It made me recall the young man I called Carl and the horrendous abuse he suffered himself and imposed on others. If I think of Carl simply as an "offender," I want to do all kinds of nasty things to him. If I acknowledge the other sides of his short life, however, and approach him as the victim he also is, I want to give him comfort and help instead. So it becomes impossible for me to find any real use for either label, because focusing on only one aspect of his present state and past life would be foolish—and likely dangerous as well. The Carls of this world have taught me something: our tendency to stick simplistic labels on the people we deal with only gets in the way of thinking realistically about how we should respond to them.

And that's one of the reasons I shudder when I see headlines screaming, "Get Tougher on Those Offenders!" I don't know how to lock up and torture only the ugly "offender-parts" of people, while comforting the hurt parts, teaching the curious parts, nourishing the starved parts, unearthing the hidden parts, emboldening the cautious parts and inspiring the dreaming parts. I worry that whatever I do to the offender-part will make it harder still to touch and encourage all the others, much less restore balances between them. In people where the dangerous offender-part has grown so severely disconnected from the others that it is dominant, then we have no choice but to do whatever we can to keep them out of circulation. I worry, however, that we are too quick to let our offender labels blind us to all the other parts of most of the people brought to court, especially young people. Put simply, I worry that our simplistic, punitive responses to simplistic, judgmental labels lead us into blind canyons where we actually *contribute* to the development of those one-dimensional and dangerous people we are sworn to prosecute.

Is this part of the reason the Ojibway woman at the sexual abuse workshop chose to tell the story of her own abuse—and her abusers—in Ojibway, because it let her recount everything in ways that did not cause all those limits to appear? Would the fourteen-year-old girl in that Family Group Conference have been greeted initially with such hostility if she had come into it known by some term that was "softer" than "the offender"? Suppose, for instance, she had been called something like "the young girl who did that thing." Would people have had an easier time seeing the whole person right from the start? In short, do our judgmental words create hurdles we have to *overcome* before we can begin to deal effectively with complex realities?

That seems to be the case when we try to approach all the complex and interwoven issues of environmental pollution. Nouns like "pest," "waste" and "weed," for instance, make it harder for us to remember that each thing we name that way is involved in complex relationships with a multitude of other things, and that their unique contributions are essential to maintaining the health of the ecosystem as a whole. Until we overcome our conviction that we can deal with them as unimportant, unlinked and "discardable" things, a conviction that is buried right inside the names we have assigned to them, we are unlikely to begin treating them with the respect they deserve and that our own survival requires. In short, what we call them seems to be getting in the way of our knowledge of them, and this limits our capacities to respond to them in sophisticated and realistic ways.

The avoidance of labels like "right" or "wrong" also seems to be a central part of Navajo teaching. Clyde Kluckhohn, for example, had this to say in his article "The Philosophy of the Navajo Indians": "The Navajo never appeals to abstract morality or to adherence to divine principles. He stresses mainly the practical considerations: 'If you don't tell the truth, your fellows won't trust you and you'll shame your relatives. You'll never get along in the world that way.' Truth is never praised merely on the ground that it is 'good' in a purely abstract sense.... The Navajos do most definitely believe that acts have consequences, but the nature of the consequences is not wrapped up in any intrinsic 'rightness' or 'wrongness' of the act itself."

English speakers, on the other hand, seem to feel an obligation to come to judgments about things and to express them at every available opportunity. With many Aboriginal people there seems to be an opposite obligation—where coming to judgmental conclusions is seen as either wrong or, as I now suspect, largely a waste of time. Further, *announcing* such conclusions at every opportunity seems to be regarded as a display of immaturity, if not arrogance.

I want to say something here, something that people will probably have to experience to understand fully. When I am submerged for some time in a group of Aboriginal people, knowing that I am not *expected* to judge everything that everybody says or does (much less declare my judgments as quickly as I can come to them!), it's as if a huge weight lifts off my shoulders. It's a weight I didn't know I was carrying until recently, the weight of this obligation to form and express opinions at all times and about almost everything. I do know, however, that when I'm in places where the opposite obligation applies, I find myself relaxing, simply enjoying the wide range of thought and opinion expressed. I even love the opinions and suggestions that my English brain would judge "loony" if I allowed it to indulge its addiction to name calling. Perhaps it's because I know that other opinions or suggestions are not offered as challenges or threats to my own, but simply offered. Perhaps it's because there's no obligation even to respond to them, much less fight back.

I'm not sure I understand it yet, but I do know one thing: everything seems much less *personal* this way, much less arrogant, much less antagonistic. It's almost as if the strict rules prohibiting *personal* attacks in the course of proper academic debate have been carried over—or even expanded—into each person's private life as well. At the same time, the competitive aspects of academic debate also seem to be prohibited. I feel much freer to "think out loud" in such a group, to push my own speculations a little harder, to follow some tangents a little further. Because I know they will be received as contributions, not weighed for judgment, attack and possible rejection, I can actually be more *honest* about them as well. In a connected way, it becomes much easier to hear what others are trying to say, because you are no longer preoccupied with trying to assess whether they are attacking or supporting you, and how you'll "have to" respond to them. The whole issue of attacks and counterattacks, judgments and defences, seems repugnant to the traditional Aboriginal ideal of civilized and respectful discussion.

These sorts of differences were underlined in an article by Susan Urmston Philips of the University of Arizona entitled "Some Sources of Cultural Variability in the Regulation of Talk." In it, she looks at how conversations are "structured" among Aboriginal people at the Warm Springs Reservation in central Oregon. A great deal of what she described seemed familiar to me. In one section, she wrote about public meetings where questions about certain issues are asked and about how those questions are handled:

> For Anglos, answers to questions are almost obligatory, even if they take the form of "I can't answer right now," or a brief shake of the head.... With questions, the speaker assumes that he will get a reply. That this is not the case with Warm

Springs Indians was pointed out to me by an Indian from another Reservation who had married into the Warm Springs Reservation. He observed wryly that it is often difficult to get an answer out of "these old people" (and I should add that the phrase "old people" has the connotation of respect). And he told me an anecdote about posing a question that got answered a week after it was asked.

In other words, answers to questions are not obligatory. Absence of answer merely means the floor is open, or continues to belong to the questioner. This does not mean, however, that the question will not be answered later. Nor does it mean that it ought not to be raised again, since the questioner might reasonably assume his audience has had time to think about it.

Ms. Philips goes on to mention a particular incident where a woman raised four issues during a meeting, but no one responded to them immediately. Instead, over the course of the next hour (in what she refers to as "sequencing"), responses and partial responses emerged in bits and pieces, from a number of different speakers—often in the course of discussing other topics. Ms. Philips described it this way: "[I]n all of this, neither the first woman nor those who responded to her ever spoke *directly* to one another...; the first woman never *called for* a response to her statements; and the 'responses'... were widely separated from the speeches to which they were a response.... It may be worth noting that with this approach to sequencing, *conflict between persons can be muted or obscured.*" (emphasis added)

And that's exactly how I feel now that I have grown accustomed to (and aware of) some of the traditional "rules" of conversation amongst Aboriginal people—comparatively free of the potential for conflict and antagonism. By contrast, when I return to the non-Aboriginal world, I keep asking myself why everyone seems to be arguing about everything. The contrast makes me constantly wonder why we can't seem to just enjoy life, with all its magical diversity, without arguing endlessly about what to call it.

Crossing over into the Verb Lane ...

Now, as promised, I want to move away from my observations about Aboriginal people speaking English and turn to Aboriginal languages themselves. After all, it is here that all the differences must really begin.

And the biggest difference? I've given a clue with all my talk about staying away from judgmental nouns and the judgmental adjectives that modify them. Let me quote a friend and teacher, a man who has invested enormous time and spirit in my education. His name is Sákéj (pronounced "Saw-gage") Henderson, a Chicksaw-Cherokee by birth, and he said this about the Mi'kmaq language: "... when you're speaking Mi'kmaq, you can go all day long *without saying a single noun*. My eyes can see nouns ... That's what my eyes are supposed to do, see nouns, and obstacles and tracks and trails. But that's not what the function of the language is. It's not to become another pair of eyes. It's supposed to be speaking to the ear and to the heart ..." (emphasis added).

Is this relative absence of nouns only a characteristic of Mi'kmaq? Apparently not. Another special friend and teacher, Danny Moonhawk Alford, a professor of linguistics from the University of California at Hayward and a fluent Cheyenne speaker, had this to say to an international religious symposium in Ottawa:

How many of you out there at first assumed that "Dances" in the film title *Dances with Wolves* was a plural noun, like "the dances with wolves"? And then you realized at some point that it was an agent-less verb phrase instead, talking about the dancing. It's like He-Who-Dances-with-Wolves, except these languages don't need the He-Who. It was the same with another character in the same movie, "Stands with Fist." These phrases are complete sentences in their own language, but most often when we turn them into names we turn them also into nouns, leaving behind and ignoring the structural meaning it also had in the other language.

Now I don't want to give the wrong impression: Native American languages generally CAN have nouns.... The major differences to be found are in their frequency and in the way nouns are constructed in Native America. They usually start from a root—neither a noun or a verb or anything else, just a root—and then you add things to it to make it into a verb, and then you have to add some *other* things to make it into a noun, maybe take some verb parts away. *But it seldom becomes a static noun, and its speakers are not cast adrift of its dynamic, verbal root.*" (emphasis added)

But how can you have a language that lets you go all day without speaking a single noun? What do you do when you want to talk about all those "things-out-there" that we deal with every day? What does it mean to say that the focus of the language is on the dancing, not the dancers? Does this relative absence of nouns in Aboriginal languages explain the reluctance to use *judgmental* nouns when English is spoken?

I must repeat my earlier confession: I speak no Aboriginal languages myself. For that reason, I will rely completely on the descriptions and explanations provided by my Aboriginal friends. I also confess that their explanations have stretched my imagination further than I ever thought possible. In fact, some would say that I have come back positively warped! In that regard, I am pleased to repeat something said by a leading American legal scholar, Oliver Wendell Holmes: "A mind that is stretched to a new idea never returns to its original dimensions."

So let's go for it.

Where Nouns Are Verb-boten ...

I would like to introduce some of the people I will be quoting from, people who have volunteered to be my teachers on these cross-language issues, and so much else as well. If anything I say makes sense, give them the credit; if anything I say is out to lunch, blame it on my inability to understand them!

I met most of them for the first time in the fall of 1991, when I was invited to be a presenter at a week-long series of workshops on Aboriginal justice at Banff, Alberta. The host was Leroy Little Bear, whom I mentioned earlier. A Blackfoot lawyer from southern Alberta, Leroy is now head of the Native Studies Department at the University of Lethbridge. He was also a member of the Alberta Task Force on Aboriginal People and the Criminal Justice System.

A second presenter was Leroy's close friend, Sákéj Henderson, whom I have just mentioned. Sákéj has law degrees from Stanford and Harvard and is now director of the Native Law Centre at the University of Saskatchewan. They and their wives, Amethyst First Rider (Blackfoot from southern Alberta) and Marie Battiste (Mi'kmaq from Cape Breton Island), have opened their homes, hearts and histories to me on many occasions since then. Leroy's wife Amethyst has recently gained a Masters in Dramatic Arts, focusing on Aboriginal storytelling, and Sákéj's wife Marie is an associate professor in the Indian and Northern Education Program at the University of Saskatchewan, with a Ph.D. from Stanford University.

One evening after the workshop sessions, Leroy mentioned that he, Sákéj and some others had been having "conversations" about some things, and that I was free to join them over a cup of tea in the third-floor common room if I wished. I followed along, expecting nothing more than a pleasant evening of chatter.

Leroy began by introducing some other people. One was Dr. David Peat, a physicist from Ottawa. David was once a coworker with an English physicist, Dr. David Bohm (now deceased), who had in turn been a coworker with Albert Einstein. Bohm was also a significant force behind the original start-up of these "conversations." I learned as well that they were a little more formal than I had thought, for they were sponsored by the Fetzer Institute of Kalamazoo, Michigan. They even had a title: "Dialogues between Western and Aboriginal Scientists." The first had taken place in Kalamazoo in 1992, with David Bohm in attendance, and the second would follow at Banff as soon as the justice workshops were completed.

Some of the other participants included Danny Moonhawk Alford, whom I mentioned earlier; Sam Kounosu, a physicist from Alberta; Rose Sergeant, a physicist from Berkeley, California; and Stan Knowlton, a Blackfoot intent on restoring knowledge of his people's huge and mysterious medicine wheels which still dot the landscape of southern Alberta. Over the last several years, three more Dialogues have been held, where I have come to hear from such people as Tobasonikwut Peter Kinew, an Ojibway of the Midewewin Lodge; Robert Yazzie, Chief Justice of the Navajo Nation; and Russel Barsh, also of the Native Studies Department of the University of Lethbridge. Each Dialogue is spread over three days and involves everyone taking their turns contributing to the issues presented by Leroy.

I will never forget how that first "informal" evening began. Leroy made the introductions, then said something like this (although I don't remember half the puns he included):

In our last Dialogue, you will recall that we started to examine the movement in Western physics away from Particle Theory towards an emerging new paradigm, one which some have called Wave Theory. At the same time, we started to speak about the two kinds of languages, English with all of its nouns, and many of the Aboriginal languages with their emphasis on verbs instead. You will recall that we were asking ourselves if those language differences could be related in some way to the differences between Particle Theory and Wave Theory. To prevent anyone taking ownership of those discussions, we all signed Wave-er Agreements, Particular-ly the physicists. No doubt they were all Patent-ly unenforceable, but we signed them anyway. At the same time, we began to speak of other things as well. For instance, we spoke of the similarities between the "new" doctrine which physicists are calling Chaos Theory, and the figure of the Trickster, which has been important in many aboriginal traditions for, it seems like, ions. And we wondered what Albert Ion-stein would have thought about that.

I remember (apart from the laughter!) looking around that little common room at all the other faces, wondering if they had any better idea than I did what Leroy was talking about. As the evening progressed, I was left with one unforgettable impression: while I could make very little sense of what was being said by either the physicists or the Aboriginal people, they seemed to have no difficulty at all communicating with each other! It was a humbling experience—but an exciting one at the same time. It was also the first time I was introduced to the sophistication of Aboriginal languages and the sense of universe that has shaped them.

While I have neither the space nor the skills to detail the lengthy conversations that took place at the Dialogues, there is one thing I can report: there seemed to be a startling correspondence between Einstein's famous $E=MC^2$ description of the universe and a great many teachings of Aboriginal peoples. I'll do what I can to summarize what I heard.

In both visions, all existence is seen as energy—or spirit—manifesting itself through matter by organizing and reorganizing that matter in ever-changing (but patterned) ways. It is, for instance, this energy or force that moves through molecules of water and shapes them all into waves. While the particular molecules of water go mostly up and down, the wave shapes travel hundreds of miles across vast oceans. According to Aboriginal perspectives, I gather that the particular shapes assumed by matter at any particular point in time are far less important than the energy pattetns causing those shapes to change. As Sákéj Henderson describes it in his yet-to-be-published book *Algonquian Spirituality: Balancing the Opposites:* "Indigenous people view reality as eternal, but in a continuous state of transformation.... It is consistent with the scientific view that all matter can be seen as energy, shaping itself to particular patterns. The Mi'kmaq language affirms this view of the universe, building verb phrases with hundreds of prefixes and suffixes to choose from, to express the panorama. The use of verbs rather than nouny subjects and objects is important; *it means that there are very few fixed and rigid objects in the Mi'kmaq world-view. What they see is the great flux, eternal transformation, and an interconnected order of time, space and events.* With this fluidity of verb phrases, every speaker can create new vocabulary "on the fly," custom-tailored to meet the experience of the moment, to express the very finest nuances of meaning." (emphasis added)

Languages that don't have fixed lists of nouns to capture all those "things-out-there"? Languages in which people are expected to develop the skills to create their own vocabulary "on the fly"? How many times have judges and lawyers watched an interpreter struggle to express an English word in an Aboriginal language and concluded that because they didn't "know" the Aboriginal equivalent, they were not good enough?

An example may help illustrate the way things are "named" in Aboriginal languages. At the 1993 Dialogues, Sákéj Henderson spoke of how the Mi'kmaq language deals with trees. They are "called" by the sounds that are made as the wind goes through their branches, in the autumn, during a special period just before dusk. In short, they are known and talked about in terms of how they interact with certain aspects of their surroundings—and in terms of how the individual observer perceives them. In a sense, it is a very "interactive" naming, with room for individual creation.

As we saw in connection with Aboriginal approaches to science, the focus seems to be less on the *characteristics* of things than on the *relationships between* things. One of the best examples of this different focus came when Sákéj Henderson dealt with the issue of referring to things by the characteristic of their gender: "No, we don't have any gender. It's a relationship.... The woman who cares for your heart—that's your wife. Your daughters are the ones who enrich your heart. Your sons are the ones that test your heart!"

The (relative!) absence of noun-like words, when put together with the absence of gender distinctions, leads to something that many non-Aboriginal people remain unaware of: the absence of personal *pro*-nouns based on gender (like "he," "she" or "it") in many Aboriginal languages. Because they don't exist there, searching for the correct ones often seems an artificial and unreasonable exercise. As a result, Aboriginal people are often as careless about getting them right as I am when I'm speaking (garbled) French and trying to remember whether a noun has "le" or "la" in front of it.

Unfortunately for Aboriginal people, however, getting those pronouns right can often be critical. I remember, for instance, an Ojibway woman in a trial giving evidence about how she had been raped. She began by explaining that she and her assailant had been going down a deserted path alone. When I asked her what happened next, she answered, "*She* grabbed me from behind and threw me to the ground, and started ripping my clothes off." The judge stopped everything immediately. As best I recall, what he said went something like this: "Now just wait a minute, young lady! You told us there was only you and the accused, on that path. And now you're talking about some *woman* grabbing you! Where did *she* come from? How am I going to believe *anything* you say!"

On the more humorous side, my Aboriginal friends appear heartily amused by the frenzied Western debate over whether God is a "He" or a "She"!

It should be noted, however, that Algonkian languages contain a constant division that is *not* part of Western thought: the division between animate (or breathing) and inanimate (non-breathing) things. Just as the French articles "le" and "la" describe everything by gender, so Algonkian languages describe everything in animate or inanimate terms. Unlike our divisions, however, the same "thing," I gather, can be first one and then the other, then returned again. In my superficial understanding, it depends partly on how the speaker relates to it. A pipestone, for instance, can move from inanimate to animate, depending on the degree to which the speaker is recognizing—and creating—its essential spirit at that moment of its existence.

The Language of the Heart

I'd like to go back to that earlier quotation from Sákéj Henderson, the one where he said that the function of language was not to become another pair of eyes, but was to "speak to the ear, and speak to the heart." What did he mean by this? I have my own interpretation, although it is difficult to express. It involves thinking about music and what we find significant about music. It is not the individual notes or sounds that appeal to us, as much as it is the way they all blend together in their changing rhythms, patterns and (to borrow a musical term) "movements." What if we took that same focus and applied it to the rest of our experiences, looking for the shifts, patterns, movements and cadences exhibited by all the things that surround us every day? What if that is what we wanted to describe when we spoke of them to others? Is that what the Inuit woman's grandfather was teaching when he took her to the shores of Hudson Bay and had her look for the five waves? And if those were the dynamics her eyes were to examine, are they also the dynamics her language has been shaped to capture?

When in English we call someone, for instance, an "offender," we use a noun to represent an unchanging state. To what extent do we do similar things with all the rest of our nouns, creating a world that appears to be full of static objects without connection to each other?

In English, for instance, we can say, "The tree died," and it seems to make sense. But would it be possible to speak about that event in a way that acknowledges that what we really have is just a conversion of matter into a different form and to other uses, with its essential energy—or spirit—remaining undiminished? Further, what if all of Creation was understood to participate in this constant transformation, whether it was a mosquito turning into frog food two days into its four-day lifespan or a cliff becoming a sand beach over eons? Our way of speaking *disconnects* segments of the transformation process, freezes them with labels like "tree," admires them as long as they stay within that label, then laments their "death" as soon as they pass on to a different form. In reality the only death has been of the noun-shape we created ourselves.

The differences between Aboriginal and non-Aboriginal understandings can be expressed in terms of Einstein's famous equation,

$E=MC^2$. It appears that the English language, with all its nouns, focuses primarily on the *mass* side, on all the "things-out-there," on the collection of water molecules sitting in the shape of a wave. The spotlight of Aboriginal languages, on the other hand, shines primarily on the *energy* side of Einstein's equation, on all the "patterns-and-changes" that exist between and among things-out-there. These are the forces that have not only built the wave-shape we presently see, but are also already shaping different water molecules into new forms for the next moment, and the next after that.

During the Dialogues, it was this Aboriginal focus on the energy side that seemed to catch the physicists by surprise, because that was the very realm they were wrestling with. It was also the realm for which they had found English so poorly suited. While English was rich in words representing the temporary shapes and formations perceived by the senses at particular instants, Aboriginal languages were richer in words representing the energy, forces and spirit that created all those shapes and formations in the first place.

My Aboriginal friends talk a great deal about what it's like to have to use English all day, and they generally describe it as a strain. If we truly recognized that we occupy a universe of constantly transforming things, people and relationships, they suggest, then we would have no choice but to discard our heavy reliance on nouns to capture and describe it. Sákéj seemed to be expressing something like that when he told us: "[In] the Sun Dance, the one thing they always instruct is never, when you get into the Sun Dance the last day, never say a word in English, or think an English thought. People who speak English and enter this realm come back deranged. So when you enter this realm, whatever you do, don't speak nouns. *Don't start looking at the objects! Look for the forces* that contain the Nakota part" (emphasis added). As Bay-be-mi-say-si, the whirlwind, said to Waynaboozhoo, the spirit of the Anishnaabe, "I am brother to the Gee-zhee-ba-sun (tornado), I am brother to the waterspout of the oceans and seas, their power is my power and my power is theirs." The focus on power, and the statement that they all shared the same power, was far more important than I had originally understood.

Whenever I came across passages like this, I found myself thinking of Aboriginal languages as poetic languages, languages that relied heavily on metaphor, where a description of one thing stands as a description of many others. The more I come to explore the language issue, however, the more I think the idea of metaphor fails to capture what's really going on. Instead, it is my present guess that those languages are really describing reality at another level altogether, an energy or spirit level, where many things can be understood to actually *be* the same. A whirlwind is not "like" a tornado at this level of description; it *actually* is one.

I encountered (I think!) an interesting illustration of this "looking for the forces" in a recent conversation with some Aboriginal people from northern Manitoba. We were talking about the plight of their younger generation, discussing possible reasons for the excessive rates of suicide, substance abuse and violent behaviour. One of them mentioned that an elder had volunteered his own explanation: in his view, the present problems could be traced to the fact that mothers were no longer breast feeding their babies. For that reason, the babies did not grow up with the sound of her heartbeat. I asked if this had been said in English or Cree, and he replied, "Cree." Taking a gamble on my own understanding of what might actually have been expressed in the Cree, I said, "So everybody knew he was talking about much more than breast feeding." The simple, almost off-hand, reply was "Of course."

I'll explain what I meant. It has to do with the way whirlwinds, tornados and dust devils can be understood as being, at their most basic levels, the same thing. I knew, for instance, that references to "heartbeat" refer to much more than the human heartbeat. Mother

Earth too, because she lives, has a heartbeat—one that comes through the drum. And at the most basic level, such a heartbeat flows through all of us, giving us all the same life. We are all connected by that heartbeat, pulsing along in a common life with it. Because of that we are never truly alone, but always connected, through Mother Earth. Unfortunately, too many people come to the conclusion that they are alone and unconnected, that they don't matter, that they have no role in anything larger than themselves, no significance beyond themselves. If they come to conclusions like this, they live desperate, lonely lives and often fall into self-abuse and the abuse of others.

It was my guess, then, that when the elder talked about children not growing up with the sound of the heartbeat, everyone understood him to be talking about what animates all heartbeats. It was not, strictly speaking, a metaphor, but a way to describe reality at a level of life, of animation, of spirit, where everything *is* the same, coming out of the same energies and manifesting identical patterns.

It was the same with the Inuit woman who told me about the five waves. I had just finished describing the young man I called Carl, and my growing realization that I could not deal with him effectively until I understood all the traumas that had affected him, his family, his community and his people. Without hesitation or introduction, she told me her grandfather's teachings about the waves. It was clear that she felt *all* of Creation, whether Carl's plight or the surface of Hudson Bay, had to be examined, understood and spoken of in terms that paid primary attention to their energies, forces and patterns, not particles, shapes or sizes. At that fundamental level, it is the similarities, rather than the differences, that are most striking—and that language should attempt to capture.

The more I explore these issues, the more I understand that the Ojibway woman's observation about her language having a "softer" way to describe people stood for much more than I was able to grasp at the time. It stood for a language that not only seems to have different *words* for things, but also seems to express a fundamentally different understanding of what is *important* about things: their constant reformation and change as the energy and spirit side of life's equation ripples through them, every instant of every day. In that sense, she told me something similar to what that Inuit woman told me, that Hudson Bay is far more than its molecules of water.

Every time I go back to the things that Sákéj Henderson, Leroy Little Bear, Danny Moonhawk Alford and others have expressed, another layer opens up. For instance, Aboriginal languages seem uniquely able to offer almost limitless opportunities for, and enjoyment of, double meanings. After all, once the dynamics or patterns common to things have been expressed, modifications still need to be made to take the listener's attention to the particular thing being mentioned. If those particulars are not accurate enough, one thing can be "called" in almost the same way as another. Pun-like double meanings, intentional or otherwise, are thus both common and treasured. Double meanings also serve a more serious purpose, for they reinforce the conviction that everything is in the process of transformation.

It was after being exposed to such descriptions of the vitality of Aboriginal languages that I began to understand how traumatic it must have been for the children when they were forbidden to speak their languages at the residential schools. In that connection, let me pass along a comment made in 1995 by one Ojibway woman from northwestern Ontario during the course of community justice discussion when, as often happens, she turned her attention to language. "Boarding school was supposed to be a place where you forgot everything about being Anishinabe. And our language too. But I said, 'I'm going to talk to myself'—and that's what I did, under my covers—talked to myself in Anishinabe. If we were caught, the nuns would make us stand in a corner and repeat over and over, 'I won't speak my language.'"

Replacing the Good, the Bad and the Ugly

In earlier pages, I spent a great deal of time talking about Aboriginal people's reluctance to use judgmental English words like "good" and "bad." That does not mean, however, that there is no place for expressing preferences. In fact, the opposite is true, for preference is pronounced, and moral teaching of primary importance. As we have seen in so many other contexts, however, when those preferences are expressed, the focus is not on "things" but on processes; not on people but on relationships.

I obtained a glimpse of how this is done in the article by Bluehouse and Zion I mentioned back in Chapter 1—"The Navajo Justice and Harmony Ceremony." At one point Bluehouse and Zion speak of the Peacemaker as he or she looks at, and listens to, each party to a dispute, then turns from the parties as individuals to consider the kind of relationship that exists between them. The Peacemaker does not ask if it is "good" or "bad," given the absolute nature of those declarations. Instead, "The Peacemaker wonders, 'Is it *hashhkeeji* (moving towards disharmony) or is it *hozhooji* (moving towards harmony)?'" The emphasis, then, is still on the movement that all things demonstrate, on the energy side of Einstein's equation. In a sense, value judgments thus appear to be relative things, not absolutes, applied to the *direction* in which things appear to be moving—towards or away from harmony.

I began this book by quoting from a justice proposal prepared for the Ontario Government by the Oji-Cree Sandy Lake First Nation. It bears repeating in this context: "Probably one of the most serious gaps in the system is the different perception of

wrongdoing and how to best treat it. In the non-Indian community, committing a crime seems to mean that the individual is a *bad
person* and therefore must be punished.... The Indian communities
view a wrongdoing as a misbehaviour which requires teaching or
an illness which requires healing" (emphasis added). Once again we
can see an emphasis on the belief that people are not forever one
thing or another, but that they can and do change. It is not just a
hopeful, liberal conviction, but a necessary reflection of a core
conviction about life. Life is change. In the same way, people are
change, and to imagine the opposite is to deny life.

As luck would have it, I ran across a quotation in the February 17,
1995 issue of the *Globe and Mail* which expresses the opposite,
static and limiting view of humanity better than anything I could
have dreamed up myself. It is a quotation attributed to a British
clergyman, Charles Caleb Colton, who lived between 1780 and
1832: "He that is good will infallibly become better, and he that is
bad will certainly become worse; for vice, virtue and time are the
three things that never stand still." While clergyman Colton does
appear to acknowledge room for movement in his universe, there
doesn't seem to be much room for changing the *direction* of that
movement. Once he arrives at his judgment about what to call you,
that's who you stay, forever!

I shake my head every time I remind myself that it was during
the decades of clergyman Colton's ministry that a great many of his
colleagues, some of whom must have shared similar convictions,
came to Canada and began their work with Aboriginal people. In
this particular respect, could two visions of the universe have been
more opposed? I can't help but see him running about the country-
side imposing all his nouns on everything in sight, dividing the
world up into two static camps of absolute opposites—the good
camp and the evil camp. How must he have been seen by all his
Aboriginal contemporaries as they glided back and forth along the

rivers, contemplating the infinite numbers of ways in which all the forces surrounding them were coming together beneath and around them, wondering how they could best fit in with and "ride" what they could not alter, even had they wished! I can see the billing now: "The Great Mystery Meets the Great Certainty!"

I also recall something Sákéj Henderson said—a statement clergyman Colton would probably have taken as clear evidence of pagan depravity: "For some reason, English-speakers seem to have chosen to live under the rule of King Noun. We Aboriginal people, on the other hand, would rather think of ourselves as being in bed with Queen Verb."

And that brings up another difference that seems to be little known, though it is of critical importance. It has to do with whether we see ourselves as a living part of our surroundings, or distinct and separate from them. It has to do with the choice between what Danny Moonhawk Alford called "surfing the flux" or trying to live within the "illusion" of stability. It has to do with whether you acknowledge and learn to ride the waves converging around you at every moment of every day or whether you fight to try to keep them all at a safe distance.

Albert and the Fish Heads vs the Plate Glass Window

I mentioned the figure of the Trickster which is so important in the storytelling of many Aboriginal peoples. Here is how Sákéj described another of the Trickster's roles during the 1992 Dialogues in Kalamazoo, Michigan: "What people miss about Trickster stories is that they're talking about a process of flux. They're talking about how things change. They change quickly and dramatically. The Trickster may have outrageous behaviour and then change again. We're teaching our children to have tolerance for change; to understand it, not to fight it."

I've struggled for some time to find a way to express how I perceive the difference between my English-speaking world and the world my Aboriginal friends tell me is given to them by their languages. I have this sense that if you decide that the first reality is constant change, if you discard your belief in the usefulness of judgmental absolutes like "good" and "bad" and choose to speak in terms of relative movement like "towards harmony" instead, then a lot of other things change as well. You start to sit in a room differently, in a car differently, everywhere differently. To end this chapter, I'll try out the metaphor I've found most useful so far. It ties together Danny Moonhawk Alford's "surfing the flux" image, the five waves, the horror of Carl's life thus far—all those things. I have used portions of it before. Every time I go into it, however, I bring back more out of it.

It has to do with the difference between standing behind the triple-pane window of your cliffside mansion and watching the sun go down over a quieting ocean—and watching instead the first beginnings of a sunrise over that same ocean, but from flat on your belly on a wet surfboard three hundred miles out from shore, as the ocean beneath you awakens.

In the cliffside mansion, there is a conviction of separation, stability and control. On the surfboard, there is the conviction of intimate and inescapable exposure to unfathomable powers which, while they might let you ride them, will never let you gain control over them. If you are alone on a surfboard as the ocean starts to stir, there is no way to know what it will bring you that day. The only true certainties are that you cannot change those waves—only the way you ride them—and that your riding will depend on how much you can accommodate yourself to *their* forces.

Curiously, each wave that comes at you—that will determine your future—comes at you from behind. In that sense, the limits of your future, of where you might come to travel over the course of the day, have been building out of your vision in the wide ocean *behind you,* and way back in time. You do not face your future. Instead, you face your past—the waves that have already passed you by. Your future is out behind you, where it's most difficult to see.

In fact, it's useless to speak of "seeing" your future at all. Instead, you have to feel it with all your other senses as it emerges beneath you. That being so, it is impossible to really predict, with any accuracy, how the new waves will show themselves under you. You can only try to open yourself to their dynamics as they emerge to your senses, to "feel" them as they appear, to make millions of minute and flowing adjustments to them, to constantly harmonize yourself with their forces to the greatest degree possible. Then, surprisingly, you can draw astounding speed from them. If you can find and maintain the precise intersection between all the forces, their combination is yours for the riding.

In the course of that riding, something changes: you seem to stop paying attention to *separate* things like the surfboard, your toes and arms, the water, the wind and so on. Instead, your consciousness of all those things is a consciousness of their power, of how they are "shaping-all-together" and of how they are (or are not!) moving in accommodating and expanding ways. If that accommodation is lost, however, if suddenly a power shift is not anticipated accurately, then the whole balance of things comes suddenly undone and all those separate things come, quite literally, crashing back again—the surfboard, the water, your own limbs and lungs and skull—in an instant display of rampant *disharmony*!

There are other aspects to this wave image as well. The wave that is *about* to emerge beneath your feet is, in a very real sense, already there, because all the forces that will transform the molecules into that wave are already there, already going in that direction. You only need to train yourself to focus on emergence, rather than on what has already emerged. This anticipation, this "moving-towards" what is already there in its energy but has not yet appeared in its mass, becomes the essential skill.

The odd fact, then, is that the surfer does not live first and foremost in a physical realm, but in another one—a realm of anticipating whatever is "about-to-emerge." Only by dwelling primarily in that realm can he or she begin to move towards the postures that will successfully accommodate what has not yet revealed itself but is unquestionably forming all around him or her.

This focus on things-emerging and relationships-changing goes far beyond the events of one particular day, week or year. The search for patterns extends far into the future and also looks at patterns that have "emerged" or "manifested" way back in time. Within the traditional understanding, there are almost incomprehensibly large waves undulating beneath the tiny ones we surf on every day, and these too—or perhaps especially—demand our attention. Think of Carl, and his desperate loss of self, and look all the way back to the first fur trader pressing for a decision on the spot and so beginning generations of insult and injury to every definition of a valuable Aboriginal self. Think too of the Ojibway obligation to look seven generations into the future before making major decisions involving change. And when you wonder about this attention to patterns, think as well of the following quotation from someone by the name of Rolling Thunder, who remains unknown to me. The words were given to me in North Bay by an Ojibway woman who never told me her name:

As long as ten years ago, I could not talk to you about any spiritual things regarding the American Indians, because after the conquest of this continent those things were hidden. We go by signs in the times, and they change as we go along. The pattern of life changes, and we were shown about six years ago that the time had come when we could travel and mix with white people, and we would find people in different places with good hearts, and we could talk with them.

The problem is that when we speak out of such different understandings of what is *important* about reality, it's so hard for us to really *hear* each other!

Just in case anyone thinks that by reading this book, they have achieved a significant level of understanding about traditional perspectives, I offer a warning: I have succeeded only in learning how little I know. As proof, let me return to the book by Ruth Beebe Hill I mentioned earlier—*Hanta Yo*. Hill suggests that neither the words nor the concepts of "waste," "weed" "or "pest" formed part of the traditional Lakota understanding of reality. Let me now give the full quotation, and the full list of words and concepts that she tells us were never a part of that traditional world-view: "Admit, assume, because, believe, could, doubt, end, expect, faith, forger, forgive, guilt, how, it, mercy, promise, should, sorry, storm, them, us, waste, we, weed—neither these words nor the conceptions for which they stand appear in this book; they are the whiteman's import to the New World, the newcomer's contribution to the vocabulary of the man he called the Indian. Truly, the parent Indian families possessed neither these terms nor their equivalents."

Understanding a universe in which those concepts do not play a role—much less the central role that Western society has given them—is likely an impossible task for English speakers like me. I am not helped by the fact that I spend so much of each year in cities, buildings and cars, disconnected from the patterns, changes and cycles of the natural order and so increasingly remote from all of their lessons.

And what is the fate of languages that depict so differently who and "how" we are? Will they disappear in favour of European languages that make us feel protected and in control, but at the same time seem to leave us with a sense of being alone and unconnected? Here is part of an essay written in 1993 by Sasheen Gould, aged seventeen, of the Eskasoni First Nation on Cape Breton Island:

> As a Mi'kmaq, I was born into a network of relationships and responsibilities. I am taught that these are to be the utmost priorities in my life. These include my family, my friends, my community and my nation. The largest of my responsibilities rests in my language. It is through my language that my worldview is transmitted and brought to the attention of whomever I communicate with. If it was not for the survival of the Mi'kmaq language, all of our rich cultures and traditions would have been lost.

Courses in traditional Mi'kmaq spirituality are now standard in Eskasoni schools. The Mi'kmaq people are also hard at work devising ways in which the "normal" curriculum can be taught in the Mi'kmaq language. The same vision is spreading across the country, and I am glad this is so. I say that not only for the sake of reviving Aboriginal health and esteem. I am also glad for myself, and for the future of my own people and their thought. After Albert Ion-stein crawled right down through the atom and came out the other side, he saw things about the universe that his (and my) language had never captured. They led him, and many others who travelled that astrophysical road after him, into a place where they too sensed the ultimate unknowability of a somehow-unified Creation—a place where the most appropriate English words sounded strange coming from their lips, because they were words like "awe" and "majesty."

Perhaps it will be the Aboriginal people who will help the rest of us catch some of the glimpses that Albert and his colleagues have found. Perhaps it will be Aboriginal people who will lead us back out of some of the noun-sense (like that, Leroy?) that seems to have stolen so much of our hearts and spirits away. And perhaps then we too can share a portion of the understanding expressed in 1995 by another Ojibway woman from northwestern Ontario when she said, sounding so much like old Albert: "Everything the people used to do was with reverence. There was no waste. They never threw anything away—like today. The fish heads, bones, all of that gives us what we as Anishinabeg need. Everything of the Creator's has a purpose. *When we throw part of the fish away, we are throwing part of ourselves away.*"

CHAPTER 6

THE FIRST STEP
TO RECONNECTION

I have spoken at length about the way Aboriginal languages emphasize Creation's complex interconnectivity and constant change. In the following three chapters I want to explore how such visions of Creation have given unique shape to Aboriginal processes for dealing with life's problems—often determining who must be involved, the ways in which they should (and should not!) be brought together, and the kinds of relief and assistance they might expect to gain.

Getting on the Right Planes ...

There is no question that those visions, and the processes they inspired, have been weakened since 1492, but they have not disappeared. In fact, they are making an impressive comeback across the country, especially where traditional languages have survived.

I regret that I cannot take each of you into the sweat-lodges, the healing circles, the ceremonies and the other emotionally charged, spiritually loaded experiences that have formed such a major part of my own learning. There is wisdom in the belief that things must be learned on many planes if they are to be truly learned at all, that we must involve our emotional, physical and spiritual dimensions as well as the mental one if we are to gain any real understanding of things. I have only these words, however, and this page, and they reach out primarily to the intellectual dimension alone.

In my own case, I thought I "understood" what the counsellors were doing at Hollow Water after talking to them on the phone, hearing their public presentations and reading all their papers. How wrong I was! Until I felt Hollow Water, and until the power, dignity and love of Hollow Water lifted me, I understood only surface things. Just as you cannot "know" what snow skiing is by reading descriptions, seeing snapshots, watching movies or even studying skiers from the bottom of the hill, so you cannot "know" Hollow Water unless you lose yourself (or at least your analytical, mental self!) within the experience itself. It is the same with almost all healing approaches I have been exposed to. My real hope in writing these pages is that many of you will be encouraged to head out on your own explorations, for Aboriginal capacities for healing have a power that words can neither encompass nor convey.

Please also remember that I'm an English-speaking criminal prosecutor, not an Aboriginal healer. I therefore have only a surface understanding of the healing art and the Aboriginal universe that shapes it. It's a struggle for me to escape the impact of forty-nine years of total immersion in Western ways of seeing and doing things. Every time I am in a sweat-lodge or a healing circle, new shadows of comprehension start to form, some so many layers below the surface that it takes months to even sense their presence, much less understand how they come together within the whole.

It makes me recall something an old woman told me some time ago: "You will have a good life," she said, "if you make it to seventy-five, look back five years to when you were seventy, and say, 'Boy, I sure didn't see things too clearly way back then!'" I can only share the way I understand things now, at this moment, knowing how limited that understanding is. What I will present, therefore, is not step-by-step instruction, for that would only mislead. Instead, I want to share how I *responded* to what I have experienced and my own sense of *why* I responded as strongly as I did.

The Disconnecting of Jeremy ...

I want to recount something from the late sixties, when I had my first encounter with suicide. The boy who did it was nineteen, a university student, and the friend of one of my brothers. He stood on the shoulder of a busy Toronto expressway for a long time one night, then leapt into the path of an oncoming car.

I'll call him Jeremy.

Until that event, I had always pictured suicides as desperately unhappy people, sobbing or screaming hysterically during their final moments. Even if that was a little melodramatic, I still felt that such a desperate act would have to be driven by some desperate pain, one that could not be withstood an instant longer.

Jeremy's suicide, however, seemed quite different from that. No one seemed to be able to point to a dramatic and obvious cause, for we knew of nothing especially difficult, abusive or threatening in his life. There hadn't been a tragic love affair, a violent or uncaring family, enslavement to alcohol or drugs, or a failure at school. There was nothing obvious that we could point to, and he had offered no real complaint. All we could see was that he had grown somewhat less communicative, less involved. But even that withdrawal wasn't remarkable or extreme. On the night he took his life he hadn't been locked up in a lonely attic room, but out playing volleyball with a group of friends. In fact, his team had won.

In an odd way, it was the winning that seemed to hold the clue. Apparently it hadn't meant anything to him. People told us he showed no reaction one way or another. It just seemed as though his heart wasn't really in it. After the game, he went back to his room, sat a while, then hitch-hiked up to the fourteen-lane freeway, stood on the shoulder watching cars and trucks whizzing past in all directions, then walked out in front of one.

I mention Jeremy's suicide because it said something to me at the time, something that seems to reverberate more strongly as I explore traditional approaches to healing. It has to do with the principle of wholeness I quoted earlier from *The Sacred Tree:* "All things are interrelated. Everything in the universe is part of a single whole. Everything is connected in some way to everything else...."

Jeremy, I thought at the time, had somehow come to believe the opposite, that he was connected to nothing, and that nothing was connected to him. It wasn't that he was running away from violent or abusive connections he could no longer bear, as I had always expected of suicides. It wasn't that he was trying to escape forever from painful things too powerful to sustain. Instead, Jeremy seemed to have come to the conclusion that he was somehow not connected to anything anymore, that nothing was touching him and he was touching nothing. In that frame of mind, making a physical disconnection through suicide would seem like a logical next step. Why maintain the charade of a physical existence if you feel effectively invisible to everyone and everything around you? It wasn't that those people and things meant pain; instead, they meant nothing at all. Even the supposedly good things, like winning the volleyball game, failed to have meaning.

I have always thought that standing on the shoulder of that freeway in the darkness must have been, unfortunately, an almost perfect metaphor for how Jeremy saw himself in the world. That world was "out there" somehow, like all the cars whizzing past, removed from him, carrying on their frantic pace without him. He, by contrast, was on the shoulder, only watching, an impotent bystander, unconnected to everything else. We know that a number of drivers did in fact see him standing there (and later told the police), but I have always imagined that he felt completely invisible to them. I have even imagined him at the moment he jumped, expecting that they would just pass right through him. In my dreams, I have also sometimes imagined his shock when they *didn't* go right through him, when he discovered, too late, that he was not invisible and ghost-like, but connected with everything, if only in that brutal, bloody and final way.

It is this issue of becoming disconnected that keeps coming back to me when I think about so much of the violence we do to ourselves and to each other. The more I spend time exploring traditional approaches to healing, the more this seems to be the one question that lies at the heart of all the other questions asked and all the healing steps suggested. Everything the healers explore seems to boil down to one issue: connection and disconnection. It's as if *some state of disconnection* (or unhealthy connection leading to a desire to be disconnected) *is assumed to be the cause of the problem,* following which there will be lengthy investigation into how that state came to be and how all the processes that created it can be turned towards reconnection instead. Healing is by turns subtle and dramatic, but underlying the entire process is this movement toward reconnection.

Looking Beyond Events

To begin the process of reconnection, healers are likely to begin a number of investigations. They might investigate, for instance, whether the person had been abused in any fashion, and as a consequence started disconnecting himself from others, carving out places where others could no longer touch and hurt him. They might want to know if he or she had been involved instead (or as well) in relationships that were good and valuable to him, but that had somehow evaporated, despite his best efforts, leaving him afraid to attempt new connections for fear that they too would lead only to eventual abandonment. They might want to know whether he had simply been raised without connections of either kind, good or bad, at a distance from the world, seeing things and people as resources only, unaware of feelings like warmth, respect and care. They might want to know if he had done things for which he had never forgiven himself, things that kept him from being connected warmly with others because his shame kept him from feeling warm connections with himself. They might want to know if he had become violently manipulative of others because the whole course of his life had told him that violent connections were the only way to say, "I am here, can you see me?"

No matter what *kinds of events* are explored, it seems that their importance is always evaluated in terms of whether they have led to healthy or unhealthy connections—or the decision to avoid connections of any sort at all. The issue is never as simple as just looking for events.

After such investigations, part of the healing process will likely involve searching for ways to deal with the anger, pain, grief, guilt or other negative feelings that have built up. As long as they remain strong, they can only get in the way of efforts to build healthy relationships—including relationships with the healers themselves. The teachings suggest that there are many different ways to discharge such emotions, and that talking is only one of them. I have been given a Cree teaching that lists seven ways: crying, yelling, talking, sweating, singing, dancing and praying. Any number of combinations may be required for a particular individual and a particular set of circumstances. Finding the combinations that are most effective for all four dimensions of each individual may be complex in itself, requiring great sensitivity on the part of the healers.

One of the most powerful healing tools I have encountered is the sweat-lodge. Those I have attended (and found personally powerful) involved the three activities of singing, sweating and praying. They did not involve talking about, or even mentioning, the particular problem you wanted help with. It seems to be understood that in some contexts talking can even get in the way of dealing with some issues because it puts you one step removed from your physical, emotional and spiritual dimensions. It is sometimes better to create processes that bypass this distraction and aim straight for the "heart" of the matter instead.

It is also understood that even the healthiest people should make regular use of such techniques—for regular cleansing of our emotional, mental and spiritual dimensions is seen as no less important than regular physical cleansing. They should all be part of each day, and should never be seen as somehow embarrassing or shameful.

While the discharge processes are being used, many other steps may have to be taken as well. For people who have known only abusive relationships, for instance, it may take some effort to convince them that healthy relationships are *possible*. As I will explore later, trust, love and respect are just words to many people, for they have never known them. Those people will have to be helped to face the events that have prevented them from knowing those feelings, to learn how to discuss them openly. Only then can they start to gain some understanding of how their relationships broke down, evaporated or degenerated into violence. In cases where two strangers have come together in a sudden, violent connection like an assault, restorative measures may be accomplished with relative ease. In cases of longstanding abuse, however, where unhealthy relationships ate themselves causing "outside" eruptions of violence, the process is likely to be much more lengthy and complex.

To change their unhealthy relationships, offenders, victims and their families learn how to change the ways they relate to others.

Manipulation is transformed into respect, fear into caring, power into partnership. The ancient teachings that help people make those kinds of changes must not only be given in words to those who have come for help; they must also be given by being *manifested* by the helpers themselves in everything they say, do and offer. The healing team must demonstrate the most fundamental teaching of all—that life is relationships and that acting in individualistic defiance of that reality will only lead everyone downhill.

No Frills, All the Spills

Once a focus on relationships occupies centre stage, some other things seem almost inevitable. As we have seen, there is the understanding that you cannot effectively deal with unhealthy connections between people by dealing with people as individuals, as having independent control of their own fates. Instead, because the connections are the issue, all the major players in anyone's life will have to be part of the process. If they are not, there is simply no way to understand or alter the connections between them.

That is not to say that there is no such thing as "one-on-one" work or that all the players in severely dysfunctional groups should be instantly brought together in every case and worked with *en masse*. As we shall see, sometimes the power imbalances between players call for intensive individual work before it is either safe or useful to bring them together. It is true, however, that the most intensive healing efforts will likely come undone if they are restricted to only one of the players involved, or if all those players are "treated" separately. If people "go home" at the end of their formal healing to all the unchanged relationships that dragged them down in the first place, there is every chance that all the good work will come quickly undone. Many times, for instance, case workers and community members have seen Aboriginal children who abuse solvents whisked away to a distant treatment centre, worked with as intensely and well as can be imagined, then sent home only to "revert to form" within a matter of weeks.

To some observers, their relapse says that the children themselves are just hopeless cases, for whom nothing can be done. To the healing people I have come to know, it says something different: that there are very few of us—children or adults—who can ever hope to sustain internal harmony if everything that touches us shrieks of discord. Think of Carl. Better, they say, to take out a core of the healthiest people, help them become as healthy as they can be as individuals *and as a functioning group,* then return them to support each other as they bring their group power to bear on the challenge of turning that discord around.

Within the narrowest definition of connection, then, it is seen as essential to include at least the immediate family and most important friends in the healing process. Recall the recommendations of the three Cree women, who spoke at the trial of the man who had beaten his wife. They made recommendations first for the Dad, then for the Mom and Dad, and then for Mom, Dad and kids together. At the time, I thought the second two steps were "add-ons"—frills that were only secondary to the goal of helping the man. Now I have come to understand that working with the individuals was just preparation for the main challenge, creating a healthier *group.*

Including families and others in the process is not an "extra" that, in times of tight budgets, can be carved away as an unaffordable luxury. Instead, including those people is seen as a *precondition* to the effective and lasting healing of individuals. When the Ojibway woman at the alcohol treatment centre pointed to the circle of chairs and the drum in her healing circle and said, "In our understanding, we heal best when we heal together," she was saying so much more than I understood at the time.

This focus on relationships is not confined to relationships between people. Of equal importance are the relationships people establish between themselves and the rest of Creation. The teachings that requite certain attitudes in one context of life require them in *all* contexts. Respect and sharing, for instance, are not attributes that can be turned on and off like a tap, or called upon only in special circumstances. They require effort and will, and must be a part of continuing relationships with *all* aspects of Creation.

At the same time, we must constantly monitor the relationships between our mental, physical, emotional and spiritual dimensions as individuals and do what we can to keep healthy and balanced connections between them. If that is not done (and it is never "done" but must be always pursued!), it is understood that the combinations of wisdom, stamina, courage and faith needed for "a good life" will not exist. In fact, the understanding is that society itself must be dedicated to maintaining the same balance. If it does not, if it concentrates on the mental and physical dimensions of existence and ignores or maligns the emotional and spiritual, then it becomes increasingly difficult for individuals to maintain their own balance as well. There is only so much each person can do to stand against the prevailing winds if those winds are ill.

With that introduction, it is now time to take you back to Hollow Water, to see in more detail how ancient understandings have been incorporated into practical techniques for dealing with the most painful realities of the late twentieth century.

My First Morning at Hollow Water: Dewing the Web

I will never forget my first morning at Hollow Water.

At 9:00 a.m. (okay, it was Indian Time, somewhere *around* nine!), the team assembled for a briefing session on the day's activities. As I expected, we all stood in a circle, holding hands, while a prayer was said. As I also expected, in that prayer thanksgiving was offered to the Creator for the sun's return once again, for the blessing of life, for the chance to bring good feelings to others, for the strength that came from the circle as the hands were closed. It asked for help in facing the challenges that would come that day. Then we sat down, all eighteen of us, at a long boardroom table. Papers were pulled from briefcases, and the business of the day began.

I should mention that no matter what "business" is being conducted at Hollow Water, it takes place within the circle format and the rules that govern it. A question is asked, or an issue raised, and then, going around the circle, each person takes a turn speaking to it. Everyone is free to speak as long as they wish, or not at all. The choice is theirs, and no one will interrupt or show impatience. No one speaks until it is their turn, and everyone concludes their turn by saying thank you to the circle for the chance to contribute.

If issues ate raised that concern someone across the circle, that person is not permitted to jump in and reply out of turn. Even when their turn comes, however, there is no *obligation* to reply. If they choose, they can wait until some other time, when they are more prepared. As I often saw, however, many issues that might have been the source of debate or contention between two people were substantially defused, buffered or even resolved before the second person's turn arrived. If nothing else, they had a chance to reflect on what was said and how they should respond with the calm and respect that the circle itself demands. I like the way circles involve everyone respectfully, and I am always happy to be a part of that process.

That first morning, however, I was in for a shock. The first question put to the circle was not "What cases do we have today?" or "What do you think we should do about So-and-So when he comes into the circle this afternoon?" Instead, the question was "How do you feel this morning?" Then, one by one, following the rules of the circle, people took their turns talking about exactly that. As I discovered, however, such questions did indeed direct everyone to "the business of the day." At Hollow Water, it's just that they have their own definition of "business."

I remember one woman speaking of how happy she felt that morning, because when she had first walked into her kitchen and looked out the window, she had seen the dew sparkling on a spider-web on the back porch. She spoke of how pretty it was, then of how difficult it was sometimes to keep seeing such good things when they spent so much time dealing with all the pain in the community. She closed by laughing about how good it was that she was such a terrible housekeeper, leaving those spiderwebs like that! Everyone laughed with her.

Another woman then spoke of how tired and worried she was. She had been up till 2:00 a.m. the night before, talking to her teenaged daughter about a school trip to Winnipeg, where some of the students had gotten some drugs and one of them had been taken to hospital with an overdose. She was worried about her daughter and about what the chief and council were going to do. She didn't want all the kids to suffer because of a few. Mostly, though, she was just worried about all the kids and the pressures they were under wherever they went. Several speakers later, someone else spoke about how happy they felt about the direction things were taking with the kids in the community, reminding the circle that just a few years earlier there had been so much more drinking and gas sniffing among them. She felt good to see those changes and felt that the best thing they could do was keep working on the violence in families, because that was the thing that made the kids take on those destructive behaviours.

And so it went, for about half an hour. In its quiet way, it was for me one of the most significant "cross-cultural" periods I have experienced. It set a pattern—and a standard—for almost every-thing else I watched them do.

Not surprisingly, that standard was based on caring for the relationships between team members, and between each of them and the workplace in general. The very fact that they work in the same place means that they are involved in relationships with each other and with the group as a whole. That is just a fact of life, as real at Hollow Water as it is on the factory floor or in the corporate boardroom. The issue is whether those relationships are healthy or unhealthy, supportive or destructive. Hollow Water is determined that those relationships be as healthy as possible. As a result, two questions become important to everyone: What did you bring from home today? and What are you taking home tonight?

… And What Did You Bring from Home Today?

As the First Principle in *The Sacred Tree* is phrased: "It is … possible to understand something only if we can understand how it is connected to everything else." Within that teaching, I could not "understand" the people who came into my first circle at Hollow Water without first understanding, for instance, that one of them had come to work intensely "connected to" her daughter's school trip, while the other came vibrantly "connected to" the dew on the spiderweb. Because they were given an opportunity to express those connections, everyone could come to an understanding of "who-they-were-that-morning." They could then begin to relate to each other in healthy ways. Had they not had that opportunity, the unhappiness of one could easily be misinterpreted by others and create tensions between them. Instead, because they all had a work-sponsored opportunity to learn about it and respond helpfully to it, they could overcome it.

In this way, Hollow Water does its best to recognize the wholeness of each person in everything they do. They know that everyone has a life beyond their workplace, a life that cannot be put into a separate compartment and ignored for eight (or fourteen!) hours a day. Each day therefore begins with a chance to carry some of that other life into the working circle, to make a transition, if you will. What is "in you" from home is, without doubt, still "in you" at work, affecting what you think, say, feel and do. To deny that is to deny reality—better to recognize that reality by making room for it at work.

Ironically, the extra time taken to smooth the transition from home to work was not just a personal luxury granted to each individual at the expense of workplace productivity. Instead, it improved work performance in a number of ways. First, by being able to get some burdensome things (like worry about your daughter) off your chest, there was some personal release. Second, other people then had a chance to contribute information or experiences (like how the situation with kids was actually improving, not deteriorating) that might help you put your own issues in perspective. Third, some people's stories of joy (like the dew on the spiderweb) seemed to be just the "pick-me-up" others needed to rise above their own problems, at least for a while.

At the same time, everyone gained a cleat understanding of who was "up" and who was "down," who might be preoccupied and who might be really focused, who had energy and who did not. They could then make allowances for each other throughout the day. They knew who might need a little extra patience or support and who had the capacity to extend them. In that way, a "levelling" took place in that first half-hour—a "wavelength-adjustment," where people were given a chance to come together as much as possible. I have no doubt that there are days when it becomes clear that too many people are burdened with too many worries that can't be "left at home," and I expect that decisions are made to stay away from issues that demand higher energy attention or optimism than people are capable of contributing.

In short, "the business of the day" follows the capacities of the people, instead of demanding things that they are jointly or individually incapable of delivering. At the same time, the help each person receives from others throughout the day makes each one *more* capable than when they arrived.

This attention to, and respect for, each person as a whole person makes each one feel that much more comfortable *going* to work! In fact, some people spoke of times when work almost seemed like a refuge from the chaos—and tensions—that existed outside it. It may be hard to believe, but I heard people at Hollow Water speak of being happy to be "back into the circles," as they phrased it, even though the topic was the sexual abuse of children. In those circles people are continuously and openly respected, supported and nourished as individuals, and they are encouraged to operate within relationships defined by health, sensitivity and care.

Then there is also, of course, the *end* of each working day to consider.

... And What Are You Taking Home Tonight?

Just as we bring our home to work, we take our work experience home with us. Instead of trying to deny that reality, Hollow Water does what it can to accommodate it. At the end of the day the team gathers for a "case debriefing," which, just like the first morning meeting, includes a circle in which people are asked "What do you feel after what you've been through today?"

I remember one woman talking about how afraid she was for a certain young girl, because her family did not want to admit the danger she was in from her father. She also felt guilty that they hadn't seen the signals and started to work on intervention earlier. Another woman, several turns later, spoke about how she too felt guilty that way, but had come to realize that they were all still on a learning path, and that they couldn't expect to see and anticipate everything fully at this stage in their development as a team. She had decided to feel happy about the fact that they had learned so *much* in the last five years. Someone else spoke about how excited they felt in one of the day's circles when certain people started to show their anger, for it meant that the circle was breaking them out of their secrets and their fears. Someone else spoke about how hard it was going to be to rescue a certain girl from her father after so many years of abuse, because she was now seeing this as normal and believed that their relationship was based on love. Someone else reminded her that five years ago none of them would ever have *known* about that abusive relationship, much less have had a chance to intervene, so strong was the secrecy about such things.

And so it went, an emotional and spiritual "debriefing" that not only canvassed all the factual issues of the day but did so in a way that acknowledged people could be touched by them, often in a burdensome way. Because of the dangers of having team members take those burdens quietly home and then inject them into their own family relationships, everyone was given the opportunity to discharge some of them, and to offer encouragement, hope and perspective to each other. From what I could see, people actually seemed to take some *good* feelings home with them, despite the painful nature of the work, for they reminded each other of the contribution they were making and that the direction for the future was now more, not less, promising for all of them.

Hollow Water gave me a new understanding of what the word "team" might mean, how many dimensions there are to the concept of "respect" and how ultimately destructive it is to think that you only need to show certain levels of respect (or even none at all) within different "compartments" of your life. Once you see yourself as a product of, and constant contributor to, all the relationships that surround you, it becomes impossible to forget that what you absorb in one place you will pass on at the next, just as what you pass on will soon affect a hundred others as well.

No matter how much you deny that fact of life, you can never escape it.

... And There Ain't No "Neutral" on the Healing Train

Do you remember the question Bluehouse and Zion told us the Navajo peacemaker asked himself? "Is it *hashkeeji* (moving towards disharmony) or *hozhooji* (moving towards harmony)?" Notice that there is no third option, no suggestion that we can slide along in neutral, affecting nothing. Instead, the understanding is that whatever we do or say has an impact on everything around us, in one direction or another.

At that first morning's meeting at Hollow Water, everyone was consciously involved in a process of healing themselves, each other and the relationships their work demanded of them. They did not operate under the impression that the way they dealt with each other could be "neutral" to their work, their workplace, their relationships with their families or the balances existing between their mental, physical, emotional and spiritual dimensions as human beings.

According to traditional thought, if we fail to organize all aspects of our lives, including our work, around making positive—or healing—contributions to our relationships, then we are actually making negative contributions instead. In other words, healing is not just a form of emotional or psychological surgery you reach for after there has been a significant injury.

Instead, healing is seen as an everyday thing for everyone, something which, like sound nutrition, creates health. In short, the healing perspective must be built into the attitudes and processes that shape every aspect of every day. If it is not, then those attitudes and processes will contribute to ill health instead, and for all of us.

I confess that at the time I did not understand how important the team members' relationships with each other were to the success of their work. I was happy to see them support each other, and suspected that such support would help keep them from burning out. I did not, however, see how essential those apparently "non-work" efforts were *when it came to bringing healing to others.*

Powering Down, Opening Up

One of the things I learned from Hollow Water is that a central part of the healing process involves showing lost, hurt and frightened people that relationships built on respect and care are *possible.* It is a sad truth, but there are a great many people—Aboriginal and non-Aboriginal—who do not know that. To them, relationships are power struggles built on manipulation, slander, injury and control, and those power struggles show themselves in so many ways.

There are all the insults meant to make the other feel small: you'll never amount to anything; your friends are a bunch of jerks just like you; if you had any guts, you'd tell your boss to stuff it; you can't even balance a chequebook; you always get taken, every store you go into; you're just as lazy as your old man.

And there are all the questions that are also just declarations of failure: Are you gonna let them get away with that? Can't you do anything right? How can you send the kids off looking like that? Why can't you get a job like Harry's? Can't you cook nothing right? Why do you always look so frumpy? Are you gonna start crying again? Can't a man get a little peace around here?

And there are the strategies of isolation: Who'd believe you over me? There's no way that woman ever sets foot in this house again! Not even your own kids will listen to your bellyaching! Your job is right here, for when I get home! You never had one friend who didn't lie to you! Your family never did give a damn about you!

In far too many cases, such barrages of soul-destroying insult are backed up by threats and open violence. And in far too many cases, children grow up believing that this is how relationships are formed. They learn to think of themselves as failures who have no right to expect better than they get. At the same time, they spend every waking moment trying not to repeat their "failures" and give their abusers an excuse to come after them again. The most damaging thing they learn, however, is how to hide the pain they feel. If they let their abuser know how much they hurt, or the things that have hurt them, it is no different from handing him a gun and telling him where to aim it to cause the maximum pain the next time. At all costs, never acknowledge how, why or how much you hurt—even to yourself.

When those people come into healing, they come fiercely connected to that definition of relationship. They live so defensively, in such terror, that they cringe at requests to let their guard down. They will not open up their hearts just because someone says they should. They do not have enough trust for that. What they need is a long, steady period of observing trusting relationships *in action* all around them. They need to feel them, to hear them, to sit quietly at their fringes for as long as it takes to start believing that people really do treat each other that way.

As I see it now, part of the genius of Hollow Water—and of the traditional teachings that shaped it—is that each person who comes to them for help finds himself in a circle composed of people who have already built relationships of honesty and openness with each other and who consistently *demonstrate* their respect and care for each other in everything they do. In other words, they get to sit, perhaps for the first time in their lives, in a "safe" place, a "hope" place and a "learning" place.

I mentioned that many members of the Hollow Water team were themselves the victims of longstanding sexual abuse. In the circle, they do not offer judgments of others, nor do they issue instructions to anyone. Instead, they primarily tell their stories to the circle, complete with all the tears, angers, frustrations, regrets, doubts and other swirling emotions that live so long within them after the physical abuse has ended. The fact that they can speak openly, fully confessing all the things that have weakened and hurt them, sends the most powerful message of all: that they are in a safe place where no one will abuse such confessions, such honesty, such revelations of pain.

It is nothing short of amazing to watch what happens as team members use their turns in the circle to speak of their own struggles, their own fears and hurts and horrors. As the people they are working with hear those stories, they start to gain some confidence that what they confess will not be used against them. At the same time, team members openly speak of the *bravery* of those who expose their secrets to others, saying that they are "honoured" by the other's tears. It took me a long time to realize what a gesture of trust those tears really are, especially when they are given by someone who has always had them turned around and used against them.

So that is one aspect of the magic that exists in the Hollow Water circles: the way they deal *with each other* teaches, in the most multi-dimensional and powerful fashion, that it is possible to have relationships built on respect and caring, not fear and manipulation.

In fact, the teachings are much more detailed than that. It is an Ojibway teaching, for instance, that healthy relationships—and "a good life"—depend on constantly cultivating seven attributes: Respect, Caring, Sharing, Kindness, Honesty, Strength and Humility. In both the group and the individual sessions, the team examines all the relationships people have been maintaining with each other, with themselves and with all of Creation. In doing so, they look at how much, or how little, those attributes are present.

It is understood that everyone is capable of improvement in all of them, at all times, throughout their lives.

I have not been a victim of abuse, not have power and manipulation been major parts of the relationships in my life. In that sense, I didn't need to have Hollow Water show me a different possibility. I must confess, however, that Hollow Water and the teachings that have shaped it have shown me something I didn't know: how far *healthy* relationships can go if people consciously strive towards the development of those seven attributes, as team members have done, The dignity, openness and love that shine through all the relationships they have built amongst each other—men and women, Aboriginal and non-Aboriginal, victim and offender—went beyond anything I had thought possible for human beings.

I remember one day, back in Kenora, telling someone how excited I was about getting a chance to go back up to Hollow Water and sit in the circles again. A puzzled look came over his face. He asked how I could be so enthusiastic about submerging myself in discussions about the sexual abuse of children! It was at that moment that I realized how deeply Hollow Water had touched me, for although the topic was sexual abuse, the forum itself was wholly defined by love, respect and faith.

So there was one of the lessons I took from Hollow Water: if you are dealing with people whose relationships have been built on power and abuse, you must actually *show* them, then *give them the experience of,* relationships built on respect (and the six other attributes) instead. That means you have to involve them in processes built on real-life manifestations of respectful relationships, not simply talk about them.

That, in turn, means two things. First, the healing process must involve a healthy *group* of people, as opposed to single therapists. A single therapist cannot, by definition, do more than *talk* about healthy relationships. Second, each person in that group must be capable of exposing their mental, physical, emotional and spiritual engagement with each other, with their own histories and with the lives of those coming to them for help. No other process has the same power to teach that healthy relationships are possible, that all dimensions of each person must be worked with and honoured, and that they too can begin the long journey towards trust. For many victims *and offenders,* their time in the circle gives them their first chance ever to take a few faltering steps in a whole new way of relating to other people, to Creation in general and to their mental, physical, emotional and spiritual selves.

I remember the words of an Oji-Cree man from northwestern Ontario who went out to an Aboriginal treatment program to deal with his alcohol problem. He was over fifty, successful in business and a proud sort of individual. Whatever was causing him to drink, however, was also causing him to abuse his wife. He came to court for sentencing after completing the month-long program and he made quite a speech. The part that sticks in my memory was this: He said, "I thought, when I went there, that it would be a place of shame. I learned, however, that it is a place of respect instead." At the time I didn't understand what he meant, apart from the fact that they had treated *him* with respect. I now suspect he was saying much more—that it was a place where he was given the teachings *about* respect and all the other attributes we must strive for if we are to live "a good life."

True Grit, True Learning

I want to repeat something here. People could have told me before going into Hollow Water every single thing I have mentioned so far, but I still would not have been prepared for either the power or the sophistication of those healing circles. You need to be there. You need to experience the way people come into the circle and go through various kinds of changes. You need to be with them as they move, for instance, from reluctant, careful (fearful?) speech, to reluctant tears, to freer eruptions of the anger, hurt and outrage inside them, and then past that, on to some emerging belief that they really can escape the prison of those emotions and start building homes based on peace and good feeling instead.

The importance of "being there" is also part of the teachings themselves. The Hollow Water team itself came to worry that merely talking about their work was not adequate, that it could not be adequately understood simply through words. In *The Sacred Tree* some of those teachings were expressed this way: "There are four dimensions of 'true learning.' These four aspects of every person's nature (mental, physical, emotional and spiritual) are reflected in the four cardinal points of the medicine wheel. These four aspects of our being are developed through the use of our volition. It cannot be said that a person has totally learned in a whole and balanced manner unless all four dimensions of her being have been involved in the process."

That teaching required Hollow Water to change how it responded to requests for "information" from other Aboriginal communities. Instead of visiting them and delivering presentations, the team now invites people to come to the community instead, to sit in the circles, to *participate* in their work. Only then can they "learn" in their emotional and spiritual dimensions what the circles are capable of teaching. It is to honour that teaching, and the people who live by it and do so much to help others, that I am not trying to write a "how-to" manual in this section of the book.

Being Lost in "Only Me"

I mentioned that many who come to the Hollow Water circles for help are desperate people who long ago decided they'd never be able to move out of their anger and outrage. In fact, some of them seem to cling to such feelings as the only familiar and constant things they can locate in their quicksand lives. When they come into the circles, however, they listen as team members tell their own stories, revealing the rage they too felt. Each of those stories then serves to validate all those feelings, in the sense of saying, "Yes, we know those feelings, they are *normal* feelings in this situation, there is nothing wrong or weak or disturbing about you." A great many victims need to hear these kinds of things over and over and over.

I am still surprised by the fact that so many victims are convinced that their horrible experience of life is unique to them. It comes out in so many ways: the belief that there must be something especially wrong with them for things this horrible to have happened; the belief that no one else knows of or could possibly understand the depth of their hurt; the belief that only they could possibly be so screwed up as to be able to feel rage, hurt, love, guilt, humiliation and pride *all at the same time*. It never ceases to amaze me how many victims feel that somehow everything was their fault, that if only they had done or thought or said something differently in their lives, this would never have happened to them.

It is also difficult for me (and for many victims themselves) to understand how they can both hate and love the people who have abused them so violently—but that also seems to be common. In my experience, the majority of victims, especially in family abuse situations, are not looking for anyone to shoot their abuser. They merely want the abuse to come to an end and the relationship to "get back on the rails" again.

These are the kinds of things, however, that many people on the Hollow Water team understand intimately, for they have experienced exactly the same things in their own lives. In fact, I have come to see their first-hand experience of such things as being critical to their success—as something else that sets Aboriginal healing approaches apart from the professionalized approaches of the West.

When team members relate their own stories, you can watch something physically change in the people who have come to them. Their shoulders, knees and knuckles seem to relax. They seem to exhale breaths that have been held for years. Their faces seem to soften as weariness and relief take the place of wariness and fear. My own reading of those signs is that they have started to sense that they might not really be alone in all the things they feel and think and know, that they might not be freaks forever trapped by their own freakishness.

Team members have developed levels of understanding and communication that can accomplish extraordinary things. Victims may only need to say a few halting words before team members grasp their full significance and then respond appropriately. When that happens, when victims see that their counsellors have understood so much after so few words, the relief is almost tangible: "Finally, people who know what I'm talking about! People who don't think I'm nuts!"

At the same time, people trapped in their own violent feelings seem to take a special message of hope when they hear team members speak of healing, of growing out of their own violent experiences. It is one thing to hear a professional tell you that such progress is possible; it is another to hear from, *and experience the stories of,* people who have travelled exactly the same road. When that happens, it is easier to find some faith that you too might be able to set foot on the higher, softer and lighter ground that others have apparently reached.

It becomes easier still when they volunteer to walk that path beside you. Once that happens, the most critical first step has been taken, the step of daring to dream.

CHAPTER 7

THE HEALING PATH HAS POTHOLES TOO!

The Instant Pudding Assumption

M any of Hollow Water's strengths flow from the fact that the team members have built respectful, honest and intimate relationships amongst themselves. That is what they show people who have known only the opposite and that is where they get the strength to be able to welcome and work with the horribly diminished and fearful people who come to them. If they had not built those relationships, they would not be able to send the messages that such people need to hear. Instead, their own unresolved anger, guilt and shame would simply be stirred into the already flammable lives of their "clients," adding an explosive trigger to an already unstable mix.

I therefore offer this caution: *unhealed people cannot bring healing to others—only an escalation of their illnesses*—and the creation of a healthy team at Hollow Water took several years of great personal dedication, a lot of pain and a sustained relearning of the traditional teachings.

In other words, it is my sense that communities cannot create healing teams as if they were instant puddings. So much more needs to be done than simply locating a dozen interested people, adding money and stirring in a few ceremonies. While Hollow Water's hard-won experience in team building might help other communities save time, there remains something that cannot be "imported," something that must be home grown in every community: a team whose members trust each other with their emotional, spiritual, mental and physical lives. There is no way to bypass the development of that trust. If the circle is not a safe place for them, it will be a place of *immense danger* to others.

That doesn't mean, however, that all members of the team have to be completely "healed" people. As they express it to me, healing is often a lifelong journey, especially where sexual abuse has existed. What it means is that all members of the team must reach a point in the healing path where they can share most of their stories with each other, without fear of each other. And as members of the team will freely acknowledge, the circles help them as well. Perhaps that's another reason behind their power: they absorb and express the full hearts of *everyone* inside them. As I discovered, there are no "neutral bystanders" in a circle. It is impossible to experience the dignified expression of a full range of human emotions by a large number of people and not be drawn into their energy, their pain, their uncertainty, their fear, their anger—all the things that define and express them as human beings coming together. It is impossible to remain "detached" in such circles.

In fact, the circles seem to weaken your *desire* to stay detached. Living that way suddenly feels like a shallow, impoverished and artificial way to spend your life. No matter what your background, the circle somehow brings hidden things up to the surface. Perhaps it's because all of us have endured things that have brought us similar *kinds* of feelings, even if they are wildly different in degree. Then, to your surprise, you find that you have things to contribute to, as well as retrieve from, the circle's power.

The issue is not, after all, so much the *degree* of illness that exists, but where the illnesses originate, how they spread, how they can be responded to, how they can be replaced. Because the circle shines its light primarily on the *dynamics* of things, there are no major or minor players within it, no people who have less or more to give than others. And, in some way I cannot express, you leave the circle feeling larger than when you went in, no matter what traumas were revealed within it. At this stage, I can only guess that it comes from feeling so joined, in so many real and visceral ways, to so many people, even when they came into the circle as strangers. Maybe it goes back to that "Am I really all alone?" question we all ask ourselves at one time or another, and the fact that all of us, whether relatively healthy or relatively ill, have been frightened by the answers that have occurred to us.

And maybe those of us raised into noun-worlds of dry and static separations have a special need of that sudden bath of salty tears and hot blood. We need to come down from our cliffside mansions and start swimming with the world—and ourselves—again. I don't know. I can only say that all my experiences with Aboriginal healing, from the healing circles at Hollow Water to the sweat-lodges and cleansing ceremonies have left me feeling larger and "wholer" than when I went in. Humbler, too, if the truth be known, because I see how little I've developed my gifts to touch others in healthy ways, how little I've understood about what we do to each other and how small my heart feels against the hearts of the healers. Not to mention the heart that drives the universe that my language helps me pretend I'm so separate from.

The Grief Sleigh-er

I want to give Hollow Water (and myself!) a bit of a rest here, and let another teaching speak instead. This one came to me from a Cree woman from Alberta.

It involved the suicide of her nephew on her home reserve. She knew that the grief could not be effectively dealt with by Western methods of psychiatry, so she went to the old people and asked for their guidance. They told her of something which, in English, she called a "Letting-Go Ceremony."

It was wintertime, and the ceremony centred on a sled with long, strong ropes tied to each end. In traditional times, certain items meant to accompany the deceased on his or her journey would have been put on the sled. In this case, the grave marker was tied on. Then the family of the boy lined up on one rope, while a larger number of people lined up on the other. A tug of war began, with the larger group pulling the sled towards the graveyard for the burial. The family group pulled in the opposite way, doing whatever they could to keep that sled from getting there, to keep the burial from taking place.

As she described it, it wasn't long before all the family members—men, women and children—were down in the snow and slush and dirt, their clothes wet and muddy, their hands raw, their backs, arms, shoulders and legs giving it everything they had. People up and down the rope were breaking into tears and groans, often repeating the name of the young man. And then, she told me, they started saying the names of other people who had passed away, people whom they had never been able to let go of before. All along that rope there were eruptions of grief at so many losses in the family, none of them resolved, none of them put to rest.

It took quite a while to make it to the grave site. By then the entire family had, quite simply, nothing left. The burial took place in exhausted silence. However, by the time of the feast later that night, everything had changed completely. "You would have thought we were Irish!" she told me. "It was almost like one of those wakes where you're supposed to celebrate, instead of mourn. It was like that for us too."

As I listened to her tell that story, so many images came flying by. I could see the struggle in the snow to keep from letting go. I could hear the cries and grunts. I could feel people reaching for strengths and pains and sorrows they never knew they had. I could also, I confess, see somebody just like me, dressed as an Indian agent or a Mountie or a priest a hundred years ago, demanding in total ignorance that such barbaric practices be forever banned.

How many ceremonies like that Letting-Go Ceremony have fallen under such prohibitions over the years, robbing people of their ways to handle the sorrows that were not only part of a healthy life but an increasingly important part of a deteriorating life for Aboriginal people on this continent? Just when they were needed the most, the ceremonies were put out of reach or so far underground that few could find them anymore. And then, to add insult to an injured people, we pointed to their substitute use of our own favourite mind-and-spirit-repressor, alcohol, as proof that they lacked civilized ways to handle the pain of life.

A great many complex ceremonies and "paths-of-grieving" that have been developed over the centuries are still known and are now being revived. I have been touched by only a few. During one of the Science Dialogues, for example, we received news that the father of one of the participants was near death. An Ojibway man of the Midewewin Lodge offered a ceremony and guided fifteen or sixteen of us through it. It is not my place to describe its details, nor do I believe it can be known through such a description. There is one thing I do wish to say, however.

As we sat in the circle and joined in certain activities, thoughts and prayers, it became clear that almost all of us had not been able to "let go" of important people who had passed from our lives. The ceremony engaged us all quickly and deeply, bringing a great deal of pain, confusion and other feelings to the surface. I think all of us—Aboriginal and non-Aboriginal—were a little surprised that we had been carrying such strong things inside us for so long—and that this Midewewin ceremony was capable of touching them so quickly.

I don't mean to say that such ceremonies resolve every doubt and relieve every burden. I don't know about that. I do know, however, that the ceremonies I have been involved in touched all four of my human dimensions and gave me a sense of moving forward. I felt "better" after them, not "cured." I also found myself wondering how much better things would be in my life—in the lives of all of us, for that matter—if we were able to regularly face things together in such dignified and thorough ways, and regularly move ourselves a little further past them.

Sorry, It's Just That I'm Engaged

And what do my personal reactions to those Letting-Go ceremonies have to do with this book and the topic of healing? Why didn't I resist the temptation to talk about them?

A couple of years ago, I would have said that personal responses had no place in discussions like this, that they should remain on an "objective" level instead. Once again, however, my exposure to Aboriginal people has caused me to look twice at my assumptions. I find myself asking where I learned to resist all mention of those feeling parts of "who-and-what-I-am." Or to phrase the question within the teachings themselves, why do I consciously strive to create such *imbalances* within myself?

That question does not suggest that people should let themselves be swept off their feet by every emotion that happens to fly by. It's not an issue of indulging them, of letting them take over, for that too would result in an imbalance. It does suggest, however, that we *pay attention* to all of our dimensions, that we become familiar with what they are telling us and incorporate them in a balanced way into our every day. Denying them or refusing to listen to them does not make them go away.

But the issue is much larger than finding ways to deal with negative feelings in a more productive way. Instead, it has to do with how we should think about all the feelings that come to us, negative and positive. It has to do with the teaching that all our feelings are to be treasured as essential aspects of living, not shoved off into the corner while we concentrate on "more important" things. In other words, we should not only permit life to engage us on that feeling level, that emotional and spiritual level, but also try hard to bring such levels of engagement about. If none of the things we do each day have the effect of engaging us on those levels, then in a very real sense they don't have any *meaning* for us either!

Let me give a very down-to-earth illustration of how this traditional insistence on looking for engagement with life can cause problems for Aboriginal people operating within Western institutions. Two Aboriginal women told me, on separate occasions, about a particular problem they faced at university: how difficult it was to follow the instructions of professors who kept saying things like "Never use the word 'I' in your papers" or "You must always write objectively and leave yourself out of it." As they expressed it to me, it seemed "false" to write that way. One of them described it as an "empty" way to write about the things she was studying. Although neither of them had been raised in outwardly traditional families, they had been raised to cherish establishing personal relations with everything about them, and to see "distancing" as a negative. It was not, apparently, a conscious approach, and neither knew how to express their problem to their professors. In fact, they were made to feel at the time that the problem was theirs, something about academics that they had not been able to grasp yet. It wasn't until they consciously turned to the teachings many years later that they came to understand that the problem had not been personal to them at all, but the result of clashing cultural commandments.

Sákéj Henderson once phrased his problem with the Western commandment regarding objectivity in this way: "Why would I want to spend time learning or doing stuff that *didn't* mean anything to me?"

The Western insistence on objectivity seems to contradict medicine wheel teachings about what "true learning" is, about how it is important to approach whatever you encounter in life through all four dimensions. The two women, as students, kept wanting to talk about why certain theories frightened them, inspired them, left them mystified, outraged, emboldened or depressed. They were told, however, that their personal reactions had no place in their work. Today, both of them are healers, one in the field of alcohol, the other in sexual abuse. They have now come to see objectivity as something that can get in the way of healing, because it involves distancing yourself from your emotional and spiritual sides, causing imbalances between them. What people need instead, they believe, is full connection, on as many levels as possible and with as many other aspects of Creation as possible.

According to Aboriginal teachings, it also appears that objectivity is, in fact, an illusion. That understanding suggests that we cannot help being engaged with the things around us, cannot help having emotional and spiritual reactions to them. We can pretend that we don't, but that's all our reaction is—just pretend. We can dress up our subjective, personal reactions in objective, nonpersonal language, but it's largely a sham.

To go back to the more important question, why do we work so hard to *deny* the fact that things have touched us? Why do we insist that people avoid referring to their personal reactions, that they use impersonal nouns and adjectives instead?

There is a strange and substantial confusion between cultures here. When I first began to hear elders, I was often bothered by the way they spoke. Instead of talking about the issues in a straightforward (read "objective") way, they made everything personal instead, always talking about their own lives. I remember thinking things like "Boy, what egomaniacs, taking up all our time by talking about themselves! I didn't come here to listen to their life stories. Why can't they get back to the issues instead?" As I have come to understand, they were indeed talking about the issues, but not in the way I was used to. They did not want to suggest they had arrived at some objective and absolute truth that others should accept. As a result, they refused to speak as if that were the case.

Looking back on the situation, I must have sounded like an egomaniac to them! I never once qualified my statements by saying that I could only give my own thoughts. Instead, I expressed everything in objective terms, as though I *had* managed to capture more of that objective reality than they had, as though my thoughts and opinions had more universal validity than theirs did. I didn't really mean that, of course, because I thought it was understood I was only offering my opinion. To a people who use extreme care to show respect for others by never appearing to claim superior wisdom, perhaps that was not understood at all.

So we have another instance of cross-cultural confusion: I thought them egotistical for talking about themselves and their personal reactions, and they thought me egotistical for presuming I could talk about anything *other* than myself and those personal reactions!

How you talk about life, then, is shaped by the commandment to seek engagement with life on as many levels as possible and to be *aware* of your subjective involvement with it. It also requires you to constantly acknowledge that others will have their own subjective reactions, which are likely to be very different. Again, that should not be cause for either alarm or argument, for there is no issue of what is "right" or "wrong." The commandment further requires that whenever you talk about your experience of life, whether at a meeting, in making a formal presentation at a conference or in speaking in a healing circle, you do what you can to convey that involvement. That, after all, is how you do the only thing you can do, which is to share your unique self.

Heart Seeking, Heart Speaking

It should come as no surprise that the issue of "correct speaking" has been given a great deal of thought in Aboriginal cultures, given that it was spoken words, not written ones, through which the teachings, knowledge, history and law were passed to subsequent generations. Nor should it surprise anyone that in a world centred on relationships, speech should be seen as a potentially powerful tool to affect and change the nature of those relationships. In traditional thought, it is not necessarily true that actions speak louder than words. As I have been told many times, even the Bible starts by saying, "In the beginning was the *word.*" Bluehouse and Zion expressed it this way in "The Navajo Justice and Harmony Ceremony": "In Navajo culture, words often have more powerful connotative force than in English.... Language is a powerful tool and an essential component of peacemaking."

And what kind of speaking creates that kind of power? Something often referred to as "heart speaking." The opposite way, naturally enough, is called "head speaking." The more I learn about what those phrases mean, the more that I see how significant the differences between them really are.

In the case of heart speaking, for instance, a public speaker prepares more by settling his heart and spirit into a respectful, honest and *feeling* state than by writing out and memorizing the specifics of what he will say. The latter deals with information and aims primarily at the head. For many traditional people, it may mean taking time before the act of speaking to make ceremonial preparations—like praying and "smudging" with sage or sweet grass for purification. If that state can be achieved, it is understood that the spiritual and emotional content of the presentation will be strong. If that is so, then the speech itself will be strong, and the audience will thus be respected, honoured—and moved.

Because speech is seen as a powerful force for engaging and inspiring people, it must be used carefully. Careless speech is seen almost as a slander and is frowned upon. With heart speaking the speech finds, develops and demonstrates its own life as it emerges from the speaker's lips, heart and spirit during the course of its delivery. In practical terms, that means not writing it down in advance, not being trapped by what a piece of paper tells you to say.

I have always found the thought of standing up in front of a group without a prepared speech terrifying. For the most part, I have always drafted them carefully, long in advance. In fact, I usually create an elaborate series of speech cards, all in point form, that give me a road map through all the information I decide I want to pass along. While I have to find my own on-the-spot phrasing for each of those pieces of information, the intellectual content is tightly scripted. I have always felt that an audience, seeing the extent of my preparation, would be honoured by the effort I put in.

I then began to pay closer attention to Aboriginal speakers. As a general rule—especially with the older people, who are the most powerful speakers of all—I saw no paper, no notes, no cards, no pages, nothing. Yes, there was information, but it was most often contained in stories that permitted the speakers to express their personal reactions to whatever had taken place, to share how those events had moved *them*. Their reactions might have been directly expressed in terms of feelings ("I felt so sad at that time"), but more often they seemed to be expressed just by describing the events in such simple terms that their sadness, for instance, seemed to "speak for itself."

In this connection, I pass along the words of Lisa Tyler from an article in *NeWest Review,* where she describes her reaction to interviewing a Cree elder, Gladys Cook: "When Gladys shares her story, her words are chosen sparingly, carefully. Her words are simple, direct, quiet whispers, with an almost reckless honesty about them. When she speaks, she expects to be heard. When others speak, she listens." The more I experienced such gifted Aboriginal speakers, the more I understood that this emphasis on trying to touch people's hearts instead of just their brains was a conscious choice. In fact, such speaking was part of the teachings themselves. Oddly enough, they reminded me of a teaching from my law school, where the professors told us that you had to make a judge *want* to come to a certain conclusion before he would "find" the law to take him there. Put the opposite way, the law itself is seldom powerful enough to take a judge to a conclusion he resolutely does not *wish* to announce. And here were Aboriginal speakers doing something similar.

Heart speaking is important for another reason: it honours the audience. Because it involves a sharing of things that *mean something* to the speaker, that giving means something to the audience too. To give only information, by contrast, and none of yourself, would be seen as a withholding of sorts.

I remember the first time I tried this heart speaking. It was in Yellowknife, on a Friday night when I was giving an "open presentation" in the community. I was feeling strong at the time, lifted by the warm experiences I had had all day with the people of the Northwest Territories. I had all my speech cards in my pocket, prepared back in Kenora a week earlier. As I stood at the front of the room, however, and looked out at all the faces, especially the Aboriginal women who had made my day so full of caring, I decided I had to leave them in my pocket. Whatever we had built together during the day was going to have to sustain and direct me through the evening.

As I began, it felt a little like the time I first stood with my toes curled around the end of the high diving board; I had to make myself lean forward, right through to the point of no return. I had no idea whether I was in for a belly-flop or not, but there was no going back!

That speech was quite a different experience for me. It took a while to get going—as if I was floundering around trying to catch a rhythm. Once I did, however, it felt like being swept up in an adventure of some sort, more like following something that was alive on its own rather than trying to breathe life into something flat and bloodless on the page. Stories led into other stories, following their own logic, not mine. I found myself going through connections I had not seen before, then arriving at destinations that touched me in ways that were new. There were moments when I could feel tears welling up, there were moments when I felt great love and joy, and there were moments when there was such pain that only silences could capture them—and they did.

I know I'm describing a speech that probably sounds far more powerful than it was as far as the audience was concerned, but it had a power of its own *for me*. That was not something that had happened before. As I went along, I realized that I was skipping many pieces of information I had wanted to pass along, but it was impossible to interrupt the flow to retrieve them. As I ended, I mentioned that I would leave various papers for distribution, and that they would be far more useful than anything I'd been able to remember during the presentation. When it was over, however, someone came up to say that while they had already read all the papers before coming, everything was so much stronger when it came across "live."

So I'm trying to get used to heart speaking, though it's not easy. It feels risky—as if you're always a little out of control (a Western fetish, as I'm coming to understand!). It keeps surprising you, sneaking up to ambush you with feelings you're not used to exposing in public, many of which you have been trained to *suppress* in public. The only problem is this: going back to head speaking feels a little like throwing out all my full-colour movies and going back to black and white snapshots instead. I think I'm getting addicted to the colour and movement; I may even be enjoying the sense of risk taking!

And what has all this got to do with healing? As it turns out—everything!

Tell Me Where It Hurts

It is not our minds that hurt, not our intellects that experience pain, not our information-storage systems that are violated. Rather, it is our hearts, our bodies and our spirits. Healing them must *speak* to them. Healing words must come from, draw pictures of and reach out for, the heart and spirit first, the mind second. The clearest example of this reliance on heart speaking comes from something I have already described about the healing circles at Hollow Water: the fact that they ask "How do you feel?" not "What do you think?" It is not an accident, but a conscious choice based on a clear perception of the healing reality. Until I saw personally how it worked in those circles, I had no idea how much more powerful that feeling question is.

In the first place, it keeps everyone's attention squarely on what's most important about what we have done: its *impact* on other people. It is, after all, that impact that we are trying to understand and reverse within the healing process.

We seem to have taken a different path in the Western justice system. When we originally outlawed all kinds of things, I assume it was because we understood that they caused harm to others and to the fabric of society itself. Once we got our lists of all those unlawful things, however, we called them all "wrongs," and things started to change. Somehow they became transformed into "wrongs-in-themselves." Once that happened, we no longer had to pay much attention to *why* they were wrong, to the harm they caused. Instead, we could just deal in those absolutes of "right" and "wrong" and discard any obligation to investigate and expose all the messy feelings that those acts inspired in all the people they touched.

It is the opposite at Hollow Water. The conviction seems to be that an offender cannot even *know* what he did until he begins to learn, first-hand and in a feeling way, how people were affected by it. As I mentioned earlier, the act itself fades into relative unimportance compared to its impact on the emotional, physical, mental and spiritual dimensions of everyone it touched. The reliance on abstract terms like "right" and "wrong" is seen as a manoeuvre that just creates more distance from the reality of our acts. Instead, every effort is dedicated to putting offenders through processes where they *cannot* stay distant from the harm they have caused. They are not permitted to hide, as they can by simply going to jail. Instead, everything is aimed at making them actually *feel* some portion of the pain, grief, outrage, sorrow or other emotions that they have caused in others.

In fact, that seems to be how Hollow Water has defined the concept of "taking responsibility for your acts." It means not just acknowledging the act itself, nor even giving a mental acknowledgment of the kinds of harm that those acts brought about. It goes much further than that. The process is aimed instead at trying to make each offender actually *experience* some portion of that harm.

Because "coming to understand what you have done" is tied to "real learning," it involves experiencing things in as many dimensions as possible. In that sense, experience is truly regarded as the only effective and enduring teacher.

Chief Justice Robert Yazzie, in one of his papers, observes that in the Navajo Peacemaker process the most important piece of paper is the kleenex, because for healing to take place "I must know how you feel and you must know how I feel." That knowledge, I stress, must be an experiential kind of knowledge, gained by first-hand exposure to all the people you have affected. We saw the same emphasis in the Family Group Conference, where people were urged to "speak from the heart" about how the crime had touched them.

When I first came across this desire to include everyone's "feelings" in Aboriginal justice processes, especially in horrible crimes like sexual abuse, I had an image of uncontrollable outbursts of anger and accusation that would only *add* violence to the situation. While I anticipated that such explosions might make victims feel somewhat better by being able to get certain things "off their chests," I was afraid that the institutional encouragement of such violence was a dangerous thing. Once again, however, there was something I hadn't seen: even the most intense and angry feelings can be expressed in ways that do not amount to acts of violence, and it all comes back to heart speaking.

Accepting the Pain; Denying the Name

As I have observed it, the "What do you think?" question has a tendency to attract judgments *about* other people. The "How do you feel?" question, by contrast, attracts descriptions of how we react *to* the acts of others. One focuses on labelling the act and the actor, the other focuses on the impact of what they did. It goes back to the difference between saying to the offender, "You are disgusting" and saying instead, "I felt disgusted after what you did."

At first glance, it looks like a semantic difference only. For a moment, however, put yourself in the shoes of the offender. How would you react if a victim kept piling judgmental labels on you, one after the other, calling you "vicious, perverted, deranged, vile, sickening" and so forth? Are they the kinds of conclusions you'd want to accept about your "whole" self? Or are they conclusions you'd want to fight about? Or, if you didn't feel like fighting, would you simply stop listening to them, let them wash over you, never really let them penetrate? What if they came at you in a voice quivering with outrage and crackling with anger? How quickly would you either stop listening—or start to fight back?

On the other hand, what if you were an offender who sat in a circle with others and listened to someone simply relive their own reactions: their sense of violation and vulnerability, their fear of strangers, their inability to sleep, their sudden eruptions into tears and shaking at work, their sense of isolation from family and friends, their feelings of dirtiness, their gnawing suspicion that there was something so wrong with them that they deserved to be hurt and hated. What if you then heard all the relatives and friends of your victim speak in the same way, from their hearts, painting pictures of their own confusions, their powerlessness to help, their fear for the future of their daughter, sister, aunt or mother? Would you be able to shut that out as easily, to just stop listening? It is the experience of Hollow Water that careful heart speaking, with its nonjudgmental disclosure of feelings, no matter how intense, is ultimately irresistible to the vast majority of offenders.

Contrary to my earlier suspicions, then, the full expression of even the most intense feelings of anger can occur in an atmosphere that is *not* violent, even if the violence of the crime itself was extreme. In a way, it seems to be related to the observation I made when I discussed Aboriginal languages and the relative absence of nouns in them, especially judgmental nouns: things should be allowed to speak for themselves, without judgmental embellishment. That, in turn, fits with another teaching I kept hearing but have had a hard time understanding: that as humans it is not our role to judge. Hollow Water expressed it this way in their "Position Paper on Incarceration": "Our tradition, our culture, speaks clearly about the concepts of judgement and punishment. They belong to the Creator. They are not ours. They are, therefore, not to be used in the way that we relate to each other."

Prohibiting the judgment of others does not mean what I first thought—that people were prohibited from coming to conclusions about whether particular acts or people have made positive or negative contributions. Instead, it means that it is not our place to judge the "wholeness" of people (even if we could), to stick counterproductive judgmental labels on them and then announce those negative labels to the world. Instead, as the Hollow Water team describes it in the "Position Paper":

> People who offend against another ... are to be viewed and related to as people who are out of balance—with themselves, their family, their community and their Creator. A return to balance can best be accomplished through a process of accountability that includes support from the community through teaching and healing. The use of judgement and punishment actually works against the healing process. *An already unbalanced person is moved further out of balance.*

Storytelling as a means of law-giving seems to be based on the same understanding—that law can be known to everyone through reciting the *consequences* of acts alone, not through communicating judgmental labels for either the act or, worse still, the actor. Once again, we see that there is an underlying unity tying together things that Western tradition has separated: how you make speeches in public, how you teach about law, what it means to have offenders "take responsibility" for their crimes. That unity comes from a fundamental belief that, regardless of the context, we all exist in the emotional and spiritual dimensions, as well as the mental and physical, and that our connections with each other must be connections on all levels, not just one or two. If we connect on one or two only, those connections will be weak, our communications will be incomplete, and the chances of "moving" each other will be much less.

I would go even further and suggest that communication and connection on the mental level are seen as the weakest of all forms of connection. Instead, real communication is more of a "felt" thing than a rational one. So heart talking stands as a central ingredient in the healing process. Diane LeResche expressed it this way in *The Mediation Quarterly:* "Sacred justice is going beyond the techniques for handling conflicts; it involves going to the heart. It includes speaking from the heart, from one's feelings.... It is helping people ease, move beyond, transform the intense hurtful emotions like anger into reorienting and reuniting with that which is more important than the issues of the conflict."

And this brings up another critical feature of traditional healing and peacemaking: the understanding that each criminal act has an impact on a *wide* number of relationships, often in ways that may not be predictable, and that justice must find ways to examine, recognize and bring restoration to most of them. If it does not, the original pain continues to spread from one relationship to another in an ever-expanding ring of disharmonies, touching, ultimately, many hundreds of people.

CHAPTER 8

THE WHIRLPOOL VISION OF CRIME

B ecause crimes involve one person reaching out to harm another, I have imagined them as causing ripples of pain to spread across the surface of a pond. My experiences in healing have given me another image instead—the whirlpool—where great numbers of people are "pulled into" the pain initiated by the original crime. Once there, their many relationships become distorted by that pain, and new pain inevitably follows. It is as if the original crime had the power to move them out of their accustomed circles and draw them ever deeper into a common vortex of injury, anger and fear. As we can see from Hollow Water, from Navajo peacemaking and New Zealand's Family Group Conferences, it is important that offenders gain a "felt" understanding of this whirlpool effect—of how their acts have impacts extending beyond the immediate victim, involving others in complex and often painful ways.

I heard a story that demonstrates how extensive the impact of crime usually is and how processes that include all the "victims" can help turn things around. It was about a drunken man robbing a gas bar at midnight and frightening the young woman who worked there. The offender, an Aboriginal man with a long record, pleaded guilty, then asked for a sentencing circle. The victim was not Aboriginal. When the judge agreed, many people who knew the offender attended. While they spoke of the abuse he had suffered as a youngster, and his addiction to alcohol, they also spoke of how he had squandered a great many chances and broken a great many promises. He had already spent much of his life swinging back and forth between alcohol, crime and jail on the one hand, and sobriety, work and promise on the other. In the end, the judge's sentence was significantly reduced, primarily because he didn't wish to do irreparable harm to someone for whom there was still considerable hope.

I mention this case, however, not because of what it did for the offender. Too often we look for alternate processes simply to create more effective responses for offenders, never paying the same degree of attention to victims and those who love them. In this case, the young woman attended the circle with her mother, and both of them spoke about how the crime had affected them.

At some later point, the young woman participated in making a video about that sentencing circle and its impact on her life. She said she was grateful to have had the chance to express her feelings directly to the offender so he could come to know just how much he had terrified her. The violence of that five-minute encounter at the gas bar had caused her to become afraid at night and afraid when she was alone. She no longer had the same confidence and sense of security as she went about her business. She appreciated being able to tell him those things directly—that he had robbed her of far more than money. She also appreciated the chance her mother had been given to express her own anger, and the fact that she now lived in much greater fear for her daughter's safety.

I gather from speaking with one of the lawyers involved that it took some time after the sentencing circle was completed for them to realize fully how much it had helped them. First, they benefited by seeing the offender throughout the day in that circle, by hearing him speak of his life, by hearing others speak about the kind of person he was—his strengths and his weaknesses. Until that day, he had been, in their eyes, a one-dimensional monster who had lurched drunkenly out of the night, threatened violence, then disappeared as fast as he had come. In that way he had been a haunting figure, not only for the daughter who saw him but for the mother who only imagined him. After that day in the sentencing circle, however, the monster had been replaced by a man. It was remarkably similar to the incident in the Family Group Conference where the fourteen-year-old girl came into the conference as an "offender" but left as a youngster whose mother expected nothing but trouble and wanted nothing to do with her. Whole people, no matter how troubled and occasionally dangerous, seldom fuel full-fledged nightmares. By bringing the victim and the offender into a relationship, the circle sentencing permitted the paralysing fear that had gripped both mother and daughter to subside.

The Aboriginal notion of "relationship" is a tricky one, for powerful relationships can be established almost on the instant—and the insistence upon "restoring harmony to relationships" is not limited to people who see each other regularly. That young woman was engaged in a powerful relationship with that man from the moment he stumbled out of the night to make his demand, and it lasted long after he left. If anything, it grew in power the longer it was left unresolved, spreading tension and conflict into her relations with her mother as well.

That was the part of the process I found most fascinating. After the crime, the mother had apparently grown terrified *on her daughter's behalf.* As a result, she constantly interfered in her daughter's life, questioning her about where she was going, whether she would be alone, what time she was coming home, where she would park her car and so forth. In turn, the daughter had grown to resent those intrusions, even though she knew they were motivated by love and concern. In that way, their relationship too had been poisoned. To my mind, one of the most significant benefits of the sentencing circle came as a result of including the mother and recognizing the impact on her as well. When she saw the offender as a whole person, and so lost her "nightmare" picture of him, she no longer felt the need to second-guess every decision in her daughter's life. Their relationship, so strained by the five-minute midnight encounter that only one of them had experienced directly, began to be restored.

Another, similar story concerned a woman who had her purse and knapsack stolen in broad daylight by an angry, drunken man in the streets of Moncton, New Brunswick. She described her feelings before being given a chance to deal with him directly in Moncton's innovative MOVE (Mediating Offender Victim Encounters) Program: "By the time MOVE approached me, I was afraid to walk on Main Street. This crime occurred in broad daylight and I had my four-year-old son with me. After the crime, every man I encountered on the street was a potential enemy—men ... I feared. I was afraid to meet this person face to face, but I was hoping mediation would solve my greater fear of being on the street."

During the mediation she learned what had led him to his theft. He had sold his car and deposited the cheque. Unknown to him, however, the cheque had bounced. He then broke up with his girlfriend and went drinking. One drink led to another, until he ran out of cash. When he went to the automatic teller and he could not withdraw anything because he was broke, everything erupted. It was at that instant, drunk, swearing and angry, that he spied the purse and knapsack, grabbed them and took off. During the mediation, he expressed his regret and joined with the victim in signing a contract for compensation. The judge included that contract as part of his sentence.

How did the woman feel at the end of the process? "We are no longer enemies," she told the offender after the mediation. She experienced all the negative emotions connected with victimization. But she credits mediation with empowering her and bringing home closure. She described closure for a victim as "that point when a crime, while still an important event in the person's life, no longer preoccupies that person's every thought." With mediation she, unlike many who stay victims for life, was able to put the incident behind her and move forward.

In this connection, I remember something I was told by Burma Bushie, one of the originators of the Hollow Water healing program and someone I count on as a teacher and friend. We were talking about Hollow Water's "Position Paper on Incarceration" and its opposition to the use of jail for offenders. I pointed out that their stand was completely contrary to the one taken by most other groups representing women victims of sexual abuse. For the most part, such groups demand that governments get tougher with the men who abused them. When I asked what she would say to them, she did not hesitate for a second. She just turned to me and said, as if it were the most obvious thing in the world: "Oh, we remember feeling that way too—before our own healing journeys began!" Then she added: "The next time you meet them, see if they'll come to visit so we can help them move beyond those feelings too."

In the vision of Hollow Water, it is entirely natural that victims speak in angry voices and push only for angry responses to their abusers. This is not a surprise, for abuse *causes* anger. The problem, as they see it, is that there is no system in place to help victims move *beyond* that anger. On the contrary, the only system available, the criminal justice system, requires them to participate in adversarial trials where they are often accused of being more "at fault" than the offender, where their truthfulness is attacked every step of the way and where their feelings are substantially irrelevant to everyone concerned. In Hollow Water's view, the escalation of anger is entirely natural in those circumstances, and the criminal justice process can be viewed as *contributing* to that anger. Many justice professionals complain that angry victims' groups are driving them down punitive roads that will only cause a further erosion of social peace; this is an odd observation, however, because it may be our own processes that feed and harden that anger in the first place.

Please note that Burma Bushie did not say those victims' groups were "wrong" in feeling the way they did, just as she would never suggest to a victim in her circles that their anger was "wrong." That anger simply "is," and it is what everyone must expect after abuse. That does not mean, however, that it must be a *permanent* condition. With help, people can move out of it, escape it, put it behind them.

But Hollow Water's definition of who must be included in the healing process does not stop with victims and their families and friends. It extends in the other direction as well, taking in the *offender's* friends and family. In some ways, their input may be even more essential for offender rehabilitation. While offenders might not care about the impact of their acts on victims and other strangers, they are much more likely to be touched by seeing the impact on those close to them.

Once the families and friends of offenders are given a chance to express their feelings, all kinds of surprises are possible, especially as far as the offender is concerned. Some may feel shame that one of their own has done such an act. Others may feel guilt that their efforts to bring up a good person have somehow "failed." Some may blame others for that failure, and those others may feel resentful about that. An essential part of offender learning, then, has to do with coming to understand how many of his own people have been touched, and in how many complicated ways, by what he has done. As this process unfolds, his "crime" gradually takes on a different shape. It is no longer just a small, over-and-done-with act that touches strangers, but a spreading and enduring force that touches many people close to him, most often in negative ways.

Within traditional perspectives, offenders must come to that awareness—and in a "felt" way—before they can begin to take responsibility for their acts. Seeing their widest impact is the only way to glimpse the larger truth—-that they are neither invisible nor alone but intimately connected in a large web of relationships, where whatever they say or do makes a significant difference, for good or bad. Only then can they begin to understand that, ultimately, the poison they spread by touching those they never meant to hurt *comes back to them*. In that connection, I repeat the Ojibway teaching passed along in 1995 by an elder in northwestern Ontario who told a community justice researcher: "If we go against the Creator's laws, then we hurt ourselves and end up hurting others who Kizha Manito loves. We end up troubled. Like someone who mocks or cripples an animal, or someone who wastes what they hunt. It's against our teachings. It comes back to haunt you." This does not mean, however, that it's either safe or productive to just bring everybody together and let them go at it. In some contexts, the nature of the relationships demands that other steps be taken first.

Long-Standing, Long-Lying, Long-Lost

There are a great many situations where quickly bringing offenders, victims, their families and other significant people together in such processes can bring only benefits to all. The cases of the gas-bar robbery and the Moncton purse snatching fit into that category. There are other circumstances, however, where quickly assembling them all in one location could be dangerous in the extreme. As in all other things, it depends on the kinds of relationships that exist between the parties themselves.

Most of the cases I've touched on so far have been about minor crimes or serious ones between strangers. The experience of Hollow Water suggests that when the crimes are serious *and the offenders and victims have been involved in longstanding relationships of abuse,* it is risky to bring everyone together without doing a great deal of preparation first. Sometimes, that preparation may take months or years.

What they worry about is the fact that abusive relationships involve imbalances of power between the parties. For whatever reason, abusers have come to depend on constantly demonstrating the power they wield over their victims. To take the case of wife abuse, the husband will have a long list of excuses ready at the drop of a hat, including "She asked for it," "She likes it" and "I wouldn't have had to do it if she hadn't put that beer in the wrong cooler." Over time, the wife begins to believe all those things as well, taking all the blame onto herself. There is only one certain thing in such relationships: whatever the wife says or does will be turned against her to demonstrate both how worthless and how powerless she is. Similarly, everything the husband does and says will be calculated to deepen her belief in exactly those same things.

If one of the husband's violent acts comes to the attention of the authorities and he is charged, what will happen if he and his wife ask to be brought into a judge-supervised sentencing circle, as opposed to a much lengthier healing process, prior to sentencing? What will happen if the judge asks them both to speak openly about the event, their feelings and their recommendations about the future? Can either of them be expected to abandon the identities and strategies that have defined their relationship for years?

Will she, for example, be able to reach under her self-blame, discard the fear that has driven her into such a negative image of herself and honestly speak of her pain, her anger and her outrage at being so constantly violated? How can she do that if she has come to believe on some level that she deserves such behaviour? Won't she continue to speak out of the longstanding illusion, created between them, that she has no cause for complaint against him?

And as for him? As a master manipulator, won't he come into a sentencing circle surrounded by his friends and supporters—all the people who either fail to see the truth or totally agree with his self-serving version of it? Feeling that he has done nothing more than what was "righteous" in all the circumstances, will he be capable of receiving news of her pain and outrage, even if she is somehow able to express it? Or will he feel instead that the justice system itself is victimizing him, calling him to account when he doesn't deserve any of it? Even if he pleads guilty, will it really stand as an acknowledgment of wrongdoing?

And if, in the end, his manipulative confessions of regret, coupled with her silence, seem to satisfy the court that they have put the violence behind them, what message does that send to her? Does it not say that he was right after all when he told her in so many ways that he has all the power and she has almost none? Isn't there a real risk that such a sentencing circle will just help him win one more round in his battle for dominance? Will she be emboldened into reporting him to the police the next time or will she come to agree with him that there's absolutely no point in reporting, because he is almost untouchable? In short, isn't there every danger that legal processes that do not recognize the power dynamics of long-term abuse may *contribute* to abusive relationships by unknowingly supporting all the lies that sustain them?

Frankly, I'm not sure I would ever have asked questions like these had it not been for Hollow Water. Perhaps because of their specialized focus on longstanding sexual abuse, they have looked closely into the issue of the power imbalances within dysfunctional relationships. Those imbalances make up one of the central issues that must be addressed within the healing process.

How is that done? To put it in general terms, the victim and victimizer must be brought level with each other. That, in turn, means working with the offender to "strip" him of all the lies he has been hiding behind, all the justifications ("The Bible says it's okay!"), excuses ("I was beaten as a child!"), victim blaming ("She deserved it, wanted it, begged for it") and minimizations ("I only hit her a couple of times, and they didn't hurt") and so forth. Until that takes place, the victimizer will not be able to acknowledge either that pain was caused or that his infliction of that pain is indefensible. At the same time, the victim must be *freed* from all those lies, lifted up again in her own heart and spirit, raised high enough that she can begin to acknowledge her pain and understand that it was not deserved. Only then will she be strong enough, and he vulnerable enough, to begin the process of *jointly* acknowledging those things. Until they are brought separately into that more level or balanced state, however, his manipulation is likely to continue, as will her inability to resist it.

And how does it take place—this "building up" of the victim and this "stripping down" of the offender? How are they brought to the place that they can come together without lies? I don't pretend to have any more than a surface understanding of such processes, and I would not try to describe them in detail if I did. What I can say, however, is that they too seem to be built on the storytelling, the heart speaking of the healers in the circle.

While many of the healers at Hollow Water are victims themselves, others are ex-offenders, men who have moved far enough down their own healing paths that they have come to understand the lies they once hid behind. They are now capable of facing the truths they refused to admit about the harm they were causing, and they are capable of expressing how hard they found it to leave the safety of their lies and expose themselves to the pain of what they were really doing. When those two groups within the team— healing victims and healing victimizers—come together to tell their stories in a heart-speaking way, the truth about abuse becomes irresistible, and the lies that fostered the abuse begin to crack and fall away. They can read people so much better than I can, relying on tiny signals of sincerity and progress that my inexperienced eye would never catch, as well as discarding the protests and declarations of those who are fooling themselves as they try to fool others.

Just as importantly, they fully understand how many demons have to be fought simultaneously in a person's path to healing, how strong the temptations are to slide back into the lies, how long a process it is to start weaving and wearing a whole new set of understandings. It's strange, when you think of it, the determination we have in the Western justice system to make sure that those who are in charge of it have absolutely no personal knowledge of the forces haunting the people who are paraded daily before them. I often wonder how much of a judge's, a jury's or a lawyer's reliance on deterrence, for instance, comes from the fact that they know *they* would be deterred by the possibility of certain punishments. As I've come to realize, however, there are a vast number of circumstances in which those punishments are not nearly as threatening to the poor, the hurt, the hopeless, the sick and the desperate. Think again of the boy I called Carl. As I asked before, does any threat of punishment from the justice system have enough power to rein in the rage and hurt that propelled him through his days? Think of the abusive men who follow and kill their fleeing partners, then kill themselves as well; if they are desperate enough to take their own lives, what influence over their actions can the threat of jail possibly have?

In Hollow Water, ex-offenders are not shunned forever, but seen as important resources for getting under the skin of other offenders and disturbing the webs of lies that have sustained them. Better than anyone, they understand the patterns, the pressures and the ways to hide. As they tell their personal stories in the circle, they talk about the lies that once protected them and how it felt to face the truth about the pain they caused. It is done gently, but inflexibly, sending signals to offenders that their behaviour has roots that can be understood, but that there are no such things as excuses. In doing so, they leave offenders with no room to hide, no way to maintain their disguises successfully over the long haul.

One of the advantages of using people who know the terrain personally is that they know what to expect from sick people. This, in turn, gives them the patience to stay with them, digging a little deeper every day. They expect, for instance, that abusers will try every manipulative trick in the book to hang on to the lies. Because of that, they are not put off by an offender's initial efforts to con them through outrage, for they expect exactly that. Nor are they put off by any other manipulative strategies, including humour and forced camaraderie, for they expect them as well. I remember watching one day as an offender joked and kidded with members of the team during a smoke break. When the team came back together, with the offender gone, someone said, "Did you see him out there? Remember when he tried to manipulate us all with his anger? And now he's trying the joking instead? Isn't that *wonderful*?" When I asked what was wonderful about that, the answer was instant: "Because he's *moving*!"

In other words, they could see progress, where I could see only a stubborn refusal to face the truth. Out of their knowledge they have created timetables, routes and strategies that fit with the realities of such deep-seated dysfunctions. They don't expect a man who has excused his abuse of others for ten years to feel remorse just because he's been caught. They don't expect victims to be able to forgive as soon as their abuser mutters the magic words "I'm sorry" and promises never to do the same things again. Instead, they expect minimization, blaming the victim and using childhood abuse as an excuse for what they do as an adult. The fact that offenders do all those things is not a reason to write them off forever; they do them because those are the things that offenders *do*!

All those stubborn and manipulative responses to being confronted with their abuse make it essential, in the judgment of Hollow Water, that the lengthy process of restoration be initiated as quickly as possible, with as few stops in jail as community safety can tolerate. Jail, it bears repeating, is seen as an environment that only serves to reinforce the reliance on power and force within relationships, to make it harder still to replace them with respect and consent instead.

Long before such offenders are confronted with their victims in the circle, however, they are confronted by team members who speak of their own victimization at the hands of others. Because their stories do not concern the offender, they are less threatening, more easily received. Over time, however, they become irresistibly personal, because the patterns of abuse they reveal are virtually identical. In that way, the stories of other victims start to crack the "tough guy" barriers that have been erected to keep the truth at bay. The real, enduring grief of those healing victims, expressed in the dignified and nonblaming atmosphere that heart speaking creates, seems to present an almost irresistible challenge to people who have grown to think of themselves as removed, independent and "tough."

This approach seems to be equally effective whether we're dealing with sexual abuse between generations or youngsters beating each other up in turf wars. Some commentators hold the view that our present criminal justice process, with its labelling and damning, actually serves to reinforce and preserve the negative identities behind such acts, rather than change them. As the Australian criminologists John Braithwaite and Stephen Mugford have said with regard to Family Group Conferences for young offenders: "Criminal trials tend to leave criminal identities untouched.... Indeed, degradation tends to harden them. It is not a major challenge in identity-management for a tough guy to sustain his identity during a criminal trial. The challenge is more difficult in an open dialogue among the different parties assembled for a community conference."

Tracing the Sources

In my experience, that challenge is more difficult still when an offender finds himself within the sophisticated dynamics of a properly conducted Aboriginal healing circle. If that circle follows traditional teachings against blaming, it has a unique capacity to draw out the most secret emotional burdens carried by everyone in attendance, including the offender himself. The common experience is that offenders ultimately react to the honest pain of others by beginning to release their own pain into the circle, thereby starting to acknowledge that their "toughness" regularly hides their own history of significant, unhealed injury. That acknowledgment is seen as the first step in altering the "criminal identity" that Braithwaite and Mugford described by breaking down the defiant individualism that has already placed them at such a distance from their society.

By contrast, the stigmatizing and blaming system of Western justice seems to encourage offenders to *deny* their emotional and spiritual dimensions, to deny their own hurt just as they deny responsibility for the hurt they have caused. As a general rule, they acknowledge responsibility only when their lawyer advises that the case against them is rock solid and a guilty plea will result in a lesser sentence. In those circumstances, such a guilty plea often says nothing whatever about understanding wrongness, perceiving hurt and harm, or acknowledging that they had choices in the matter. As a result, it is not unusual to see offenders spend their entire time in custody proclaiming that they were not really "guilty" of anything at all. In their own eyes, still relying on the web of excuses and justifications that sustained them in the first place, they haven't done anything "wrong" at all. To make matters worse, they are surrounded their whole time in jail by people who live within identical webs of self-deception. You can hear them all yelling "not guilty" in unison!

Hollow Water's approach, however, seems to take that denial complex into account. In fact, the team members seem to begin with an expectation that an accused will be psychologically unable to acknowledge responsibility for his acts, in the sense of gaining a felt awareness of the actual harm they have caused to real people. Instead of confronting offenders with a complete and detailed set of allegations, as well as a requirement that they immediately confirm or deny each and every one of them, as the court often does, the Hollow Water team is prepared for a much slower process of increasing confrontation and acknowledgment.

I mentioned that it is common for offenders to start acknowledging a history of their own abuse once their "tough guy" shell starts to crack. It is important to note that such histories of victimization in offenders are never taken as excuses or justifications for what that offender has done. Rather, they are seen as forces the offender has *given in to,* forces he or she has a responsibility to confront, deal with and resolve. The belief is that no matter what demons drive us, we are all able to overcome them, provided we are humble enough to acknowledge our fears and pain, to seek help in cleansing them and to seek guidance in how to deal with them better. Those who claim that they were overpowered by their past are told, in effect, that they were overpowered by their own pride instead, by their refusal to get down to Mother Earth and acknowledge their need for help and teaching. So while past victimizations will be exhaustively dealt with so that their influence is diminished, they will never be permitted to stand as an excuse.

Blended into all the storytelling offered by the healers are descriptions of how they too had to struggle hard to understand, much less begin to live by, all the teachings about how a good life may be pursued. As anyone who has been exposed to the teachings can attest, there is not one single aspect of existence that has not been contemplated exhaustively. I have mentioned *The Sacred Tree* and quoted several of the Twelve Principles that are understood to have application throughout life and in almost every context. I can hear the healers finding ways to talk about how difficult they found it in their own lives to both understand and then start living by the other five principles which *The Sacred Tree* expressed as follows:

- Human beings can always acquire new gifts, but they must struggle to do so. The timid may become courageous, the weak may become bold and strong, the insensitive may learn to care for the feelings of others, and the materialistic person can acquire the capacity to look within and to listen to her inner voice. The process human beings use to develop new qualities may be called "true learning."

- Human beings must become active participants in the unfolding of their own potentialities.

- The doorway through which all must pass if they wish to become more or different than they are now is the doorway of the will (volition). A person must *decide* to take the journey. The path has infinite patience. It will always be there for those who decide to travel it.

- Anyone who sets out (i.e., makes a commitment and then acts upon that commitment) on a journey of self-development will be aided. There will be guides and teachers who will appear, and spiritual protectors to watch over the traveller. No test will be given that the traveller does not already have the strength to meet.

- *The only source of failure on a journey will be the traveller's own failure to follow the teachings of* The Sacred Tree.

I can hear the healers searching for ways to put those teachings to offenders in ways which tell them that their childhood abuse, though important, cannot be used to escape responsibility for what they have done to others. I can also hear them volunteering to be the guides and teachers that were promised.

Given those kinds of teachings, we should no longer be baffled when Aboriginal groups criticize the Western system for doing so little to help victims deal with the pain and anger their initial abuse aroused and for putting them instead through processes in which such emotions expand and harden. In their understanding, this only means their spiritual, mental and physical health will be slowly consumed as well. Nor should we be baffled when they complain that our treatment of offenders goes in the same direction. According to those teachings, the more they each go out of balance with themselves, the more they will contribute imbalance to their families, communities and countries. The Western system is seen, both in what it does and what it chooses not to do, as undermining the very society it is meant to protect. As Hollow Water's "Position Paper on Incarceration" expressed it: "Our children and the community can no longer afford the price the legal system is exacting in its attempts to provide justice in our community...."

I was told something recently that underlines, in a simple but powerful way, everything I've said so far. It is the story of a recent "discovery" by some Mi'kmaq people determined to restore their language to everyday use. They have "found" an ancient verb tense that has fallen into disuse and is remembered by only a few of the elders. It is a tense specifically designed to say to everyone: "This event has been concluded to the satisfaction of all." In English, they have called it the Forgiveness Tense, for it allows people to speak about "crimes" for the lessons that they contain, while at the same time making it clear that the victims have been appeased and healed, the "criminals" restored to full honours in the community and the event "put behind" the community. When the "discovery" of that Forgiveness Tense was relayed to Ojibway people in Ontario, they did their own digging—and found their language had the same tense!

A Forgiveness Tense: what a great idea!

Another aspect of the teachings about healing must be stressed: it is understood that people have to heal themselves. No one can do it for you. When the healing turns its focus on the relationships between people, the same holds true: only the parties to those relationships can heal them. Justice processes that do not recognize those realities and make those demands of people are seen as both superficial and misleading. As suggested in *The Sacred Tree,* there will be healers to assist, but they are guides and teachers only.

And who will those guides and teachers be?

Up the Healing Mountain, Hand-in-Hand-in-Hand-in ...

As I mentioned earlier, Aboriginal healing processes constantly stress values like respect, sharing, humility and so forth. It has to do with an understanding that the Healing Path is not something that "sick" people need, totally "healthy" people supervise and the rest of us can largely ignore. No one ever "accomplishes" healing in their own lives. Instead, it is a path we must all walk on, throughout our lives, constantly striving to create healthier balances and relationships. We all have healing contributions to make to others along the path, and others always have healing contributions to make to us. The process seems to be based on the understanding that none of us are likely to achieve the degrees of kindness, honesty, strength and humility we are capable of as individuals, nor show to others the degrees of sharing, caring and respect they deserve. It is as if we are all climbing the same mountain, working towards developing the same qualities, trying to create the same ways of relating to others. While we did not all start with the same blessings, strengths, teachings and guides, we all have a duty to climb as high as we can.

Within this vision, people who have been involved in abusive relationships are not seen as being on a *different* path than the rest of us. Instead, they are seen as having been pushed farther down the same life path towards wholeness that the rest of us are travelling. The issue, then, involves showing them that they too can make the climb, convincing them to have the courage to try and reaching back a hand to help them.

The matter of courage is raised in many contexts: the courage to cry, the courage to offer help, the courage to acknowledge fear, the courage to face nightmares, the courage to humble yourself on Mother Earth. I am learning how frightening those kinds of things really are—especially when you feel alone. It is hard enough for me to do those things, with all the blessings I had in my birth, my health, my family, friends and teachings. As I mentioned before, it involves acknowledging how vulnerable you are, where you hurt, where you can be hurt. I have a fear of doing those things, even with my most charmed life. I cannot imagine the terror that must exist in the hearts of those who started farther down the mountain than I did and who have been kept there by every abusive relationship that crippled them.

It is this need for personal courage that seems to lie behind the teaching that no one can heal you but yourself. Only you can find the will to take all those first steps towards trusting others, towards taking hold of the hands that reach down to help you. The healers can show you how they trust each other, how they don't let go of each other, but they can't force you to reach out yourself. They can only demonstrate, teach, encourage and receive. Everything else must come from the individual who needs healing.

At the same time, the teachings seem to hold that we must find ways to remind ourselves, each step of the way, that we are not important in ourselves, but only through what we bring to the relationships that surround us, including our relationships with the nonhuman parts of Creation. This is my understanding of the attribute of strength, the strength to acknowledge that while all the relationships that surround us do not *need* us, we have a responsibility to contribute to them positively as long as we remain within them. Sometimes it takes getting back down to Mother Earth on your hands and knees, naked and in the darkness as in the sweatlodge, to feel that small again, to focus once again on accommodating and respecting all the life around us. Sometimes it takes days of starving your physical body (which I have not yet done) while your spirit is opened up—made vulnerable—to the forces of Creation that flow through every rock and tree, that are so much more powerful than your own. Sometimes it takes sitting in a circle with people who have, despite horrible beginnings in their lives, found the courage to move farther up that healing mountain than you ever imagined anyone could go. Whatever it takes, this combination of humility, strength and courage seems to be the only way to open you up enough to start learning who and what you might become.

This is as close as I have been able to come to some understanding of the word "spiritual" as it is used by Aboriginal people. It doesn't mean what I first thought—allegiance to a particular religion or religious institution. Nor does allegiance to those sorts of things either guarantee or *prohibit* the development of a spiritual dimension. My beginner's exposure to Aboriginal spirituality has me reaching for ways to capture something that English words almost deny: a felt evaporation of my separate self into an awesome and frightening interconnecting with the energy—the *spirit*—that forms and fires all of Creation. I have felt it rarely, and it has usually taken me by surprise. It contains an element of terror, at least at first, because losing my separate identity—my illusion of control, as Danny Moonhawk Alford put it—means losing how I've always seen myself. When Descartes said, "I think, therefore I am," he not only gave me a purely thinking "I," but a very separate "I," as well. To a certain degree, making connection involves a loss of that "I," and it's scary.

As I am beginning to find, however, there is another "I" that is available, if hidden under the weight of all our nouns. It comes only if you quiet yourself enough to hear a connecting song within you, the song of the E-side of Einstein's famous equation. In some places, like the healing circles at Hollow Water, it is a loud and joyful chorus of brave and feeling people learning to celebrate the interconnecting of hearts that lived for so long in separate, silent terror. It took the music of their circle, of their unfolding kindness, humility, sharing, strength, honesty, caring and respect, to bring some sense of the spiritual to the surface in me. I recognized it, somehow, as the same song that the Northern Lights sing, that hums through every meadow, that erupts with every dawn. I knew it from those connections forged over many years as a fishing guide in northwestern Ontario, and I knew it from being beside my wife at the births of our children. I had just never experienced the way it sounds when it comes through the hearts of strangers gathered to become something helpful and sustaining to each other. Thank you, Hollow Water.

I referred earlier to the very simple way of speaking I have often observed among traditional people, where events are allowed to speak for themselves. I propose to close off my discussion of healing processes by following that example, letting Hollow Water speak for itself.

The Hollow Water Sentencing Circle

In a 1994 interim report, CHCH team members outlined in point form their suggestions for how the court should be structured when it finally comes to sentencing victimizers. These suggestions have been accepted by presiding judges, and are now well established. Remember that a great deal of healing work will already have been done by the CHCH team in the months between the entry of a guilty plea and the victimizer's return to court for sentencing. Remember too that the victim and offender will not be brought together at the time of sentencing unless the team believes they are *ready* to face each other with relative honesty. As I noted earlier, nearly two hundred people attended the first such "community sentencing" to participate in this unique process.

I will follow the headings the CHCH team used in their interim report, starting with "Rationale." All the italics, however, are mine.

Rationale

1. In our conjunctive relationship with the legal system we see our role as one of representing our community. We do not see ourselves as "being on the side of" the crown or the defence. The people they represent are both members of our community, and the pain of both is felt in our community.

   Until now, our efforts have focused on (1) attempting to help both crown and defence see the issues in the court case as the community sees them, and asking for their support, therefore, in representing the community's interest, and (2) providing the court with a Pre-Sentence report which outlines the situation as we see it, informs the court of the work that we are doing with the victimizer, and offers recommendations on how we see best proceeding with the restoration of balance around the victimization.

Now, however, we believe that it is time to expand the community's involvement in this process. *We believe that it is time for the court to hear directly from the community at time of sentencing.*

2. Up until now the sentencing hearing has been the point at which all of the parties of the legal system (crown, defence, judge) and the community have come together. Major differences of opinion as to how to proceed have often existed. As we see it, the legal system usually arrives with an agenda of punishment and deterrence of the "guilty" victimizer, and safety and protection of the victim and the community; the community, on the other hand, arrives with an agenda of accountability of the victimizer to the community, and a restoration of balance to all the parties of the victimization.

As we see it, the differences in agenda are seriously deterring the healing process of the community. We believe that the restoration of balance is more likely to occur if sentencing itself is more consistent *in process and in content* with the healing work of the community. Sentencing needs to become more of a step in the healing process, rather than a diversion from it.

The sentencing circle promotes the above rationale.

Purpose

As we see it, the sentencing circle has two primary purposes: (1) it promotes the community healing process by providing a forum for the community to address the parties of the victimization at the time of sentencing; and (2) it allows the court to hear directly from the people most affected by the pain of the victimization. In the past, the crown and defence, as well as ourselves, have attempted to portray this information. We believe that it is now time for the court to hear from the victim, the family of the victim, the victimizer, the family of the victimizer, and the community at large.

Participants

As we see it, the following need to be included, if at all possible, in the sentencing circle:

1. the victim;
2. those support people working with the victim, including his or her individual worker, group workers, psychologist, as well as members of his or her support group. If the victim is not able to attend, we see the individual worker taking the role of the victim representative;
3. the family of the victim;
4. the victimizer (offender);
5. those support people working with the victimizer, including his or her individual worker, group workers, psychologist, as well as members of his or her support group;
6. the family of the victimizer;
7. the community. This would include members of the Community Holistic Circle Healing team as well as whoever else from the community wishes to participate;
8. the court party. This would include the judge, crown and defence; and
9. RCMP. This would hopefully include the members responsible for the investigation as well as for policing our community.

Preparation for the Sentencing Circle

1. Advance preparation will include:
   a. tobacco being offered to the presiding judge;
   b. the preparation of the pre-sentence report by the CHCH team, and distribution to crown, defence and judge;
   c. meeting of the CHCH team with the chief, mayors, and councils to develop and implement a process for ensuring community participation;
   d. circles with victim, victimizer and family/ies the day before the sentencing circle;
   e. the sweat-lodge being available to any interested participant the evening before the sentencing circle.

2. In the morning of the day of the sentencing circle, preparations will include:
   a. a pipe ceremony;
   b. the hanging of the flags;
   c. the smudging of the court buildings;
   d. the placement of the community drum and eagle staff in the courtroom;
   e. serving of breakfast to participants from outside the community; and
   f. offering of tobacco for a prayer to guide the sentencing circle.

The Structure

The courtroom will be set up in such a way that seating will consist of two circles, an inner one and an outer one. The inner circle will be for those participants who wish to speak. The outer circle will be for those ... who wish to just observe and listen. It is hoped that most participants will choose the inner circle.

Sentencing Circle Process

The process of the sentencing circle will be as follows:

1. personal smudging;

2. opening prayer;

3. court technicalities (e.g., confirmation of pleas);

4. outline of "ground rules" that will govern the sentencing circle, by presiding judge;

5. first go-around: "Why did I come today? Why am I here?"

6. second go-around: participants speak to the victim;

7. third go-around: participants speak to the victimizer (offender) about how the victimization has affected self, family, community;

8. fourth go-around: participants outline expectations to victimizer, and/or state opinion as to what needs to be done to restore balance;

9. judge gives decision re: sentencing;

10. closing prayer.

Following the judge's decision and the closing prayer, participants will be invited to stay and use the circle for sharing/debriefing purposes.

Seating/Speaking Order of the Inner Circle

The judge will occupy the seat at the northern point of the circle. On the judge's immediate left will be two CHCH members who will play the role of process facilitators. To their left will sit the victimizer, followed by his or her individual worker, then four members of the CHCH team, then the victim, followed by his or her support workers, then all the other participants of the circle. Seated on the judge's immediate right will be the crown and defence lawyers.

The first person to speak in the circle will be the person on the immediate left of the judge. Speaking will follow a clockwise direction and will end with the presiding judge.

The Rules That Govern the Circle

The following shall govern participants' conduct in the circle:

1. only one person may speak at a time;
2. the Laws of the Creator shall govern the person speaking. Those laws are: (a) Honesty, (b) Kindness, (c) Sharing and (d) Respect;
3. a person may only speak in turn. There are to be no interruptions while a person is speaking;
4. if desired, a person may pass when it is his/her turn to speak;
5. all other participants should be attentive to the person speaking.

Conclusions

1. use of the sentencing circle promotes sentencing *as a step in the healing process;*
2. because those most affected by the victimization are involved and have input in the decision, the healing process of individuals, family and community are enhanced;
3. the victimizer is both held accountable and supported by those most affected by the victimization;
4. inclusion of the formal court party confirms the conjunctive relationship between the community and the legal system, as established through the protocol with the Attorney General's Department for Manitoba and supported by the federal Department of Justice.

Hollow Water is now conducting its own "review circles" at six-month intervals after the sentencing circle. They are structured in an identical fashion, but do not involve the court party. Their purpose is to reinforce community expectations with victimizers, maintain accountability to the community and review the progress of the healing plan. In effect, these reviews correspond to periodic visits from a Probation Officer, with the community-at-large assuming that supervisory role.

As of the spring of 1995, the healing circle team members at Hollow Water have worked with forty-eight offenders, eighty-three relatives of offenders, sixty-two victims of sexual abuse and one hundred and fifty-three of their relatives. Many of them are still actively in the formal healing process and will be for some time. In only two instances did offenders reoffend—and, as I mentioned, one of them is now a valued member of the team itself.

If things can ever truly "speak for themselves," then that enviable rate of recidivism sings a powerful song indeed.

Skirting the Issue

I listened to a Cree elder speak of her life one day. She talked about one of her grandsons, about how he always asked her the "tough" questions. One day he asked her if the Creator was a man or a woman. She answered that she wasn't sure the Creator had to be one or the other, but maybe something else instead. He then asked if she had ever *met* the Creator, and she answered that no, she hadn't met him, not the way she would meet other people on the street. Then he asked how she could be so sure that the Creator existed, if she'd never met him. At that moment, a gust of wind billowed through her skirts and she had to hold them down with her hands.

"Maybe it's like that wind," she told him. "I can't see that wind. I can't tell you what that wind looks like. But I know that wind is there, because I can see what it does."

I have the same problem talking about healing. Maybe you just have to go stand in that healing wind for a while.

CHAPTER 9

AT THE CROSSROADS: RESPONDING TO THE ABUSE OF POWER IN SMALL COMMUNITIES

A boriginal communities in Canada appear to be at a cross-roads with respect to justice. On the one hand, they can negotiate transfers of jurisdiction over justice with federal and provincial governments and then develop formal justice institutions like tribal or "community courts" based primarily on Western notions of adversarial proof and the passing of a criminal sentence. On the other, they can focus their time, energy and resources in the way that Hollow Water did, building healing capacities that operate separately from, but perhaps linked to, the outside courts. Every Aboriginal community in Canada is asking itself serious questions about which path to follow. The fact that many of them start their analysis from *within* severe community dysfunction presents special challenges. Ironically, it is traditional approaches which may show the greatest promise.

Aboriginal people frequently tell me that, in their view, substance abuse, vandalism, youth suicides and minor assaults are primarily surface problems erupting out of homes filled with violence and sexual abuse. Understandably, communities want to deal with the roots of those problems. I suspect, however, that many people, Aboriginal and non-Aboriginal alike, will be reluctant for a very long time to transfer jurisdiction over such serious matters to "community courts."

Getting to the Roots of Abuse

First, such offences normally result in harsh penalties in the Western system. A community that asks for a punishment-based "community court" with jurisdiction over abuse-related offences is also asking for the power to impose such penalties. As I noted, it is likely that the government response will be to insist that such jurisdiction come only with all the procedural protections that guard against someone being improperly convicted and then punished. In effect, this means that communities wanting the power to impose Western penalties will have to provide Western safeguards too—including Western-trained lawyers and judges. Once that happens, the whole notion of *community* courts goes up in smoke. I suspect that a great many Aboriginal people will voice the same concern, for it is their people who will become exposed to the risk of long jail terms.

I have heard a strong chorus of Aboriginal women arguing something else as well: that the outside system, as bad as it is, should not simply withdraw until it is known how "community courts" might use their new-found jurisdiction. There is a fear in many communities that certain power groups would use power over justice only for their own benefit, by prosecuting their blameless enemies and *not* prosecuting their abusive friends. As I tried to explain in Chapter 1, the consistent and all-pervasive denigration of virtually everything Aboriginal over the course of many generations has created an alarming number of broken communities, where traditional virtues have been eroded to the point that power and fear are in the driver's seat. Handing a punishment-based criminal justice power to such communities would only *increase* the scope for possible abuse.

There are many voices, then, asking that the jurisdiction of any "community courts" be restricted for the foreseeable future to less serious matters, like substance abuse, property crimes and minor assaults. To the extent that a community focuses the bulk of its scarce time, energy and resources on the creation of "community courts" with such limited jurisdiction, however, they run the risk of being unable to deal effectively with the root *causes* of both minor and more destructive behaviours.

Furthermore, I suspect that many Aboriginal people will oppose the creation of such "community courts" on philosophical grounds as well, if it looks as if they are going to be used only in the Western way, to deal out punishment instead of healing. Such people see no merit in trying to gain the power to punish; rather, they seek ways to prevent the punitive approaches of Western courts from thwarting their attempts to heal.

I am reminded of something said by a well-known elder (whom I will not name) at an all-chiefs meeting in his region. The chiefs were celebrating their creation of an Aboriginal police force, complete with Western training at a nationally recognized police academy. Apparently the elder did not share their enthusiasm. As it was reported to me, he told them something like this: "To my understanding, this is not the direction for self-government for our people. With this kind of policing, all you have brought us is the capacity to start oppressing ourselves."

There are many who look at "community courts" in the same way.

Opening Up the Secrets

In choosing between "community courts" and a healing approach, I suggest that it is also important to ask which route is more likely to break the horrible silence about sexual abuse and family violence that grips so many communities. My experience as a prosecutor for seven years leads me to understand that victims are often reluctant to report their abuse to the police. Whether Aboriginal or non-Aboriginal, there are issues of shame here on the part of victims, who sense that somehow it was *their* fault. When the abuse is within families, there are extra pressures of divided loyalties, and fears about what the criminal process will do to all the other members of that family. There is also the possibility that Aboriginal people face special pressures not to involve the police, for with them comes exposure to the untrusted outsiders, with all their adversarial ways and punitive powers. Perhaps there is also an issue of communal shame at work here, reinforcing the "conspiracy of silence" that surrounds sexual abuse.

As a result, a great many community problems are not reported to the police at all, and many violent acts, especially within families, never make it to court. I can't prove it, but I suspect the Western system deals with only a small fraction of the violent crime in Aboriginal communities. Aboriginal groups commonly report that severe violence, sexual or otherwise, has touched over 60 percent of all people in their communities. I have already mentioned Hollow Water's estimate that 80 percent of their population, women *and* men, have been the victims of sexual abuse.

In my view, this is one of the most striking and unacknowledged failures of the Western justice system: *a great many victims, especially Aboriginal victims, choose not to use it.*

Another seldom-acknowledged problem within the Western system occurs *after* victims disclose their abuse to the police and charges are laid. In my experience, whenever suspects exercise their rights and call for trials in Aboriginal communities, they stand a higher-than-average chance of being acquitted. Aboriginal victims and witnesses alike often seem unable and/or unwilling to testify in a convincing manner, especially before non-Aboriginal judges and juries. *That is, if they testify at all.* It is not unusual to arrive on court day to find that victims have taken off, literally, for the woods. And if they appear and take the witness stand, it is not uncommon for them to refuse to say a single word about the offence. The Hollow Water team members have also considered that phenomenon, and have this to say in their "Position Paper on Incarceration": "Crown Attorneys, to make their case, put the victims—often children—on the witness stand and expect them to participate in a process that in many ways, as we see it, further victimizes them. The court room and process is not a safe place for the victim to address the victimization."

In my view, each "not guilty" verdict following a victim's reluctance or inability to testify convincingly is corrosive in itself. Abusive people laugh at the system which could not touch them, while victims and witnesses shrink into even greater fear after realizing that their disclosure took them through agonizing processes for no purpose whatsoever. Even when they do testify if they survive cross-examination with their story unshaken, it has commonly been given in such a small, flat and unemotional voice that it seems to be "missing something" to non-Aboriginal ears. Judges and juries are understandably careful about convicting people for sexual abuse, with the normal result of a long period in prison, and the testimony of frightened Aboriginal women often is not strong enough to move them "beyond a reasonable doubt." It is not pleasant, as the representative of our system who has guided those victims into court and through their testimony, to see the hurt, confusion and outrage that engulfs them as soon as "not guilty" verdicts are announced. Some have absolutely refused to speak with me after court. To add injury to that insult, there are many communities where victims who have reported their abuse to the Western system are ostracized, punished or driven right out of the community for good.

These are different kinds of "failures" of the Western system in Aboriginal communities, and they do not get the same coverage as the high rates of Aboriginal incarceration. Perhaps for that reason, they don't seem to be part of the equation when proposals for reform are evaluated. They are, however, an important aspect of the grim reality of justice in most Aboriginal communities. To the extent that proposals for "community courts" continue to promise identical failures, the secrets of abuse will remain, and the illness will continue to spread from one generation to the next.

In my view, Aboriginal people performing Western justice roles seem to end up just as powerless as non-Aboriginal justice professionals when it comes offering victims, offenders and witnesses something powerful enough to lure them our of their present states of denial and silence. It seems to take the healers to do that.

Even the healers, however, face enormous problems in gaining the trust of their communities, so deep are the suspicions that decades of abuse have spawned.

The "Why Should I Trust You?" Issue

Virtually all Aboriginal justice projects speak of common goals involving attempts to reverse the tide of substance abuse, family violence, sexual abuse and suicide that has swamped too many communities. That does not mean, however, that communities will automatically look with enthusiasm on every justice proposal put in front of them. The history of many communities is in fact the history of losing power, first to outsiders and then to those at home who emulated the outsiders. In many of those places, significant power is already concentrated in the hands of small subgroups, and the powerless are all too familiar with how it has been used against them in the past. As a result, any justice proposal that involves the transfer of even more power into those hands will set off alarm bells instantly. Many people begin their response to anything new from a stance of deep suspicion. In that respect, Grand Council Treaty Number 3 (the elected governing body of twenty-six member communities in the southern portion of northwestern Ontario) speaks about such control issues as a *cause* of violence in its member communities: "Control issues were also mentioned as presenting problems. There are certain people in First Nations communities who believe they have more power than others and expect to control other people. They seem to have no conscience when it comes to hurting others in pursuit of their own personal gains."

No matter how much justice proposals speak in high terms of healing, of self-government and a return to traditional wisdoms, there will be a substantial number of people in the community who greet those pronouncements with scepticism and sometimes fear. If that is the starting point within the community, it is important that those offering justice reforms realize the validity of those reactions and offer proposals that attract community confidence instead. The establishment of "community courts," with their transfers of jurisdiction over offenders, is only likely to increase community fear and suspicion. By contrast, healing programs that do not involve increasing anyone's power over anyone else will have the opposite effect. For the same reason, projects of *any* kind, if they are proposed by those in power—be they band councils, select elders or particular families—may inspire the same sort of suspicions and have the same negative effect on nourishing community support.

Preventing the Abuse of Power

In Chapter 3 I mentioned being part of a large discussion group, composed primarily of Aboriginal women, where the issue was raised of retaining the protections of the *Canadian Charter of Rights and Freedoms*. A number of them spoke about instances of sexual abuse by well-connected older men that were successfully hidden from the authorities, and they seemed unanimous in their insistence that the charter be maintained to protect them—especially in the context of criminal justice—as the movement towards self-government gained momentum. I also mentioned everyone's surprise when a young woman from the Yukon presented a different perspective, telling us that her community saw reliance on the charter as "one more step down the whiteman's path." Instead, she advised, her community was trying to escape the hierarchies of power that dominate Western organizations and were imposed on Aboriginal people, primarily through the *Indian Act*. It was their hope, she said, that they could create a system of more traditional governance, without such hierarchies, where no individuals held such power over others. If that could be accomplished, with all groups participating in the decisions that affected them, it was their hope that protections like the charter might not be necessary.

Her quiet analysis made me wonder, for the first time, if it might be our particular justice system that itself creates the need for such things as the charter. Would all our complex mechanisms to protect people's rights be required to the same degree, or at all, if some other system were adopted instead? At that point, various features of our system seemed to come to my attention, including:

- the fact that we have given immense powers over the fates of our citizens to *individual* human beings—our judges—as opposed to broad-ranged groups of people from within the community;

- the fact that we have given our judges the right, if not the duty, to *impose* their resolutions upon others, against their will if necessary; and

- the fact that we have instructed them to use their powers to *punish* citizens called before them, and to *generate fear* in the population at large in the name of general deterrence.

In short, it does seem possible that the structure of the system we have designed creates its own unique need—the need for powerful measures to protect citizens from abuse *by those who operate that system.* After all, it is a system built around single individuals legally imposing painful consequences on others against their will.

We have, for instance, created the right of appeal from the decisions of individual judges, through several levels of court, right to the Supreme Court of Canada. We have done our best to insulate judges from political or other interference, giving no one the power to tell them what to do and making it illegal for people even to try. We demand that our judges not hear cases where there is even a suggestion that they have private knowledge of the facts or private relationships with any of the people involved. As we phrase it, the judge must come as "a complete stranger" to each case and each accused. There then exists a maze of procedural and evidentiary protections which few lawyers can grasp completely—all of which may stand as grounds for appealing against a citizen's conviction.

Because we are so familiar with those protective aspects of our justice system, we keep asking about them during justice discussions with Aboriginal communities. How, we ask, can anyone "come as a stranger" to any case in a tiny community? Doesn't everyone know almost everyone else? How can anyone sit in judgment over others when they will continue to live side by side as neighbours long after the case is over? Just as importantly, how can people be insulated from political interference in such small communities, given that band councils control everything from housing to jobs to welfare, all of which can be used to *punish the families of people who displease them?* Even the issue of using elders in sentencing decisions causes us concern, for our system tells people to disqualify themselves if they know the people coming before them.

Is it possible, when we ask how such safeguards can be provided in small communities, that we are preoccupied with problems that uniquely arise within *our vision* of a criminal justice system? *Would another system, with a different structure, keep those kinds of problems from arising in the first place?* I don't have the answer, but I think I have at least found the question!

We know, for instance, that in traditional times decision-making processes seldom involved disinterested strangers coming in from the outside to render impartial justice. Were things structured so as to avoid the potential for abuse that our system now contains? What kinds of structures are we talking about? If we go back to some of the traditional peacemaking perspectives already discussed, we see that they could indeed serve to limit the kinds of problems our system presents, and that our safeguards are designed to handle. They include:

- the requirement that decision making not be entrusted to solitary individuals, but be shared among a wide range of people, representing diverse groups, all coming together in a common process;

- the requirement that they focus their efforts on a restoration of health to each of the parties and to their relationships with each other and with the community rather than on punishing the offender and creating fear in the general population;

- the requirement that they focus on fostering healthier relationships, which will themselves give rise to workable solutions, rather than on the creation and imposition of detailed plans by strangers who will have no continuing involvement in their implementation, save when they prove unworkable.

In short, since our safeguards do not seem possible in Aboriginal communities, what seems to be called for are justice processes structured very differently from ours—*precisely what traditional peacemaking visions seem to contemplate!*

While their exact form will likely vary widely from culture to culture and community to community, it seems reasonable to expect that such processes will demonstrate nonadversarial *team* approaches, aimed not at punishment and deterrence but at *rehabilitation* measures designed and implemented primarily by the *parties themselves*. The result will be a system that, by its very nature, does not require the same kinds of complex procedural protections to guard against improper pressures and the abuse of authority. In the end, an Aboriginal charter designed for Aboriginal processes might look wholly different from the one that governs all of us at present.

I want to step sideways for a moment, however, to suggest that a truly Aboriginal approach to justice may *properly* contain certain kinds of pressures that our system would think of as totally improper.

I recall, for instance, a young man charged with smuggling liquor into his dry reserve community. His lawyer urged him to plead "not guilty," because the search methods by which the alcohol was found were in breach of his rights under the *Charter of Rights and Freedoms*. After a month-long adjournment, the young man came back to court, without a lawyer, and entered a plea of "guilty" instead. He explained that he had consulted with the elders who had spoken of their wish that the community be alcohol-free for the health of all. Because of that, he told us he had chosen not to "use the whiteman's law to go against the wishes of the elders," even though he knew he could have.

There are other pressures to plead guilty as well. One comes from the cultural perspective that the proper thing to do is always to acknowledge your misdeeds as quickly as possible, then ask for assistance so that you can both make amends and avoid repeating them in the future. Another comes from the fact that pleading "not guilty" forces others to come forward and speak publicly against you in a hostile or critical manner, a burden that should not be placed on them if at all possible.

A more dramatic illustration of pressure involves the sense of collective responsibility that traditionally holds entire families responsible for the actions of their members. I recall, for instance, a case where a highly intoxicated young man asked for and got the keys to his parents' car, then rolled it, killing a passenger. He was charged with impaired driving causing death. There was, for a short while, some doubt about whether he was actually driving the vehicle at the time or whether he'd handed it over to a third person. But in the eyes of the community, we learned, it did not particularly matter who the actual driver was. The real responsibility lay with the family that had permitted their drunken son to have their car in the first place. That being so, it was appropriate that they be held responsible by a conviction being registered against their son, whether or not he was the actual driver at the time, for his shame was their shame.

For those who squirm at such notions of wider responsibility *it must be remembered that the traditional purpose for allocating responsibility was not to pick out someone for punishment, but to identify issues that needed to be addressed, as well as the people whose attitudes and activities had to be reoriented if the issues were to be resolved.*

A system geared not towards punishment but towards a restorative response can easily carry a much broader notion of responsibility and may cherish many different justice "truths" from those we have come to hold dear in our own. As I am just beginning to suspect, a great many of our central justice concepts may have achieved that status only because they are necessary in *our* system, where we constantly run the risk of punishing an innocent person.

For instance, our belief that each individual is the complete master of his fate is only that: *our belief.* In traditional eyes, as

I have suggested, such an idea is considered both simplistic and, from a social point of view, dangerous. Rather, every action is seen as flowing out of a large, complex and powerful web of lead-up events. To ignore those factors entirely is seen as baffling. To assume that individuals are always powerful enough to swim alone against the currents established by those events is considered to be both arrogant and short-sighted. A society that makes such assumptions and then deals with its problems by examining only the isolated acts of solitary individuals is seen as somewhat naïve and at risk of experiencing an escalation in problems.

"What Will Get Us Back on Track Again?"

From everything I have said thus far, it will be apparent that I believe traditional perspectives and understandings remain far more vibrant and alive than many people—including some Aboriginal people!— suspect. It's not just a question of people being traditional in the sense of going to ceremony, participating in pow-wows or consciously studying the teachings. It's also a question of how much the "small" details of each day are shaped and guided by those perspectives and understandings. Does it feel proper to write university papers in a purely objective style? Should you respond philosophically to having all your plans suddenly thrown upside down or should you get angry instead? Traditional perspectives encourage reluctance to think judgmentally, to use judgmental words or to speak before the other person has finished. They suggest that telling other people what they should be thinking, saying, doing, buying, reading, watching and so on just doesn't feel "right" somehow. Especially where first languages are still spoken, such preferences are still strong. So too is the understanding that all things are interconnected and that all people are, as Sasheen Gould of Eskasoni phrased it, "born into networks of relationships and responsibilities."

My question, then, is this: how can communities be expected to create justice processes that speak in ways that their very languages deny? How can processes centred on power, rights, pain, force and individualism feel comfortable—feel safe—to people whose philosophical homes remain built on accommodation, responsibilities, comfort, teaching and mutuality instead? As traditional perspectives continue their revival across Canada, won't Western-based justice processes encounter escalating resistance?

It has taken a long time for me to start seeing things that way. To a large extent, my thinking was trapped within the Western paradigm of what justice was: a primarily reactive enterprise centred on police, lawyers, judges, jails and probation officers. For that reason, I saw "Aboriginal justice" in essentially the same terms, with the same sorts of players performing the same sorts of roles, but modified in various ways to make them more "comfortable" for Aboriginal people. It appears that *many Aboriginal communities have found their thinking trapped within that paradigm as well,* for it has been the only approach many of them have known for years and the only one they probably thought the Canadian government would respond to with enthusiasm. If, however, traditional justice really does involve different players (healers, helpers, teachers and guides) using different processes (grieving, healing, bridging and restoring) for different goals (the restoration of harmony between and within people), then why work hard to capture control of a system that is structured in a completely opposite fashion?

Hollow Water has never held itself out as a "model" of some sort to be copied across the country, and I don't mean to present it in that light. What it has taught me, however, is that a group of people determined to create a healing response *in their own way* can fundamentally change how justice is done in their community, without ever trying to gain jurisdictional control over how it is being done at present. As an (anonymous) elder within the English-speaking tradition phrased it: "There's always more than one way to skin a cat!" and the degree to which the healing way has skinned the Western justice cat is the topic of the next chapter.

CHAPTER 10

CHOOSING THE HEALING PATH

May We Help ... Ourselves?

Ironically, building healing capacities within the community may prove to be the fastest, cheapest and safest way to get the Western justice system to "step aside" in Aboriginal communities. The team at Hollow Water, for instance, did not seem to ask, "How do we get control over this or that aspect of the system?" Instead, they seemed to put the question this way: "What can we do to help all the people whose problems get funnelled *into* that system?" By coming at it from that problem-solving perspective, they began to create their *own* ways of protecting and supporting victims, bringing abuse out into the open and making victimizers take meaningful responsibility for their acts. As those ways began to show themselves as powerful alternatives to the methods of police, lawyers and judges—all of whom share the same fundamental goals—they gained the support of those "outside" professionals. In time, they have all "stepped aside" to a startling degree, giving the team more room to grow stronger still.

The role of the police, for instance, has changed dramatically. Victims now make their disclosure to the team instead of to a police officer. Further, it is the team that has the first confrontation with the suspect; no longer do the police simply arrive suddenly at someone's door, arrest them and take them away, leaving everyone else lost in fear and confusion. The team then escorts the suspect to the police for the laying of charges and the taking of a statement. The police, in other words, have "backed off," leaving the community free to orchestrate its own interventions and to do things in ways that support, rather than obstruct, the initiation of long-term healing processes for everyone. The more Hollow Water demonstrates success in their approaches, the happier the police are to work with and support them. After all, their goal is the same as the team's—to help create a peaceful community. It's just that the Hollow Water team has offered new ways to help reach that common goal.

The same is true in New Zealand, where the police are the strongest supporters of the Family Group Conferences, simply because they really accomplish things. In Hollow Water, no one had to gain jurisdiction over the police or create their own versions of them to change the way in which policing was conducted in their community. Instead, they worked with them in ways that held better promise of achieving goals that were common to all.

The same can be said of Hollow Water's impact on the entire bail system. They did not start by demanding jurisdiction over bail decisions, by trying to get their own people appointed as justices of the peace to conduct bail hearings or by trying to change the law that governs them. That law focuses on the same concerns the community has: protecting the victim and the community, making sure the accused will not disappear and taking steps to keep him or her out of further trouble until matters are firmly in hand. What Hollow Water did was create alternate ways to achieve those goals. By involving families and the community, they were able to propose new plans for supervision of the accused and for separate housing for the parties if that was necessary. People who used to go to jail while awaiting trial now remain in the community. There is little loss of community protection in the short term and a much greater chance of creating the long-term protection that comes from true rehabilitation. This came about not because the bail process changed hands or changed philosophy, but because the community presented better alternatives to satisfy common goals.

The role of the Probation Officer at Hollow Water has also been altered. In the past, probation officers prepared pre-sentence reports on their own, going into the community to gather information and suggestions. Hollow Water started out by working with them, collecting information and coming up with suggestions as a team. Now the families and community members are coming into court and speaking for themselves instead, and it is *their* plan, created with the assistance of the team, which is presented to the court. Similarly, the team has taken over many of the Probation Officer's supervision and control duties after the offender is sentenced. Once again, Hollow Water did not ask for jurisdiction over probation, demand to have their own people appointed as probation officers or succeed in bringing changes to probation law. Instead, they created more thorough and effective ways of achieving the goals they shared with probation services.

Without question, Hollow Water has also affected the way the lawyers do business as well. The Crown Attorney was once the person who "spoke for the community" and, to a certain degree, for the victims of crime. Now those victims and the community at large speak for themselves. Just as importantly, Hollow Water has provided the Crown Attorney with sentencing alternatives that did not exist before. Until they created their healing program, the Crown Attorney's concern for protecting the victim and the community, especially in cases of sexual abuse, left him only one option: jail. The work of the team has now created new ways to ensure that that protection continues, without the use of jail. Similarly, the very public nature of the sentencing circles has created another

way to satisfy the law's demand that there be a strong public denunciation of such offences: standing before two hundred of your
fellows, each of whom has a chance to speak to you and all of whom
are going to hear any promises you make and demand that you keep
them, is a more effective denunciation than sitting in a jail cell,
perhaps hundreds of miles away.

If a stumbling block persists as far as the Crown is concerned, it
comes from the law's demand that jail be imposed as a deterrent to
both the offender and others. The community insists, on the
contrary, that deterrence cannot be permitted to get in the way of
healing and that jail is an ineffective deterrent in such cases anyway,
given the other traumas already driving each offender. Primarily
because of strong victim support for healing sentences thus far, the
Crown has been able to give less weight to the goal of deterrence
and support the healing proposals instead.

The behaviour of defence lawyers has been similarly altered, for
they are no longer demanding and then conducting lengthy adversarial trials. Nor, when a guilty plea is entered and it comes time
for sentencing, are they doing all the talking. Instead, their clients
are expected to participate themselves and are given assistance by
the team to get ready for that participation.

In a sense, the two lawyers have become professional bystanders
to a community-driven process, where their role is to make sure
that none of the parties are being deprived of any of the procedural,
charter or other rights without their full, informed and express
consent. That is an important thing to remember about all those
rights: people are free *not* to insist on them. That is exactly what
the majority of offenders in Hollow Water do, so they can escape
the punishment-based system that spawned them and move instead
into one aimed at rehabilitation. Once again, Hollow Water
neither sought nor gained jurisdictional control over the lawyers
or their functions. Instead, by creating sentencing options that

could be supported by people from the community and from the court, they significantly reduced the circumstances where their adversarial and advocacy skills were called for.

One of the most significant changes, however, has to do with the number of trials that are held and the number of times that victims, witnesses and offenders are forced to suffer the stress and trauma of such adversarial events. For many reasons, including the desire to maintain the support of the healing team, offenders routinely plead guilty and acknowledge what they did. As a result, one aspect of the Western system judged most objectionable by Aboriginal people has become a rare occurrence. This too was accomplished not by gaining jurisdiction over the Western system, then changing it, but by presenting offenders, victims, the community and the court with a sentencing alternative to jail that all could endorse. That sentencing alternative has also permitted judges to change their sentencing patterns, with the result that jail is used far less frequently than before.

Hollow Water's focus on healing, then, has resulted in fundamental changes to the roles, behaviour and influence of all the mainstream justice players, from police and probation right through to the lawyers and judges. Adversarial trials have given way to cooperative problem solving aimed at the restoration of harmony, and punitive prison sentences have been replaced by community healing programs.

If that can happen in the context of sexual abuse, one of the most serious and complex areas of criminal justice, what changes are possible if less serious matters are approached from within the same philosophy? New Zealand's experience with Family Group Conferences strongly suggests that substantial improvements are possible regardless of the offence. Further, it does not seem to matter whether the case involves Aboriginal or *non*-Aboriginal people, or an urban or rural community. In *all* cases, the move away from adversarial and strictly punitive process seems to bring benefits to all concerned.

The progress of Hollow Water suggests that Aboriginal communities wishing to get the non-Aboriginal justice system out of their affairs as quickly as possible might be wise not to put all their energies into negotiating issues of jurisdiction and control over people and processes they wish to replace. No matter how much jurisdiction they achieve, and in how many areas, they will encounter exactly the same problem that Western professionals now face and the one Hollow Water tackled first: how do we deal *more productively* with the people who commit crimes and the people who were hurt by them? Again, it appears to come down to creating alternatives.

Grand Council Treaty Number 3 in northwestern Ontario seemed to be speaking from within a similar vision in their 1993 *Final Report on Community Consultations.* They included a list of twenty-six short-term and thirty-one long-term goals, focusing on such things as the need for community self-help groups, family therapy sessions, workshops related to family violence, training in work skills, training in parenting skills, and treatment centres and after-care programs for survivors of addictions and abuse. They also asked for "more support and constructive guidance" from chiefs and councils. The report's final recommendations included the following statement: "Funding for the development of community driven and culturally appropriate *alternatives* to the existing penal and corrections systems must be instituted ..." (Recommendation no. 22) (emphasis added).

None of the fifty-seven proposals for change spoke of seeking greater control over the legal system and then funnelling such issues through it. This does not mean that Treaty Number 3 will never seek involvement with, or control over some aspects of, the Western system. It does suggest, however, that their first focus may be upon matters other than gaining control over a system from which they want to escape.

At an earlier point, I ventured the thought that the healing approach might be a way for Aboriginal communities not only to change the behaviour of the Western system, but to dispense with it entirely for the vast majority of cases. This may not be as far-fetched as it sounds. For one thing, the healing that Hollow Water promotes is community healing aimed at the *causes* of criminal acts. To the degree that it succeeds, the numbers of those criminal aces will diminish. As that happens, the Western justice system will retreat on its own, without the need for constitutional change, legislative enactment or jurisdictional transfers.

Patricia Monture-Angus, a Mohawk law professor, teacher and friend, raised that issue in her article "Justice as Healing: Thinking about Change":

> Healing is also about taking responsibility. It is about re-learning how we are supposed to be. Without knowing what traditional responsibilities are, then the right to self-determination really means nothing. Healing is about learning to act in a good way....
>
> Many of our people know how to do "time." Jail "junkies" like myself know how to get them out. What we do not know is how to stop the revolving door of justice from recapturing them. We need to know how to keep our people out of institutions. That step requires healing our communities as well as providing healing opportunities for those who now fill Canada's criminal justice system.

But there is another aspect to Hollow Water, something rather startling, which is just beginning to show itself now that healing alternatives are the centrepiece of community justice activities: some victims are disclosing their abuse only to the team and refusing to disclose it to anyone from the Western system. They are asking that their "cases" be resolved entirely within the community, with no outside involvement at all. Where that takes place, and where the victims and witnesses indicate they will not testify in the outside system even if charges are laid, the Western system is powerless to maintain a role. In the Queen's system of criminal justice, you must register your complaint with her agents before the Queen can act. In the long term, then, it may not be the justice system that retreats from the community; instead, by building preferable alternatives, the community may retreat from the justice system.

Lest anyone think that is fanciful, it is worth noting that large corporations are doing exactly the same thing in some jurisdictions, abandoning the antagonistic, costly and time-consuming Western courts in favour of privately chosen mediators whose decisions they pledge to respect. The same movement is afoot in other matters as well, from disputes between neighbours to marriage breakdown. People are leaving the courts.

For a long while I have been worried about how Canada's superior courts would treat programs like Hollow Water. I worried that they would refuse to abandon their historic insistence on deterrence through jail, even when communities presented them with new programs for victim, community and offender rehabilitation. I now suspect that such a refusal, if it did occur, might not mean the end of programs like Hollow Water. If victims choose the community healing program instead of the court, there won't be much the court can do about it!

But focusing primarily on the creation of effective healing may not only be the fastest way to get the Western justice system out of Aboriginal communities. Surprisingly, it may also be the *cheapest*!

Delivering the Biggest Bang for the Buck

It is well known that governments across Canada are facing extreme financial pressures. Failure to take that reality into account in assessing the strengths and weakness of various justice proposals serves no one well. Simply on the financial side, there may be a lesson to be learned from Hollow Water: first put your money into developing the healing capacity, and only then, *as necessary,* into transferring jurisdiction and building Aboriginal case-processing systems.

Hollow Water asked the most powerful question first: once we know we have an offence, what do we want to *do* with all the people involved? It was only after they settled on their healing vision that they turned their attention to the kinds of case-processing approaches that might support it. The sentencing circle is a good example. It did not take shape until they had identified what their needs were *within* the healing vision, and until they could see what kinds of processes might work *against* that vision. If, by contrast, a community starts by securing jurisdictional transfers and establishing all the case-processing machinery without knowing what they really want them to accomplish, it may be wasted effort. In fact, what they spent so long building may end up *getting in the way of* the ultimate growth of community healing capacities. To use an old metaphor, it would be like designing the justice cart before you have the experience of the healing horse that will pull it, or any real knowledge of the mental, emotional, physical and spiritual terrain it must pull everyone across.

At Hollow Water this problem did not occur, since the team was built primarily out of people who were *already* receiving salaries as players in the healing field. I think here of community-based child welfare workers, NADAP (Native Alcohol and Drug Addiction Program) workers, community health representatives, mental health workers, band family service workers, nurses and nurses' aides, teachers and teachers' aides and so forth. There appear to be many such workers in most communities.

One of the original Hollow Water team members, for example, is now advising a band in northwestern Ontario, and as part of the preparation work he has identified over twenty such people already employed in healing jobs on that reserve, and an almost identical number of outside professionals with reserve responsibilities. It appears that the people are already in place in many communities. The lesson of Hollow Water is that they need to work in a different way. It was as I learned about how they restructured their efforts that I first began to get a practical sense of what the word "holistic" means.

Hollow Water saw, for instance, that while the different community workers knew the troubled families and people, they did not know how to work as a team. Team building, as they discovered over time, involved at least four essential steps: (1) breaking all the separate chains of confidentiality that kept each worker from sharing information and from being manipulated by dysfunctional clients; (2) designing common training in all the issues they faced as a team, rather than continuing with conflicting strategies from their separate fields of expertise; (3) requiring outside professionals to learn about and support their holistic team approach, as well as to share their own skills openly with team members, before permitting them to play an active role in the community; and (4) securing the time and resources to embark on continuing team and individual healing so that they had strength enough to maintain a safe place for others, as well as for themselves.

To meet those goals, the team undertook some twenty-two community training sessions for its members, covering such areas as Circle of Life Cultural Awareness, Suicide and Prevention,

Nutrition, Team Building, Human Sexuality and Intervention in Alcoholism. They also built in a continuing program for their own healing.

If Hollow Water felt they were unable to bring effective help to others without first going through such intensive team building, team training and team healing, it raises an important question: is it wise for communities to build *punishment*-based justice systems without first ensuring that the people who operate them are not un-healed people mired in their own denial? If such people are dangerous when it comes to healing others, how dangerous might they be when they bring their pains, angers and outrage into performing roles in a system based on *punishment*?

In other words, no matter which system a community ultimately decides to create, it seems that the first focus must be on healing the people who will operate it. Ironically, it seems almost more important that the people chosen to operate a punitive Western-based system possess those virtues, given the power they will be given to impose their will on others. Once those healing people are in place, however, it will be interesting to see which direction they actually recommend to their communities.

It seems to me that the healing route promises something else as well—something of special importance in Aboriginal communities: a chance for elders to once again be restored to their special roles.

Restoring the Elders and Their Role

At present, a number of Aboriginal justice projects in Canada involve elders. In Sandy Lake in northwestern Ontario, for example, two elders sit as a panel to advise the judge on sentencing for the more serious matters, and they now sit as their own "community court" for contraventions of band by-laws, primarily surrounding intoxicants. In Attawapiskat, such an "elders panel" held its own court for several years, dealing completely with all matters referred by the area Crown Attorney.

The question I want to raise is this: is this the *kind* of involvement that is most appropriate—and most sustainable—for elders? Is it appropriate, for instance, that they be the ones asked to assume the roles that Western judges perform or should they be making their justice contributions in other ways? Did they take on those roles because they wanted them or because everyone decided it was the only role outsiders might understand and accept? Is there a chance that by encouraging elders to sit on justice panels, for instance, we run the risk of attracting those who enjoy exercising power over others and of sending further into the shadows those who wish only to teach and guide?

I ask those questions because I continually had the impression that most (but not all!) elders were uncomfortable with the coercive role of a Western judge, and because my exposure to traditional teachings over the last few years suggests that their traditional roles were very different indeed. I recall, for instance, an elder who came to the court one day in a small northern community and was introduced to us as such. When the judge turned to him on a particular case and, out of respect, asked him what he would recommend as a proper sentence, his response caught all of us by surprise: he replied that it was not for *him* to tell someone else what was right!

It is my view that communities should work hard to regain an understanding of the traditional situation of elders before pushing them into Western justice roles. If those roles require them to do things that in fact diminish their qualities as elders, then we have done no favours for anyone. If, for instance, we require them to act like our judges and impose sentences on others, we may be asking them to abandon the very qualities that earned them their respected position in the first place. If their traditional role was to inspire, teach and help others make appropriate choices *on their own*, then turning them into judges may be the worst thing we could do.

It may be that when such elder-as-judge projects were first formulated, it was thought that elders would not have to play a coercive role. I confess that I held that hope myself. I hoped, naïvely, I suppose, that their example and their wisdom would be enough to turn things around for most offenders. I have since learned that many of those who most *need* the wisdom and assistance of elders are precisely those who have never learned to respect it—or to respect anyone else's, for that matter. Carole LaPrairie raises exactly that issue in her "Exploring the Boundaries of Justice: Aboriginal Justice in the Yukon," prepared for the Yukon Department of Justice: "Indeed, the group over whom elders would exercise control in justice matters are the group likely to hold them in the lowest esteem. Those who most often identify elders as the appropriate group to assume control over justice by forming elders' panels and elders' councils are the middle-aged people who hold elders in positions of respect and authority. The groups most often involved as offenders in the criminal justice system, youth and young people, do not necessarily share these perceptions" (emphasis added).

I do not dispute that the elders have a great deal to contribute to the young people in their communities. They most certainly do. The issue is whether that contribution is best made from a position as a "judge" in a courtroom context, within the Western justice paradigm, where some degree of force appears inevitable as long as significant healing options do not exist. Until it does, they are required to fall back on fines and lectures, neither of which appears to be turning the tide.

Another issue arises in relation to having elders assume a judging and sentencing role—one that was also addressed by Carole LaPrairie in her report:

The potential for discrepancy between the values of the younger and the older community members in justice hearings and decision-making is considerable. Few communities are untouched by events of the past two decades where women's issues, victims rights, and alternate life-styles have gained respectability and recognition. The social changes evolving from these events may be more in the psyche of the younger than the older members of the communities. The use of elders in justice systems, *to the exclusion of other age groups,* may reflect values not representative of contemporary community values. (emphasis added)

Clearly, the restoration of elders' values is important for a return to community health in many respects. It may still be asked, however, whether court-like sentencing hearings or community healing groups are the best places for younger people to receive those values.

Grand Council Treaty Number 3 commented on the position of elders in their *Final Report On Community Consultations,* prepared in 1993 as an initial step in developing a strategy to deal with family violence:

There have been a number of goals and recommendations that state that some persons would like to return to traditional ways through the guidance of the elders. With due respect to the elders and with recognition of the great contributions they make, it must be brought out that elders themselves are victims of abuse. It is important that the elders embark on a program of personal healing. A commitment such as this by the elders would provide an *example* to other people and it would be a necessary and beneficial undertaking for their personal well-being. (emphasis added)

As this comment makes clear, elders are themselves members of communities pulled apart by abusive behaviour for many years. It is foolish to expect that they would have survived unscathed. It might instead be wise to anticipate that many of them have been deeply affected by the fact that they were unable to *prevent* the cycle of abuse that afflicts their communities. In that way, some may have special reason to slip into a state of denial about that abuse and be unwilling to come to grips with it honestly. A final concern about using elders as substitute judges within a Western-based justice system is the issue of their age and health. When projects rest on such few shoulders and those shoulders are advanced in years, the projects themselves become fragile.

Using elders in a healing context, by contrast, may allow for very different dynamics. First, they can do what they are accustomed to doing, which is to guide, encourage and nourish. Second, they can learn from others involved in the healing processes about the complexity of the issues that face their communities—thus enabling them to contribute with a greater appreciation of today's realities. Third, their advice and guidance can be accepted or declined by others as they see fit, an option not available when elders act as judges. Fourth, they are free to choose the issues and people they feel comfortable with, and to decline others, regulating the demands made on them, rather than falling prey to an uncontrollable caseload. Fifth, because they will not be forced into carrying the ultimate burden of success or failure with each accused, they might not be subject to the accusations of inadequacy that only undermine the respect necessary if the teachings are to be passed to new generations.

Even more importantly, elders involved in healing forums would be able to bring their *personal* knowledge of an accused out into the open as a contribution to understanding. This stands in direct contrast to the obligation imposed on elders in our court system, where they are required *not* to get involved in the proceedings, when they recite their personal knowledge of an accused. That manoeuvre greatly perplexes all those who thought elders were involved because of such first-hand knowledge—including me.

And finally, if an elder fell ill or died, the continuance of the overall initiative would not be threatened, though their absence would be a loss to all.

The Need for Education ... Creating a New Partnership

The goal of creating healthy communities, however, requires something more than bringing healing to those who are already suffering within painful lives. It also requires measures aimed at education and prevention—activities that healing teams may be uniquely able to deliver. Education was clearly important to the Ojibway people of Grand Council Treaty Number 3 in northwestern Ontario, who participated in family healing consultations in the treaty area's twenty-six member communities in 1993. As their interim report acknowledged: "One woman that was interviewed exemplified the acceptance of family violence as a way of life when she stated, 'My husband beat me all the time and I lived through it—so these younger girls should be able to take it too.' Unhappily, this view seems to be alive and well in many First Nations in the Treaty Number 3 area. One participant stated that she remembered women being beaten in public and no one would intervene. She said, 'I thought this was a normal thing and everyone did it.'"

Case processing in the Western system is primarily reactive, responding to situations of abuse that have already taken place, and it is unlikely that "community courts" would be greatly different. While a healing focus also performs that reactive function, it may do so in ways that can also help meet educational and prevention goals in the community. As the healing process draws in all those affected by particular cases, those people also gain insights into community problems. If the team also operates community workshops to increase understanding, as is done in Hollow Water, the knowledge spreads further still. And unlike a court, healing circles are able to do all this in a nonthreatening manner that is more likely to promote open and honest discussion.

Another aspect of the education goal must also be considered: giving people the teaching they need to live *good* lives, not just escape painful ones. A healing team that makes itself knowledgable about healing strategies also makes itself knowledgable about health-*keeping* strategies and can share that knowledge with everyone in the community, especially the children. In Hollow Water, for instance, it was primarily thanks to the team that sweat-lodges, sacred fires and fasting have been restored to the community—all of them teaching and learning places and all of them open to anyone who wishes to participate. To give but the smallest illustration of their educational potential, I know of a seven-year-old boy who is now able, in the sweat, to sing one of the traditional songs that honour women. His father was never taught that song, for there were no sweats and the teachings had gone underground. To me, these things too are essential for community healing and can only come when a community puts its feet firmly on that path.

While I have spoken of the Western system "retreating" from Aboriginal communities, I find it hard to imagine a complete and absolute retreat as the end result. Instead, I acknowledge that I see places where a continuing—though very different—partnership may be of benefit to everyone concerned. For one thing, I suspect that the *threat* of jail may serve a useful purpose within healing programs by keeping the pressure on offenders to remain within them. By all accounts, honestly facing the pain you have caused is itself an intensely painful process. In a way, the outside system could substitute for the traditional threat of being banished, except that offenders who did not remain in the healing program would be banished to the outside courts rather than the wilderness.

Perhaps more importantly, I suspect that there will always be certain categories of cases that will demand the complexity, thoroughness and even the adversarial nature of the Western system.

On the one hand, there are those people who declare that they are innocent, who are disbelieved by the community, and who invoke their right to a trial. For the sake of protecting the innocent, the indignities imposed on witnesses by conducting trials may be a necessary evil. I suspect, however, that a healing approach will prompt the guilty to admit their crime, rather than force the Crown to prove their guilt in a trial, and that the frequency of trials will diminish dramatically.

On the other hand, we will also have some guilty people for whom the healing route is simply not a viable option, as far as society is concerned, either because they are not ready for it or because, as with psychopaths, they are not capable of it. Like it or not, there are people who present such a danger that any society, Aboriginal or otherwise, has a right to keep them out of circulation for as long as it can. That right, in my view, should be exercised within the adversarial protections of the Western system. If a community wishes to use a Western remedy and lock them up, it seems only fair that they have the benefit of Western protections as well—including the right to make society prove its case against them beyond a reasonable doubt under all the existing laws of evidence.

In my experience, it is not true that all Aboriginal communities want to abolish the use of jail absolutely. In the first place, they know by experience that some people get totally out of control and pay no attention whatever to efforts to help them. Sometimes, as one young man said of his own time in jail, it's necessary to do something drastic to people "just to get their attention," so they can start to think about their lives. In his case, he credits jail with helping him escape from an unhealthy pattern of dangerous friends, substance abuse and escalating violence. While communities may want such people to get treatment during their incarceration and to be freed as soon as the treatment has taken hold, they nevertheless want that person taken out of the community, at least temporarily. Sometimes it takes an untouchable outside force with no vulnerability to community pressures to do that.

I have also heard it suggested that in some circumstances the shame of being taken out to jail may be necessary to send certain messages to the community. I recall, for instance, a workshop in which I raised a hypothetical case to get people talking about whether jail should ever be part of a justice system. I gave them a fictional scenario in which an elder had been charged with sexually abusing his stepdaughter. Half the participants in that workshop were Aboriginal women, and I expected expressions of shock that I would even suggest that an elder was capable of such behaviour. To my surprise, I received virtually identical stories from three women from different reserves across Canada. In their view, virtually no one has escaped the violence, abuse and self-abuse that characterizes so many of their communities, elders included. While they all felt that a jail term should not be so long as to destroy the man or his chances for rehabilitation, all felt that a clear denunciatory sentence was required, given the flagrant abuse of his position.

That perspective may change as the healing perspective becomes better understood. I think here, for instance, of the shaming that has occurred in Hollow Water when offenders have stood before two hundred members of their own community, listening to each of them speak directly to them about what took place and about their expectations for the future. Until such options are created elsewhere, however, the need to send messages of shame by watching offenders being escorted out to jail remains a consideration in the minds of many people.

Canada has, in my view, a sophisticated system of case proving, which is second to none in the balance it draws between the rights of the accused and the powers of the police and prosecutors to investigate crime. Too much power in their hands creates state tyranny, while too little would lead to the tyranny of fear and chaos in the streets. I would hate to see it be put out of the reach of Aboriginal people who want to have their claim to innocence fairly tried, or Aboriginal communities who are faced with people for whom healing is not a practical alternative.

I must confess, however, that I have another reason for wanting to maintain a partnership of sorts: I'd like all Western justice professionals to have the opportunities I have had to feel the power and promise of the healing approach. For the sake of our own people, families, communities and country, the larger society needs to learn as much about it as possible. Our society is riddled with its own secrets of abuse, its own intergenerational cancers that no one reports to anyone else. My experience as a human being and as a prosecutor suggests that the "crime" problems afflicting the Aboriginal and non-Aboriginal societies are not so much different in kind as in degree, and that the difference is much less than most people suspect. While I see Aboriginal communities across the country showing signs of beginning the long trek up to health, the signs of anger and violence in non-Aboriginal Canada seem to be increasing. More disturbing still is the fact that most of the suggestions for dealing with it seem *driven* by anger and violence. As long as that persists, I worry that these proposed solutions can offer only more of the same.

To be clear, I don't see the thoroughly professionalized, adversarial and punitive justice system that we now have as an overriding problem in itself. The problem may instead arise from the fact that we shove almost everything into it—from schoolyard fights to serial murders, as if they all raised identical issues and concerns. It's as if the labels "crime" and "criminal" have gotten in the way of acknowledging how different we all are, and how different are the circumstances that cause some of us to fall short of—or intentionally defy—society's norms. In my view, this "one-process-fits-all" system is simply not capable of dealing realistically with the full range of human problems that it is presently forced to absorb. Simply put, we overuse it to an immense degree, and in the process diminish our capacity to maintain any *other* ways of responding to social problems.

Just to prove that I'm not alone in such concerns, I am pleased to report that the courts themselves are asking similar questions. The Ontario Court of Appeal, for instance, took the unusual step of adding a "PS." in the case of *R. v. McDougall* (1990) 1 O.R. (3d) 247. In it, they quoted approvingly from two earlier reports on criminal law by national bodies. The first was from a 1977 report of the Law Reform Commission of Canada called *Our Criminal Law:* "The fact is, the criminal law is a blunt and costly instrument—blunt because it cannot have the human sensitivity of institutions like the family, the school, the church or the community, and costly since it imposes suffering, loss of liberty and great expense." The second quotation came from a 1982 report of the Criminal Law Review Committee of the Federal Department of Justice, entitled *The Criminal Law in Canadian Society:* "The criminal law should be employed to deal only with that conduct for which other means of social control are inadequate or inappropriate." At the end of its PS., Mr. Justice Doherty, writing for the entire Ontario Court of Appeal, had this to say: "Those other avenues [the family, school, church community, etc.] often can more effectively deal with these situations than can *the blunt broad-axe of the criminal law*" (emphasis added!).

I will concede that the court was probably not thinking their words would be used in connection with something like Hollow Water, with a community approach for the noncustodial treatment of crimes like incest. Then again, they weren't *familiar* with a community like Hollow Water, nor with how far a determined community, using solid teachings, could go in pulling its people out from under the shadow of that blunt broad-axe and guiding them into more restorative approaches instead.

When they do become familiar with it, I hope they remember what they said!

CHAPTER 11

GETTING STARTED ON THE HEALING PATH

Caution: Assumptions at Work

I n this chapter, I want to look at how communities and outside governments might work towards creating healing alternatives to ultimately take the place of the present criminal justice system for the vast majority of cases. I use the word "community" loosely, because I think there are indeed "Aboriginal communities of interest" within urban centres that can play an identical role.

In approaching this topic, it seems fair to list some of my assumptions at the beginning, for there will be those who disagree with them.

First, I assume that Aboriginal communities across Canada have different histories, political dynamics, social problems, cultural characteristics, economic resources and administrative capacities. For any of those reasons, an approach that works in one community could prove a failure in the next. Any formula for promoting justice reform must therefore be flexible enough to permit a wide range of unique community responses. Second, the Western preference for single solutions, standardized processes and monolithic institutions may be part of the *problem* when it comes to recognizing Aboriginal hopes regarding justice—and in other social contexts as well. Whenever we use the phrase "an Aboriginal justice system," we seem to be setting a demand that Aboriginal justice must, like ours, include huge numbers of communities "signing on" to a single process. As I understand it, traditional wisdom suggests that it is wiser to give smaller groups the opportunity to tailor justice processes to their individual realities instead.

Third, I make the assumption that in many communities a sudden, overnight withdrawal of the Western justice system would not be followed by the immediate substitution of effective Aboriginal approaches, but by significant violence. Many communities face levels of social illness that would challenge anyone's justice system, Aboriginal or otherwise. Several hundred years of assimilative efforts have driven traditional processes—and the teachings that gave them spirit, focus and detail—substantially underground. While the present system does indeed have its failings, it remains preferable to the confusion, chaos or outright tyranny that I fear would erupt in many communities if it disappeared overnight. Contrary to the pronouncements of some, I do believe that things could be worse than they are, especially for women and children.

Fourth, while many people are returning to traditional teachings and finding strength in ceremonial observances of those teachings, they may not form the majority at this time. Effective justice processes will have to accommodate a wide range of perspectives, traditional and nontraditional alike.

Fifth, I suspect that progress will not be an overnight affair, but will require a great many stages of increased community activity and responsibility instead. I strongly doubt that anyone can foretell what shape things might take in any particular community as time goes by. For that reason, I suggest that both Aboriginal and government groups must accept what some on each side will perceive to be compromises. Governments must be prepared to give up power *without* seeing a blueprint for the exact ways that newly transferred power will be put to use. For their part, Aboriginal groups must accept a process of increasing practical responsibility that may not be immediately "recognized" in statutory or constitutional form: if no one knows what something is going to look like, it's hard to draft a statute that recognizes and transfers it in advance.

I make one further assumption as I survey the Aboriginal justice field—one that requires a section all its own: as much as I believe things could indeed be worse if the Western system made a sudden and complete retreat, I suspect that too many people in government are demanding far too much of Aboriginal proposals for justice reform.

The "Not Unless You Do Better Than We're Doing" Syndrome

Everyone agrees that vulnerable groups like women and children require protection—and even special attention—during this time of transition. That does not mean, however, that Aboriginal justice proposals must somehow demonstrate, in advance, that they are *risk-free* as far as those vulnerable groups are concerned.

In my view, Aboriginal justice proposals must be measured not against a perfect justice system, but against the *present* one. In that vein, seven years as a prosecutor in remote Aboriginal communities has caused me to suspect that the present system is far less "perfect" than most non-Aboriginal Canadians, including many within government, might assume.

In the last chapter I spoke of my concern that the vast majority of violent acts, especially within families, are not reported to the police at all. I also mentioned the frequency with which trials end with a finding of "not guilty," leaving abusers feeling all-powerful and victims even further at risk. These clear failures of the Western system are seldom acknowledged as proposals for reform are considered. They are, however, an important aspect of present-day justice in most Aboriginal communities. As a result, it seems to me that justice proposals that promise greater community support over time—and greater victim disclosure starting now—must be seen as distinct improvements.

I think we should take the same approach whenever we are faced with reoffending behaviour by people who have been given the benefit of sustained community healing. When that happens, as it will, the recidivism rate of that particular healing program must be compared against the recidivism rate for people sent to jail instead. Even if the rates are identical, the healing approach must be counted as an improvement if it has given greater numbers of victims the courage to come forward in the first place and get help for themselves.

I probably have many more assumptions as well, but those are the ones I've been able to locate so far!

Now let's begin the real challenge: looking for the safest and most efficient ways to increase Aboriginal involvement in all the human problems that end up as cases in the Western justice system—while at the same time helping Aboriginal people develop the capacity to escape that system in the long run.

Escaping the Three Bear Categories

Over the last decade, I have taken part in a number of negotiations about transferring jurisdiction over criminal law to Aboriginal communities. Almost without fail, they never seemed to get very far before the complexities overwhelmed everyone. If it were a tango, it would be easy to teach: take one step forward, two steps back, then repeat *ad nauseum*. Such discussions often begin with everyone talking about which offences should remain under outside control and which ones should be "handed over" to the community. Sometimes the dialogue breaks down right there, with the community saying "No way, you're not handing them *over* to us, you're handing them *back* to us! They were ours in the first place, and we never gave them up!"

If discussions continue past those hurdles, the next step usually consists of making long lists of offences, then breaking them down into what someone called the "Three Bear Categories": offences that are "too serious" to hand over/back, offences that are "*sometimes* too serious" to hand over/back, and offences that are "just right" to hand over/back!

Canadian law already has some categories like that. First, there are the "summary offences" like wilful damage, causing a disturbance, minor thefts and community by-laws dealing with intoxicants. They are usually seen as "just right" offences by government negotiators because their maximum penalties are the least severe (six or eighteen months in jail, depending on various factors, and/or a range of fines), and because they do not give the accused the right to a jury trial.

Then there is the group of "too serious" offences, called "indictable offences." They include such crimes as murder, aggravated assault and break-and-enter. Because they carry the highest penalties and give the accused the right to a jury trial, they are seen as least suitable for handing over/back, at least for the time being.

Then there is the third and largest category. It contains offences called "hybrid," "dual" or "Crown election" offences. For them, the Crown Attorney can choose whether to prosecute in a "summary" way or in an "indictable" way instead. Sexual assault is such a dual offence, for it can involve anything from improperly touching a girlfriend through her clothes at the school dance right through to rape. Because of that variety of possible circumstances, the Crown Attorney is free to choose which category best represents the seriousness of the act itself. When it comes to hybrid offences, governments usually talk about the community gaining jurisdiction only over the ones designated least serious by the Crown. That option, however, doesn't give the community much of a chance to say how *it* feels about them, and the negotiations start to stumble a little.

But that's just the beginning of the problems. For one thing, those three categories seem too rigid. Break-and-enter charges, for instance, are indictable offences, yet what we call "pop-and-chip B&Es" are common and (almost) everyone agrees that it would be better if the community handled them. At the same time, what about a really serious B&E with a really dangerous offender? Many would want that to stay in the outside system—but how do we agree in advance on the kinds of circumstances that would point one way instead of the other? If it's not possible to determine this ahead of time, who gets to decide as we go along? Once again, governments want the final decision-making power to stay in the hands of the Crown Attorney.

If I read government concerns accurately, part of the problem has to do with the very legitimate fear of sending people to jail without being certain that all their legal rights have been protected. Even a six-month jail term for summary offences is a heavy blow. Government negotiators take the view that people facing the possibility of Western penalties like jail should have the right to every Western protection. That, in turn, means things like the right to the presumption of innocence, to proof beyond a reasonable doubt, to trial before an impartial tribunal and to a qualified lawyer of choice, to name only a few. If those protections are guaranteed, however, then each tiny community would seem to require the services of Western-trained lawyers and judges, taking us one step forward and two steps back!

At that point, the only way around it is to have a system where the community gets control over all offences—*except where jail is required.* But who will have the right to decide on that issue? If it is the Crown, how does that increase community responsibility for justice?

Finally, there is the community insistence that many (if not most) of the least serious matters like drinking, minor assaults and causing disturbances are merely symptoms of more serious issues like family violence or sexual abuse. If justice activities are restricted to those less serious matters, community people rightly complain, they are only being trusted to put bandaids on surface blemishes, while the underlying diseases are left exclusively in outside hands.

For all these reasons, many justice negotiations seem increasingly pointless to everyone involved. At the end of each day, participants seem to leave with a sense that discussions about the agenda for cooperative change has been made more daunting still. At that stage, frustrated Aboriginal leaders often feel there is no choice but to simply demand the transfer of *everything,* citing the inherent right to self-government and certain constitutional provisions. "Just hand it *all* back!" is the frustrated rallying cry.

Over the last year or so, however, a more promising way of analysing the criminal justice system has begun to emerge. Appropriately, it was traditional Aboriginal teachings that suggested where and how to look for it.

Shutting Our Thing-Seeing Eyes

As I mentioned earlier, Aboriginal people have regularly spoken to me about their verb-based languages. They describe their "verb-world" as one where each person's primary focus is not on each separate thing but on all the movements and relationships *between* things. The Aboriginal or verb focus is on the many *processes* in which we all participate, at every instant in every day.

When that kind of analysis was applied to the way justice discussions have (not) been proceeding, certain patterns became clear. For instance, when we thought of a "justice system," our Western-trained, "thing-searching" eyes saw only offences—long lists of them, all precisely defined, all subdivided according to their seriousness. We then treated those lists of offences as if they *were* the justice system. Since our task was to begin the transfer of that justice system, we thought in terms of transferring jurisdiction over those offences. As soon as you begin to look at the justice system through "process-searching" eyes, however, it shows itself as a collection of four *processes* through which those offences, and the people who committed them, are manoeuvred.

We have, first, the *bail process,* where decisions are made about releasing an accused back into the community while his charges are being dealt with, often with conditions like abstention from alcohol to protect others and to keep him or her out of further trouble. We then have the *plea-discussion process,* where the lawyers and the offender consider the strength of the evidence, the accuracy of the charges, the seriousness of the damage done, the needs of the accused, the victim and the community, and the kinds of sentence that might be appropriate. If an accused pleads "not guilty," we have the *trial process,* where witnesses are called and tested, arguments are made over procedure and evidence, and a verdict is reached by a judge or a jury. Finally, if there is either a plea or a finding of "guilty," we have the *sentencing process,* whereby the judge imposes a sentence intended to achieve a balance between the four goals of sentencing: protection of the public, rehabilitation of the accused, specific deterrence of the accused and general deterrence of other people who might be tempted to copy his or her behaviour.

This shift to a process-based analysis seems to offer ways of avoiding some of the problems that will continue to plague us as long as we stay with an offence-based approach. For one thing, it provides a way to guard against the possibility of innocent people being punished through jail or fines. Within the process-based analysis, the risk of innocent people suffering any penalty at all, no matter how "light," arises only in the *trial* process—after they have insisted on their innocence by pleading "not guilty." That being so, the trial process can be separated from the others, then moved for the time being to the bottom of the discussion agenda.

Contrary to first impressions, that is not the avoidance technique it appears to be. In the first place, trials are not the dominant criminal law process. Over 80 percent of all charges in Canada result in guilty pleas, not trials. As a result, while trials may take a great deal of court time, it is the bail, plea-negotiation and sentencing processes that touch the vast majority of *people* who are charged with criminal offences.

Second, if the courts support effective healing processes as alternatives to jail or fine, the frequency of guilty pleas is likely to increase dramatically, and trials will be reserved for those who are truly protesting their innocence. In that connection, effective community involvement in the plea-discussion process could further reduce the number of trials by ensuring that only valid allegations are acted on.

Finally, putting the trial process aside means that justice discussions about Aboriginal involvement in the system no longer have to be restricted to the "less serious" matters, for the other three processes do not involve the same concern about punishing innocent people.

In the end, the trial process, which now appears to raise so many thorny issues, may be far less important than most of us have assumed. Instead, the justice system's greatest impact on Aboriginal communities may flow from the bail, plea-discussion and sentencing processes. In the next section, I will canvass how those processes can be dramatically improved *by anyone's standard,* by gaining strong Aboriginal involvement. Once communities become involved in these matters, they can more easily shift from them into strictly healing processes instead. I offer what follows not to *maintain* Aboriginal communities within Western processes, but to create the capacities and confidence necessary for these communities to ultimately escape them altogether.

... Bail Me Up, Scotty

The bail process is critically different from other processes in Canadian law: in making bail decisions, we cannot consider either deterrence or punishment. At this early stage, the offence has not been proven and the accused is presumed innocent. Instead, the principles that govern the bail process can be summarized as follows: (1) accused people are not to be held in custody unless all other ways of protecting society (and ensuring his or her attendance at court) are likely to fail; and (2) every effort should be made to design release conditions that will protect the community, help the accused stay out of further trouble and, if possible, assist him or her in getting started on a healthier path. In my experience, these kinds of principles drive *all* aspects of traditional Aboriginal approaches to justice. It is only when the Western system begins to add goals of deterrence and punishment to the mix that we start to drift apart.

There are a great many Aboriginal complaints, however, about the ability of outsiders to make sound decisions from the perspective of Aboriginal people.

1. Outsiders familiar only with urban centres, where accused people have often either skipped town or gone into hiding, sometimes fail to understand that Aboriginal people in remote communities remain both visible and, more importantly, tied to their families and communities in ways that make such behaviour much less likely, even where serious crimes have been charged.

2. Outsiders earning a lawyer's income can easily fail to realize that what they think of as a "low" bail deposit may amount to a complete denial of bail to people living a subsistence life in a substantially nonwage economy.

3. Outsiders coming from an increasingly jail-oriented climate will regularly fail to anticipate that their determination to keep accused people in jail until their trials are held will not meet with the approval of many Aboriginal communities. Instead, they may find such decisions provoke anger since in many places people feel obliged not to treat offenders as enemies of the community, but to offer them support, guidance and patience.

4. Outsiders may not be aware that each crime is seen as touching a wide range of people, that community leaders need to start working on the resolution as quickly as possible and that these leaders will not be able to do so if the accused is removed.

5. Outsiders brought up in the Western concept of family may have some difficulty understanding that extended families in Aboriginal communities often feel a strong responsibility for the care of their own and that they will freely offer alternate accommodation and supervision to satisfy everyone's interest in the safety of all parties to a case. This means jail is less necessary as a means of protecting the community.

6. Outsiders often cannot know whom to trust as representative of community views; they can thus unknowingly support those who are already abusing their power.

7. Outsiders may not know of, or be able to make the best use of, elders, spiritual leaders and other people whose involvement at this early stage might have the greatest positive impact on the accused and all those involved with him.

8. Outsiders cannot know how bail discussions might be procedurally structured—perhaps within a circle format—so as to maintain the greatest dignity, foster the greatest goodwill and send the most powerful community messages to the accused, the victim and all those who must be part of the recovery.

9. Outsiders often fail to foresee the practical results of their decisions. One of the conditions often imposed in exchange for release, for example, is the surrender of all firearms. For many Aboriginal people, the safest place they can be is out on their traplines, away from alcohol and the tensions within the community. Being deprived of a firearm, however, makes that impossible. As a result, a condition imposed to improve safety may thus have the opposite effect, leaving someone at home in exactly the same circumstances that led to the initial offence—but even angrier because he *cannot* go back on the land.

I suggest, however, that the benefits go much further than how individual bail decisions are made. Community involvement in the bail process would naturally serve as a catalyst for the overall shift towards the creation of a healing response, by bringing together all the people who must be involved in turning things around. At this early stage, the custody issue would clearly cause family members collectively to begin examining the needs of the accused, the victim—as well as their own needs. They could then begin to assemble the resources necessary for everyone's assistance, not only during the bail period but also during any probation period after sentencing, should matters come to that.

... Making Room in the Discussion, Please ...

Until recently, plea discussions involved only the Crown and the defence lawyer jointly analysing the strength of the admissible evidence, and deciding what charges would be proper, as well as discussing whether a guilty plea would be appropriate and, if so, whether they can agree on suggesting a particular range of sentence to the judge. Because trials are costly, judges are now supervising many such pretrial hearings, seeking to encourage as much agreement as possible. In those hearings, they review the case with the two lawyers and give their opinions on points of law, on the likely verdict and on the range of sentence they consider appropriate if a guilty plea is entered. If the lawyers come to an agreement, that same judge can then open court, receive the guilty plea and impose a sentence within the agreed range. Every trial avoided in this way results in substantial savings of judge, lawyer and support-staff time, and a substantial reduction in overall costs to the system as a whole. If there is no such agreement, there will have to be a trial before a different judge, one who has heard nothing whatever about the case.

From an Aboriginal justice point of view, one of the exciting things about pretrials is the fact that they are not governed by detailed law. Instead they can be as informal as the participants desire and can include as many people as they consider appropriate. As a result, there is nothing to stop them being structured in ways that show greater respect for Aboriginal approaches to dispute resolution.

One example demonstrates how pretrial hearings lend themselves to Aboriginal approaches to justice. An Aboriginal child welfare agency received allegations that a young man had been sexually abusing his adopted younger sister in a remote community. They brought a Child Protection Application in family court, and the judge took the initiative of arranging for a pretrial in the community. Because it was a pretrial, she felt free to structure it as the participants thought best, and they chose a circle. The circle included not only the lawyers and people directly involved in the allegations, but elders, community leaders and other family members as well.

That circle was more than a place to hammer out an agreement. It presented an opportunity for the various allegations to be explored in as nonconfrontational a manner as possible, for a wide range of people to be able to understand what took place and how it had affected each of them and for the process of reconciliation to begin. At the end of the day, it not only resulted in an Agreed Statement of Facts and an agreed solution on the Child Protection Application. It also resulted in the abused girl being able to go around the circle giving hugs of appreciation to everyone, including the stepparents whose son had abused her.

While the boy was not present at that circle, he later accepted the Agreed Statement of Facts as the basis for pleading guilty to criminal charges of sexual assault. The victim was spared going through a trial, and the detailed plans for long-term reconciliation and rehabilitation created in the pretrial circle were included in his criminal court Probation Order as well. At the conclusion of this "Pre-Trial Circle," I was told that the Aboriginal participants spoke about how the process had respected their way of raising, discussing and resolving such difficult issues.

Community pretrials, whether in circle form or otherwise, may thus have great potential for accomplishing *everyone's* justice goals during the transition phase toward community control. Clearly, the cost-saving goals of the Western system are advanced every time a trial is avoided, as is the goal of sparing victims and others from having to endure a trial. Just as clearly, Aboriginal justice objectives are also advanced: pretrial circles create community-specific processes for respectful, safe and comprehensive disclosure and resolution.

As a separate issue, it should be noted that many of the charges in the North occur when the accused is so intoxicated that he or she claims no memory of the event. At present, offenders must choose either to plead guilty on the basis of police summaries or to call for a full-blown trial so they can hear from the witnesses directly. If they choose a trial, their plea of "not guilty" really just means "I don't know." That all-or-nothing scenario could be avoided through a more informal pretrial process, where witnesses relate what took place either directly to the accused (though perhaps in a less adversarial manner) or indirectly, to a group whose word and judgment the accused accepts. This would also decrease the number of trials called for by those who feel they cannot rely on witness statements taken by the police.

At the same time, such nonconfrontational forums could also be important for victims. At present, their usual experience is that they are forced to wait for months in suspended animation until the trial is held, at which time they discover that the justice system values them not as human beings in need of assistance but as weapons in a legal war against an accused. Community pretrial forums give victims an *early* opportunity to disclose their trauma, fears and needs to a trusted group (with or without the presence of the accused, as circumstances suggest). Establishing these forums for all Aboriginal communities would be a first step towards attaining a justice goal frequently neglected by the Western justice system: victim rehabilitation and re-integration.

And that takes us to the issue of sentencing, the stage in any justice process where we might expect the clearest expression of a particular society's cultural perceptions and values.

... A Few Sentencing Paragraphs ...

It is the sentencing process, perhaps more than any other, that draws the most fire from Aboriginal people. As we have seen, this is not just because it is based on the foreign goal of punishment instead of on the Aboriginal goals of restoration and rehabilitation. Objections are also made to the fact that sentencing hearings are conducted in an adversarial fashion, with sides being taken, hard-line positions being entrenched and the accused being treated as an adversary of his own community. At the same time, the professionalization of the system has robbed people of the chance to take and develop responsibility for their own lives—a central feature of New Zealand's FGCs, Hollow Water's healing circle and Navajo peacemaking. As Bluehouse and Zion have expressed it: "The word *hozhoojigo* describes a process of planning—another Navajo concept. It means 'to do things in the right way' or 'go in the right way' by identifying practical means to conform future conduct with values. The entire process is called 'talking things out,' and it guides the parties to a noncoercive and consensual conclusion to restore them to harmony in an ongoing relationship with a community. The relationship is central.... The method is effective because it focuses on the parties *with goodwill* to reintegrate them into their community ..." (emphasis added).

As a Crown Attorney, I suspect that few accused people have ever felt that the Western courts focused on them "with goodwill." What they heard instead was how they would have to "pay the price" for their misdeeds. Just as importantly, most (but not all) victims I have encountered in Western courts take a similar position. Instead of expecting that I will "express goodwill" towards the accused, they expect me to deliver as much anger and outrage as I possibly can. Worked right into the fabric of our society seems to be the conviction that justice involves the retroactive, judicial creation of a balance of hurt, and the belief that this will somehow set things right again.

Diane LeResche has given perhaps the best overall description of the differences I have encountered: "[Aboriginal peacemaking] brings peace through good feelings, not through fear. Peacemaking involves deep listening, not defending, arguing, forcing. It includes the widest circle of people concerned, each having a voice if they wish, not just the immediate 'parties' and their representatives.... It is *relationship*-centred, not *agreement*—centred ..." (emphasis added).

Bringing Community Teams to Life

To date, justice initiatives have tended to focus on creating justice teams in individual communities by funding a justice coordinator from that community, then giving that person the responsibility for pulling a team together. In my own assessment, that process has a number of drawbacks:

1. Being from the community in question, the coordinators carry a lot of baggage. They are identified as a member of one community faction or another, with the result that they often find it difficult, if not personally perilous, to reach out across the factions to assemble a team that transcends them. In fact, very few qualified individuals are likely to want such jobs in the first place, so exposed are they to charges of favouritism and accusations of wanting to look like a "big shot."

2. As individuals, they almost invariably find the workload, tensions and frustrations so extensive that they burn out.

3. There is a substantial risk that such training will be wasted as coordinators burn out or move on to less stressful work.

4. Bringing adequate training to such individuals in each reserve community is an expensive proposition, for it often involves training not only in the Western court system but also in traditional *Aboriginal* approaches to dispute resolution and healing, so "successful" have Western agencies been in forcing Aboriginal people to forget—and deny the power of—those approaches.

The goal, to be clear, does not involve training Aboriginal people to take on, and be controlled by, Western processes involving bail, plea negotiation or sentencing. Instead, Aboriginal people could become involved in a day-to-day way in the *issues* that each of those processes grapples with. In the end, I suspect that the participation of "teams" of Aboriginal people in all those issues will ultimately lead to the creation of healing or peacemaking *systems*—perhaps unique in each community—that are so strong and welcome that people will choose not to take their problems into the Western one. If that occurs, the result will be full community control over all but the rarest of matters, where trials are necessary. At the same time, the "outside" system would remain "on stand-by" at all stages, ready to provide back-up as necessary.

In my view, what we should all be searching for—and finding—are Aboriginal people who are willing to take on training and coordinating functions in a *number* of communities, so that respected community healing teams can be nurtured on a case-by-case basis, over time. While they would probably begin their duties within the compartmentalizations of the Western system (bail hearings, plea negotiations and sentencing, among other things), they would, I suspect, rapidly insist on a more holistic description of their challenges, as would the community members with whom they worked.

For the moment, let me call such people Community Justice Trainers. I see them being given training in four separate areas:

1. training about the Western justice system, such as that provided in Justice of the Peace and paralegal training programs (including bail hearings, summary offence procedures, client interviewing, legal terminology and the like);

2. training in traditional teachings such as circle of life, cultural awareness, the medicine wheel, peacemaking techniques and so forth—with course content determined by the culture of the region to be served;

3. training in the principles of team building and community development; and

4. to a lesser extent, overview training issues like intervention in alcoholism, suicide prevention, and the dynamics of family violence and sexual abuse.

To avoid some of the problems identified earlier, they should not be *from* any of the communities they serve, though they should certainly speak the same language and be personally familiar with other communities of similar size, geography and social history. In that way they should find it easier to preserve their independence from local power groups, enhance their acceptability to all factions and assure everyone of their impartiality as they move into the creation of *community* justice teams.

I think it is especially important that such teams "come into being" in the course of grappling with the real issues that actual cases present, rather than through academic exercises intended to prepare them for such issues in advance. As anyone directly involved in the justice system will attest, the combinations and permutations of human problems, as well as the potential responses to them, are virtually limitless.

It is also important, for reasons outlined earlier, that such teams be composed primarily of community people with a demonstrated commitment as healers and, if at all possible, an existing paycheque to support them in such activities. These people would not only be able to lend long-term help (and credibility) to the team's efforts, but they would also bring significant knowledge to bear on each particular case.

Community Justice Trainers would have a number of roles to play. They would educate both the community and outside justice professionals as to the benefits of such holistic community involvement at all stages of the Western process. They would seek out and involve the widest range of community people committed to bringing healing about and help them obtain the common training the trainers thought most important. They would learn which forums or processes (circles, family councils, intermediaries, etc.) were most culturally appropriate to dispute resolution in the particular communities they served and would work towards revitalizing them in the context of real cases. They would provide community teams with information not only about the purposes and rules of Western court processes, but also about traditional processes for considering the same kinds of issues.

Using bail issues and the circle format as an illustration, the trainers could perhaps begin by acting as the circle "supervisor"— making certain the appropriate parties were present, conducting the opening and closing in traditional fashion, welcoming the participants and explaining the need for community safety and the challenge of looking for noncustodial ways to provide it. They would add teachings about the order of speaking and the kinds of speech to be avoided and they would coach trainees in ways of drawing out the fullest contributions of all present. While it would be the trainer's duty to guide discussions towards productive conclusions from the point of view of the community (while still keeping bail issues in mind), it would also be their task to show team members how to accomplish that goal using *respectful processes of discussion,* according to the traditions unique to that region.

In this way, community members would gain first-hand familiarity with the benefits of a coordinated, holistic approach to community problems. Then, with the power of their own traditions (such as the Medicine Wheel Teachings), they could create justice processes as productive today as they were generations ago. In time, as the team and the community gained confidence and strength, the need for the trainer's contributions would disappear.

Who knows? Perhaps the combined experience of all such trainers would give them unique capacities to sit together as regional dispute-resolution circles for matters that communities did not wish to handle on their own. They might also make up regional "appeal circles" for people who did not feel heard or supported at home. At the very least, they would be invaluable in helping to educate Western justice workers about Aboriginal processes, and they would be in a good position to learn the workings of the Western system.

As I now see it, there is no reason why justice in Aboriginal communities has to come from the same premises, perspectives and processes that prevail in the Western system. If they wish to dedicate their attention and energies towards a search for—and healing response to—the dynamics that gave rise to the "crime" before them, why should we object? Aboriginal people are not telling us that the Western way is the "wrong" way—only that it is not their way. We are not being asked to change our methods of dealing with crime, but only to step aside so that Aboriginal methods can come to the service of Aboriginal people once again.

Who knows what we can all learn if that takes place? It just may be that the Western system has confused procedural complexity in proving someone guilty with analytical sophistication about how to *respond* to that person and their crime. Is that why the Ontario Court of Appeal said that "the blunt broad-axe of the criminal law" should be used as an instrument of last resort, because it is indeed a "blunt and costly" instrument?

After fourteen years in the legal trenches, it seems clear to me that, from anyone's perspective, there are substantial failures in the Western system, especially when it comes to helping victims get their lives on track again and to addressing the reasons behind an offender's failure to respect the integrity of others. When these are precisely the issues that Aboriginal people want to tackle, why would we not support them in every way we can?

CHAPTER 12

AND FINALLY ...
THE STARTING POINT

We know you have a *legal* system;
we're just not sure it's a *justice* system.

—CREE ELDER, ALBERTA, 1991

Over the last three years, part of my job has been to read research studies about "traditional Aboriginal justice." Many of them were prepared by Aboriginal groups and, after a while, a pattern appeared: the researchers would spend a great deal of time speaking with elders, then bring back reports that seemed to me to be totally off the mark. Most of them left me feeling perplexed and disappointed. I had expected the researchers to do their best to uncover and describe the methods that Aboriginal people used to settle disputes or deal with troublesome individuals in traditional times. In many reports, however, those topics seemed almost beside the point, and the discussions wandered all over the social map, touching everything from child rearing to hunting and fishing, storytelling, naming, cosmology, ceremony, the importance of family and clan structures and the impact of residential schools. Why, I asked, did those reports spend so much time trying to describe how the whole society functioned, when all we asked about was the justice system? Why were things going in such unexpected directions? Who was responsible for *choosing* those directions?

I should have known the answer because, as in so many other cases, it was the elders who were responsible. The researchers went to the elders with their long lists of questions, and it was only after the elders became involved that things got turned around. It now seems clear that, no matter what the researchers thought they wanted to learn about, the elders would tell them only what they felt their people *needed* to hear. And what elders across North America seem to be saying, in a great many ways, is that discussions about justice have been starting in the wrong place—within Western definitions of what justice is, where it comes from and how it is maintained. As one Ojibway elder phrased it, "How can we negotiate justice with the people who brought us the *in*justice?" As I have now come to understand those words (and I may be wrong here too!), Western justice professionals seem, perhaps because of their unique training, to be *incapable* of grasping the concepts of justice the elders wish to see restored to their people.

When I looked back on it, I saw that a number of Aboriginal groups had said quite openly that their vision would not be much like ours. I still marvel at how long it took me to understand what they were driving at. In July 1994, for instance, Grand Council Treaty Number 3 held an Ojibway Elders' Justice Conference in northwestern Ontario as part of their research into traditional justice. Their interim report on what the elders spoke about contained the following: "We realize that way of life does not correspond in any way with the current justice system, so our approach in trying to research the material we wanted would have to come from a different angle. It would appear that trying to identify a justice system *as most people understand* it is going to be virtually impossible ..."

"[T]he Anishinaabe system was not a *correctional* system in its entirety, but one of trying to impress upon the individual through constant discussions by the community elders, medicine men and leaders the error of their ways ..." (emphasis added).

WHAT WAS IT that those Ojibway elders *did* want to tell their researchers about? Clearly, it was traditional teachings, understandings about life which they felt everyone needed to think about and live by if they wished to have "a good life" for themselves and for others. For instance, the Grand Council Treaty Number 3 report contained the following passage: "Respect for each other and a universal appreciation for the power of the creator kept everyone walking down a path that encompassed honesty, truths, respect for everything in their immediate life or ecosystem, whether it was your fellow man or beast or plant life. It was a holistic respect for everything that the Anishinaabeg could see, smell, hear, taste and feel."

If we move to the other side of the continent, to the Salish people of western Washington, we come across similar kinds of messages. Their Northwest Intertribal Court System did its own research into traditional justice in 1991. In an article summarizing their findings, the following caution appears: "As one elder emphasized, in earlier times people would not even have used terms such as 'dispute resolution process.' Instead, they concentrated on how to get along together to *minimize* the outbreak of disruptions in family and community life. The research included a search for patterns and values that reinforced social cohesion and *discouraged* open disputing, as well as looking for specific processes for handling disputes once they did occur...." (emphasis added).

The Salish study carried on to discuss ways in which social health was promoted, and the following passage demonstrates the kinds of issues that Salish elders wanted to speak about: "Children learned from birth the proper attitudes and behaviours that promoted appropriate dispute *prevention and resolution:* to respect their elders and teachers, to refrain from boastfulness, and to value qualities of self-discipline, self-control, generosity, peacefulness and hospitality.... Their teachers were usually the family elders who taught by example, lecture, storytelling and recounting family history. This training prepared children for their role in a society that was structured to *minimize* open disputing" (emphasis added).

So there it was: within traditional Aboriginal understandings, a justice system involved far more than simply controlling how disputes were handled after they broke out. *Instead, the primary emphasis was on teaching individuals from birth how to live together in ways that avoided or minimized them in the first place.* I had been seeing that emphasis everywhere, but had not been able to see it for what it was—a different definition of what justice really was, and where you had to start if you wanted to talk about it.

Once I became aware of that larger definition, I saw it everywhere I looked. I found, for instance, a similar approach in a 1995 report on traditional Dene justice in the Northwest Territories. While it indeed spoke of how particular transgressions were handled, its primary focus was on the kinds of values that were taught, how they were passed on and how they contributed to the creation of a peaceful and enduring society that had minimal need of "corrections" processes. The following passages from the introduction set out the issues that Dene elders felt had to be reported if their "traditional justice system" was to be understood: "Traditionally, the Dogrib people lived on the land following a seasonal round of activities which maintained them economically, spiritually, socially and politically.... Their ties to each other, to the land and to the spiritual world were strong and reciprocal.... The traditional legal system ensured that people understood what the rules were and that they were *expected* to follow them; that is, socialization ensured that the rules were the base for the normative way of behaving...."

I'm not sure why it took me so long, but it is now clear that the elders have been giving their researchers—and the rest of us—one single, coherent and powerful message: justice involves far more than what you do after things have gone wrong. Instead, it involves creating the social conditions that minimize such wrongdoing. In short, a "justice system" in their eyes does indeed encompass much more than a "legal system," as the Cree elder suggested in his own way. It involves instead all the social mechanisms that reach people from the moment of their birth how to live "a good life." In fact, "good life" is often an expression that has the same meaning as "the law."

Once I started to understand that a much wider definition was at work, I could see places where my attempts to narrow the discussion and speak only of a narrow, reactive process had been resisted. The 1993 *Report of Grand Council Treaty Number 3,* for instance, said the following: "Justice in the English legal lexicon ... means the system of law, courts, penal and appeal procedures of the Euro-Canadian system. *There is no direct relationship with our systems.* Justice to our people means allegiance to the integrity of our spiritual principles and values. Simple in meaning, but difficult to practice; to be pursued rather than attained ..." (emphasis added). That passage expresses the dynamics as well as any I have come across: no matter how hard justice researchers try to restrict the discussion to processes of correction, of *re*action, the elders will concentrate their replies on *pro*active measures instead—all of which are contained in traditional teachings about how life should be lived.

Chief Justice Robert Yazzie of the Navajo Nation Judicial Branch phrased his understanding of the difference this way in his 1994 paper "Healing as Justice: The American Experience": "European explorers often said, 'Indians have no law.' Why? They couldn't see the police; they couldn't find the courts; they didn't see uniforms, jails and all the trappings of power. But they also couldn't see the clan mothers who are so important to our Native legal institutions.... We deal with each other in ways to *avoid* confrontation and the use of force. Force, coercion and ability to punish are not necessary to have law."

I also remember something a Cree man said at a justice conference in Alberta in 1991. I quoted him in *Dancing with a Ghost,* but I'm still gaining new insights into what he told us when he asked: "Why does your law, from the Ten Commandments to the Criminal Code, speak only about what people should not *do?* Why don't your laws speak to people about what they should *be?*"

Slowly, I began to gain some understanding about why I always heard phrases like "living a good life" or "doing things the right way": people were talking about what "law" and "justice" really meant. They had little to do with simply responding to disorder after it occurred or with creating long lists of acts which were known as "offences." Instead, they involved proactive teachings about how people *should* approach the living of their lives, as individuals and as members of a group. At this point, I want to say something as plainly as I can: despite initial reluctance, I have come to the conclusion that traditional teachings formed a sophisticated body of community governance that has an equal right to be called "law." It has taken me a long time to come to see things that way, and it has been a difficult process.

For instance, I think I was bothered by the fact that such teachings were not written down. I therefore assumed that they couldn't have been clearly known to everyone, and as such couldn't have the force of real "law." In that respect, I didn't understand that there was no need to write them down because they were stated everywhere, in every activity, at virtually every hour of the day. As I have tried to demonstrate, they were even embedded in the very structure of language. As it has been expressed to me, if you are speaking in many of the Aboriginal languages, it is impossible to speak *about* life without also speaking about how it *ought* to be seen and conducted.

Second, I was also caught off guard by the fact that traditional law focused primarily upon teaching what people *should* do as human members of the cycle of life, rather than on creating lists of what they shouldn't do, followed by complex processes of proof and punishment. There were lists, of course, and very clear prohibitions against a great many things, but such "list making" seems to have been secondary to "lesson teaching," including very practical storytelling about the kinds of things that would happen if those laws were broken. I was not used to laws being expressed that way, in terms of duties, rather than prohibitions.

I also admit that I had a hard time dealing with another declaration I kept hearing from Aboriginal people across the continent—the declaration that Aboriginal law does not come from human beings, but from the Creator. To make matters still more difficult, I was also told that the Creator's law is observable everywhere you look—as soon as you leave the city behind and take yourself back to Mother Earth. Statements like those were, for me, both far-fetched and fanciful. Without being aware of it, I had grown up believing that nature's only law was the law of the jungle, and that *that* law promised only unregulated aggression and social chaos. When I looked out into the forests and streams, I could see nothing at all that might contribute to a moral code for human beings—until, that is, my many friends began to give my eyes (and heart and spirit!) the education they needed, the education I have tried to share in these pages.

LOOKING BACK, I can now see that I wasn't alone in confusing two notions of what "justice" might be. As strange as it may seem, many Aboriginal researchers seem to have been caught in a similar kind of trap. For one thing, the impact of colonization has been so severe that they, and thousands like them, have been cut off from traditional teachings—often for several generations—and left to absorb Western approaches instead. To make matters worse, many were chosen to do this justice research not because of their knowledge of traditional law, but because they had already taken some training in the Western system, whether as lawyers, courtworkers, police officers or justices of the peace. As such, their exposure to Western approaches was even more pronounced, and their definitions of justice had taken on an even stronger Western bias. Understandably, many of them approached the elders in the same way I did, expecting to hear about strategies and processes that looked like Western ones. In fact, some of them seemed just as confused as I was when the elders politely ignored their Western-oriented questions and spoke instead about values and teachings, about how to live a "good life" and about how those teachings have come "undone." I must admit, however, that they were much faster than I was in coming to understand *why* their elders refused to play that game! This was especially true for those who retained their own languages. As a result, their reports brought back information none of us had expected at the beginning—but I was the only one who couldn't understand why.

I heard a Cree man express his understanding of the kind of search that must take place as Aboriginal people look for their own ways of dealing with life. In his case, he was talking about regaining Aboriginal control over the education of children, but the same dynamics appear within justice issues as well. He and a group of twenty other Aboriginal educators had spent a week in workshops, and the task they had been given was to come up with a better curriculum for Aboriginal schools. At the end of the week, however, there was no "curriculum" in the sense of a list of subjects to be taught. Instead, each group had produced, in various forms, a vision of the kinds of *values* that should be manifested during the course of each school day and in the context of each school activity. In that one week, all the workshop groups had come to an identical conclusion: they couldn't start by creating a list of subjects.

As that Cree educator phrased it, he felt that his people had to take "two giant steps backwards" to precolonial understandings, to learn from the elders about what the traditional values and laws were, and how they were incorporated into daily life. Then, he said, it would be possible to "get our feet on solid ground again." And only then, as he put it, could his people take "even the first small steps forward" in creating the kind of education system that the communities require today. In my experience, that appears to be the strategy emerging across the country, whether the context is justice, health, family law, education, child rearing or any other aspect of life. The belief seems to be that, whatever processes are created or restored to deal with today's issues, they must be firmly grounded in the values—in the *laws*—of traditional times.

As much as it might surprise non-Aboriginal readers (and many Aboriginal ones too, I suspect), this approach is being taken even where the activity seems much more straightforward than law or education. Charlie Fisher, my friend and teacher from the Treaty Number 3 area of northwestern Ontario, prepared a paper on trapping to help discussions with the Ministry of Natural Resources (MNR) in May 1995. A couple of excerpts show how much traditional understandings are seen as *the* most important aspect of trapping:

> For Anishinaabe people, trapping is not simply a satisfying way of livelihood. Trapping in the Anishinaabe way is first and foremost a spiritual activity. At its most basic level, it means:

(1) Giving respect for the land and animals in the Anishinabe way so that life on the land will be renewed; and

(2) giving respect for those people who have the sacred knowledge of how to trap in a sustainable way based on Anishinabe teachings and knowledge.

When we talk about respecting the land and animals, we do not mean them in any way like the whiteman does.... Our knowledge of trapping is a unique knowledge.... I believe that it is vitally important because *it expresses our sense and experience of the lands.* Our knowledge of trapping has its spiritual and sacred aspects.... Our knowledge has a spiritual and cultural form....

In terms of Anishinabe people, these animals are better understood as our relatives. Many of them are clan dodaems of our people. *We have our own ways of speaking about them and relating to them....* Our knowledge of our animals is often expressed in the language of our ceremonies. But it reflects a great complexity and sophistication which the MNR bureaucrats and scientists do not know about. Our knowledge has arisen out of relationships to our lands and animals.

All of the white man's "science" used to make management decisions for quotas was based on *their* relationships to the land. It was against *our* relationships to our land and each other, as Anishinabe people, on our lands. It still is. *This science is not objective.* It is a tool of the whiteman that reflects *his* understanding of the land. It reflects *his* social relationships to the land.

I include these passages to demonstrate that there is a rising chorus of voices asking that traditional laws, practices and understandings be taught and demonstrated once again *in every aspect of community and family life,* including trapping. It causes Charlie considerable pain to see his own people break their own laws, in trapping and in every other context. He, like many others, is doing what he can to make them a part of life once again, to educate his own people once again into Aboriginal ways of approaching life. As we have seen, the awareness and application of those laws is capable of giving life a special unity and significance, something much harder to maintain when life is artificially subdivided into separate areas like "criminal justice," "health," "education," "family law" or "resource use."

Looking for traditional teachings, I should point out, does not mean an insistence on reviving every traditional *process* as well. Adjustment of those processes is clearly called for, given changed realities. As the writers of the final report of the Traditional Dene Justice Project in the Northwest Territories stated in 1993: "Many of the *practices* from the past cannot address current problems. However, if the *values* attached to those practices could be reclaimed, and new practices built on them, then it could work" (emphasis added).

When I first read that section, it reminded me of a request that an Ojibway grandfather made to the court in a remote community in northwestern Ontario. He asked that his troubled grandson be sentenced to accompany him into the bush that winter. "It's not," he said, "that he will always live in the bush. He will not. But the bush is where he can learn the things he will need to know if he is to survive in your cities." As I am only beginning to understand, the bush can indeed be the "teacher" of a value system, and the teachings themselves can indeed be carried into twentieth-century life. In fact, as the healing program at Hollow Water demonstrates, those teachings may be *essential* if today's challenges are to be met successfully.

To return to the "justice compartment," however, studies into traditional justice make one other thing very clear: traditional values must not only direct how society organizes itself so as to keep wrongdoing to a minimum, but must also direct how society responds to any wrongdoing that does occur. In other words, the reactive aspect of the justice system must itself be bound by those same laws and cannot be permitted to act in ways that defy them. The processes of law cannot *break* the law.

For instance, as we have seen, an important part of many teachings involves family responsibility for the health and behaviour of its own members. It is understood that if families carry out their responsibilities to prevent improper behaviour in the first place and to correct and compensate any misbehaviour that does transpire, then there won't be the same need for strangers to get involved. In that sense, the institutionalized justice system of the West, with its vast armies of paid professional strangers ready to impose their solutions at the drop of a hat, are seen by many Aboriginal people as a sign of substantial social failure. Their very existence means that the family and the community are no longer strong. Further, their continuing existence serves only to *undermine* the potential of families and communities. As Elder Vi Hilbert expressed it in the Northwest Intertribal Court System's report on Salish justice: "I think it would have been *disgraceful* to have somebody else resolve your problems. Your own family needed to help clear your mind and clear your heart if you were having a problem" (emphasis added).

In its own way, that passage partially explains the near-silence of traditional justice reports on what we might call "institutional" justice: as long as families, clans and other groups obeyed traditional law by remaining involved and capable, the need for outside, institutional resources was minimized. It also hints at the reason we didn't hear much about "sentencing" in those reports, if by "sentencing" we mean the imposition of a result by a neutral third party: it was understood that the people who were part of the problem carried the duty of creating their *own* responses.

It is worth repeating a certain portion of the Bluehouse-Zion article from *The Mediation Quarterly*. "[T]he judges and lawyers of the Navajo Nation are attempting to bring individuals into the dispute resolution process so they can resolve their *own* problems.... [T]he alien Navajo Court of Indian Offences ... and the Bureau of Indian Affairs Law and Order Code, made Navajos judge others, using power and force for control. That arrangement is repugnant to Navajo morals" (emphasis added). As the article goes on to explain, the Navajo are looking once again to traditional values—or law—as the foundation for both a just society and for a "reactive" justice system. It contains, for instance, a lengthy discussion of the Navajo concept of *k'e*, described as one of "the two dynamic forces of traditional law": "*K'e* translates into English as compassion, cooperation, friendliness, unselfishness, peacefulness and all the other positive values which create an intense, diffuse and enduring solidarity. Navajo ceremonies, stories and traditions, and for that matter the language itself, teach and reinforce those values...." Once again, an article on justice begins with a discussion of values, and only then talks about processes for responding to problems. Further, when it does speak about such processes, it demands that they too follow traditional law.

In that same issue of *The Mediation Quarterly,* another article deals with certain discussions that took place between urban Aboriginal leaders representing five First Nations in British Columbia. They had all been part of a mediation training program which they felt had been "culturally biased" in favour of Western approaches. The article, "Mediation around the Medicine Wheel," by Marg Huber, summarizes how they approached their search for more appropriate processes instead. As we might expect, they found themselves quickly turning their attention towards the values set out within traditional teachings:

Identified values important in *dealing with conflict* included cooperation, sharing, equality among people, harmony, consensus decision-making, non-interference in individual matters, privacy, patience and modesty. Values inherent in *communications* included moderation in speech, careful listening, physical communication (non-verbal) and quietness. Other values important in the *Aboriginal way of life* included family and community, cultural heritage, self-determination, respect for elders, a holistic approach to life, relativity of time and spiritual connectedness. (emphasis added)

I should mention that they located each of the many values they discussed within the traditional teachings of the Medicine Wheel. Further, each of those values then inspired the creation of particular processes designed to deal with certain aspects of disputes in specified ways. As Huber went on to say: "The contributors unequivocally agreed that if a mediation process were to be successful in helping people make and manage change, it would need to be grounded in Aboriginal spirituality. The spiritual focus would enable participants to heal through understanding and make decisions based on dignity and respect."

As all these passages illustrate, a great many Aboriginal discussions about justice (or education, health, trapping, parenting, etc.) are being reoriented so they begin not with processes but with a search for traditional values. Once those values have been located and identified, the discussion then shifts to methods for fostering them within each aspect of life. Only then is it appropriate—or even possible—to turn the discussion towards devising processes for responding to people who have lost or denied the teachings, and those processes themselves must demonstrate allegiance to the teachings.

Finally, it must be noted that there is a spiritual foundation for all those values, and for all the processes constructed on them.

It appears, then, that we have two different perceptions about where the primary spotlight should be aimed when it comes to "a justice system." To use a broad generalization, while the Aboriginal spotlight seems to shine primarily on the creation and maintenance of a peaceful society, the Western one highlights processes designed to respond to actual disorder instead. Not being aware of the fact that the two spotlights illuminate different aspects of the same overall problem, we of the Western system are puzzled when Aboriginal responses to our justice questions fail to shed light on the kinds of things we expected to see, but show us very different things instead.

The best metaphor I can think of involves Western doctors asking Aboriginal people to "Please research traditional methods of dealing with heart disease." My imagination then sees traditional medicine people putting 95 percent of their attention into describing the kinds of diets, work habits, teachings of moderation, strategies for healing and stress reduction and so forth that *prevented* heart disease from becoming a major health concern in traditional times. Only then might they mention, almost in passing, how traditional healers might have responded to an actual case of heart disease.

Would Western doctors answer in protest by saying, "No, no, that's not what we asked about!"—as I did when the context was justice? Or would they be quicker to say "Ah-hah! When you speak of 'a health care system,' you put your emphasis in a different place than we do, and we'd be pleased to learn more about your approaches"?

THIS WIDER VIEW of justice does appear to be gaining ground with some Western justice professionals as well. There is, for instance, the 1993 report of Parliament's Standing Committee on Justice, under Chairman Robert Horner, M.P., who has been quoted as saying: "Listen, if anybody told me nine years ago that I'd be study-ing the social causes of crime, I would have said they were nuts. I'm an ex-member of the RCMP and I'm strictly for law and order. But I can tell you that we just can't continue to build more jails and spend more money on police budgets and have crime increasing the way it is." The committee report itself focused primarily on preventative strategies, including social programs for youth, battling poverty, child abuse and illiteracy. As the report concluded: "If locking up those who violate the law contributed to safer societies, then the United States should be the safest country in the world."

I can see the elders nodding their heads, supporting the view that society cannot spend the bulk of its time, money and energy responding to the symptoms of social illnesses, and proportionately little on creating social health in the first place. As some have expressed it to me, it is almost as if Western society has *resigned* itself to the level of social illness that presently afflicts its families and communities. I must mention that, in my experience, very few elders would ever express thoughts like that in such a direct and critical fashion. I am much more accustomed to having them quietly raise the possibility that our two societies simply seem to have "different" understandings about what justice is!

Their resistance to focusing on our kinds of questions when asked about justice, then, amounts to nothing less than a polite but insistent refusal to endorse or adopt, for their own people, the reactive justice emphasis that is so prevalent in Western societies. And, as I am just beginning to understand, that refusal is much more than a matter of preference. Instead, it comes out of under-standings about Creation and about the role of humanity within it, that show significant differences from those upon which the Western system has been built.

Moon Boots and Swim Fins

I want to pass on a metaphor which someone gave me to illustrate what took place when Aboriginal understandings came into collision with those of the European world. I have extended it, but I think that's what I was *supposed* to do!

The man who gave it to me asked me to imagine that our two cultures are represented by a skin diver and a moon walker. Because they lived and worked in different environments, they developed different footwear to suit their needs. The moon walker created heavy boots, because there is less gravity on the moon. Without them, he would float off into space. The skin diver needed his swim fins to propel him through the denser atmosphere of the ocean. Without them, his ability to move about was severely restricted. As long as each stayed with his own footwear, in his own environment, they could move easily and well. If, however, the skin diver were forced to put on weighted moon boots, he would be at risk of drowning. Similarly, if the moon walker changed to swim fins, he would likely float off into space. In either case, each would be likely to come to grief if forced to wear the other's footgear.

Suppose, the metaphor continues, the moon walker was not *aware* that the skin diver operated in a totally different environment, just as the first settlers to arrive in North America were unaware of Aboriginal world-views, languages, spirituality, governance and the like. Suppose as well that the moon walker, believing in the "rightness" of his own ways, tried his best to get the skin diver to kick off those fins and wear moon boots instead. Suppose, like the settler nations coming to North America, they used everything from persuasion and ridicule right through to legal prohibition. After a time, the skin diver might finally be pressured into taking off his swim fins (at least while the moon walker was watching!). When he did that, however, he would not have traded environments at all. Instead, he would have been robbed of his capacity to swim successfully in his own.

Given enough time, his reduced mobility and his loss of power, confidence and self-esteem would destroy even his *wish* to move. He would begin to lose even more of the access he once enjoyed to his own environment, his capacity to explore it and rejoice in it. Instead, he would begin to live cut off from anything that gave life its purpose, its thrill and its potential for awe.

Within that metaphor, the Western world has indeed done everything it could to force Aboriginal people to discard their traditional footwear. Our imposition of residential schools is but one example. When children disappeared into those non-Aboriginal institutions, everything was new. Instead of being encouraged to develop personal qualities and wide notions of responsibility, they found themselves trained into unthinking acceptance of codes of "right" behaviour established by others. Instead of a "Natural Law" of interdependence requiring that they connect with each other as co-adventurers, they were trained into seeing each other as rivals and competitors. Instead of learning about humility and deference, they were trained to start thinking of themselves as "better than" or worse than their fellows.

Breaking Aboriginal Law

A report by the Grand Council Treaty Number 3 on their 1993 Elder's Conference contains the following passage: "If one follows respect, the conclusion is that no system is more valid than the other; but the Euro-Canadian validity is forced upon our ways. *The Euro-Canadians are breaking our laws day in and day out, as they accuse us of breaking theirs*" (emphasis added). When I first heard such claims, I found them offensive and perplexing. Now that I have been exposed to the kinds of perspectives I have tried to express in these pages, I can only acknowledge their substantial validity.

One of our most serious breaches of traditional law involves something I mentioned earlier: our belief in absolutes like "the truth" or "the right answer." As long as we hold that belief, we continue to declare that there is only *one* true way of thinking, of seeing, of speaking, of knowing, and that it is *our* way. Traditional law makes no such assertion, and attempts no such imposition. Instead, it grants that each person, family, community and nation should be as free as possible to put their own wisdoms into practice within their own spheres of activity. Ironically, it is our very system of Canadian law that seems to be the greatest felon where traditional law is concerned. As I now see it, traditional wisdom and law stand in substantial contrast to our Western approaches in at least seven respects.

First, according to Western law, offenders can be effectively dealt with on their own, whether within deterrent or rehabilitative contexts. Traditional wisdom suggests that we are all substantially the products of our relationships. Traditional law thus commands that justice processes *involve* all people within the webs of relationships that surround every offender and every victim.

Second, Western law seems to assume we are captains of our own ships and that each of us is equally capable of moving out of antisocial behaviour on our own, just by deciding to do so. Traditional wisdom suggests that each of us rides a multitude of waves, some stretching back centuries, which we cannot fundamentally change and which will still confront us tomorrow. Further, it suggests that each of us is confronted by very *different* wave combinations, some much more powerful and destructive than others. Traditional law thus commands that a justice system focus on healing and teaching offenders so that they become more, not less, capable of dealing with their unique and continuing realities.

Third, Western law focuses very narrowly on particular acts, for it is acts that are alleged, subject to proof and, if proven, substantially controlling of the court's disposition. Traditional understandings suggest that such acts are no more than clues signalling relational disharmonies between individuals, between individuals and other aspects of Creation, and between the physical, mental, emotional and spiritual dimensions of each individual. Traditional law thus commands that these be the areas of investigation and intervention, and that acts no longer occupy centre stage.

Fourth, Western law puts the parties through adversarial processes that inevitably add to the level of antagonism between them. Traditional wisdom suggests that antagonism within relationships is in fact the cause of those adversarial acts, and traditional law thus commands that justice processes be structured in ways to reduce that antagonism and bring health and understanding back to those relationships.

Fifth, while Western law labels and stigmatizes offenders, to others and to themselves, traditional wisdom suggests that we are all in constant processes of reformation within ever-changing relationships. Traditional law thus commands that justice processes be structured to help people begin to believe they are *more* than their anti-social acts, that they too have worth and dignity, and that they too are capable of learning how to cope with the forces that surround them. In short, while our punitive law treats offenders as enemies of the community, traditional wisdom suggests that such alienation is part of the problem, and traditional law commands that every effort be made to *overcome* that conviction, not add to it.

Sixth, according to Western law, "taking responsibility for your act" means little more than acknowledging the particulars of the illegal act, then paying a proportionate price in punishment. Traditional wisdom suggests that acts are important only for their consequences on the mental, emotional, spiritual and physical health of all those affected, including all those within the *offender's* relationships. Traditional law thus commands that justice processes be structured so as to incorporate the "felt" responses of all those people in respectful, dignified and "non-blaming" ways and to help the offender truly "take responsibility" for his act by coming to feel some portion of the pain he has caused all those other people.

Seventh, according to Western law, "solutions" are best provided through reliance on professional, third-patty strangers like judges, psychiatrists, probation officers and the like. Traditional wisdom suggests that the only people who understand the complexities of their relationships thoroughly enough are the people actually involved. The proper role for third-party professionals is to act as regulators of respectful processes, teachers of values upon which respectful relationships can be developed, and real-life demonstrations of what those relationships look like in action. Traditional law thus commands that the responsibility for problem solving be restored to the parties and that the experts step down from their thrones.

And, as I hope to have shown, all such laws can indeed be found "hidden in every leaf and rock," where every relationship speaks of interdependence, of intersustenance, of symbiosis. In the face of such laws, it only seems appropriate to contemplate a human duty to strive constantly to attain a state of mind—a spirit—that both acknowledges and manifests such understandings at every instant, and in every act.

The Teaching of the Four Colours

I want to close with a story, and with a teaching.

I'll tell you about the teaching first. I heard it from two different tribal groups, Cree and Ojibway. It has to do with the four colours of people who are understood to reside on Mother Earth: the black, red, yellow and white-skinned peoples. Each group has unique gifts to bring to everyone else, and therefore unique responsibilities as well. The oldest group (for the teaching says that we are not, as peoples, all of the same age) is the people of the black colour. Their unique gift has to do with the power of sound in Creation. In that connection, it must be recalled that, for the Aboriginal peoples of Australia, what we think of as the physical landscape must be *sung* into existence. It is their obligation to study, preserve and use wisely the power of sound in the universe. Next oldest are the people of the red colour, the Aboriginal peoples of the Americas. Their special gift involves understanding the complex relationships between the four orders of Creation and all the zillions of "things" that exist within them. Their special responsibility thus involves preserving the health of Mother Earth, her lifeblood the waters, and the plant, animal and human realms. The people of the yellow colour are understood to be younger still, and their special gifts and responsibilities have to do with understanding the workings of the human mind and body.

And what of the fourth group, the one I so often hear described as "our white brothers and sisters"? In both the Cree and Ojibway accounts, the special gift of this group, currently the largest in North America, has to do with bringing about effective communication and understanding between all the peoples on Mother Earth, for without that there can be no real sharing of the gifts that each bring for all to use. I have often heard Leroy Little Bear close his sessions by thanking his "white brothers and sisters" for the gift of the English language, so the Blackfoot could learn from the Mi'kmaq, the Cree from the Navajo and so on.

There is, however, a fly in the ointment. It has to do with the fact that the people of the white colour, though immensely powerful, are also the youngest. Amongst the Kogi people of

Columbia, for instance, European peoples are known as "Little Brother." In fact, white people are, in a social sense, seen as boisterous adolescents who act primarily on impulse and do not yet understand either the richness or the fragility of life, much less their responsibility to keep it in good health. As such, there remains the unhappy possibility that our common family home will not survive Little Brother's adolescence. With all our strength, energy and self-centredness, we might still bring the walls tumbling down on everyone.

I hope this book will be received as my attempt to honour that teaching. It is one attempt to carry out my responsibilities as "Little Brother"—to help facilitate communication between the colours so we can all come together to make a healthy whole.

The Story of Sir Walter

And now, the story. It is one I will always remember with warm feelings and a chuckle.

I was making a presentation at a special program on Aboriginal justice at the Banff Centre in Alberta. The course leader was, once again, Leroy Little Bear. I had just spoken of the Western rule of evidence called the "Hearsay Rule," which, in most circumstances, prevents people from describing things they were not present for, but only heard about from others. I mentioned that it dated all the way back to the time of Sir Walter Raleigh and to his demand that anyone who had an accusation to make against him had to "say it to my face" in open court. When judges agreed with him, that was the end of "gossip" in court, and the beginning of face-to-face confrontations and challenges between offenders, victims and witnesses.

At that point, Leroy raised his hand and politely asked if I could remember when that rule of evidence was made. I ventured to guess that it was over three hundred years ago. Leroy, I am sure, knew the date exactly. In his casual way, however, he responded by saying: "Oh, I see. So it's a fairly *new* rule for you, then. Can you tell me, how is it working out?"

Appendix

Special thanks are offered to P. Lane, J. Bopp and M. Bopp, the authors of *The Sacred Tree*, whom the author of this book was unable to locate for acknowledgment.

The Twelve Teachings of the Sacred Tree

1. *Wholeness.* All things are interrelated. Everything in the universe is part of a single whole. Everything is connected in some way to everything else. It is therefore possible to understand something only if we can understand how it is connected to everything else.

2. *Change.* All of creation is in a state of constant change. Nothing stays the same except the presence of cycle upon cycle of change. One season falls upon the other. Human beings are born, live their lives, die and enter the spirit world. All things change. There are two kinds of change: the coming together of things (development) and the coming apart of things (disintegration). Both of these kinds of change are necessary and are always connected to each other.

3. *Change occurs in cycles or patterns.* They are not random or accidental. Sometimes it is difficult to see how a particular change is connected to everything else. This usually means that our standpoint (the situation from which we are viewing the change) is limiting our ability to see clearly.

4. *The seen and the unseen.* The physical world is real. The spiritual world is real. These two are aspects of one reality. Yet, there are separate laws which govern each of them. Violation of spiritual laws can affect the spiritual world. A balanced life is one that honours the laws of both of these dimensions of reality.

5. *Human beings are spiritual as well as physical.*

6. *Human beings can always acquire new gifts, but they must struggle to do so.* The timid may become courageous, the weak may become bold and strong, the insensitive may learn to care for the feelings of others and the materialistic person can acquire the capacity to look within and to listen to her inner voice. The process human beings use to develop new qualities may be called "true learning."

7. *There are four dimensions of "true learning."* These four aspects of every person's nature are reflected in the four cardinal points of the medicine wheel. These four aspects of our being are developed through the use of our volition. It cannot be said that a person has totally learned in a whole and balanced manner unless all four dimensions of her being have been involved in the process.

8. The spiritual dimension of human development may be understood in terms of *four related capacities.*

    First, the capacity to have and to respond to realities that exist in a non-material way such as dreams, visions, ideals, spiritual teachings, goals and theories.

    Second, the capacity to accept those realities as a reflection (in the form of symbolic representation) of unknown or unrealized potential to do or be something more or different than we are now.

    Third, the capacity to express these non-material realities using symbols such as speech, art or mathematics.

Fourth, the capacity to use this symbolic expression to guide future action—action directed towards making what was only seen as a possibility into a living reality.

9. *Human beings must be active participants* in the unfolding of their own potentialities.

10. The doorway through which all must pass if they wish to become more or different than they are now is the *doorway of the will (volition)*. A person must *decide* to take the journey. The path has infinite patience. It will always be there for those who decide to travel it.

11. *Anyone who sets out* (i.e., makes a commitment and then acts on that commitment) on a journey of self-development *will be aided.* There will be guides and teachers who will appear, and spiritual protectors to watch over the traveller. No test will be given that the traveller does not already have the strength to meet.

12. *The only source of failure* on a journey will be the traveller's own failure to follow the teachings of *The Sacred Tree.*

Reprinted, with emphases added, from *The Sacred Tree* (1984), Four Worlds Development Press, Four Worlds Development Project, University of Lethbridge, 4401 University Drive, Lethbridge, Alberta, Canada T1K 3M4.

Notes

p. 13   "Mrs. P. gave evidence…" *R.* v. *P. (JA.)* (1991) 6 C.R. (4th) 126, pp. 131-32.

p. 14   "It is of interest that …" Ibid., pp. 129-30.

p. 14   "In this case I heard evidence …" Ibid., pp. 141-42.

p. 16   "First, the emphasis was on reaching …" Teresea Olsen, Cabrielle M. Maxwell and Allison Morris, *Maori and Youth Justice in New Zealand* (1993), qtd. in F.W.M. MacElrea, "Restorative Justice: The New Zealand Youth Court—A Model for Development in Other Courts?" *Journal of Judicial Administration 4* (1994): 36.

p. 18   "… The primary objectives of a criminal justice …" F.W.M. MacElrea, "Restorative Justice": 36.

p. 19   "The worst stigmatic attack …" John Braithwaite and Stephen Mugford, "Conditions of Successful Reintegration Ceremonies: Dealing with Juvenile Offenders," *British Journal of Criminology* 34(2) (1994).

p. 20   "… In Wagga, a standard question …" Ibid., p. 13.

p. 20   "This would tend to suggest …" F.W.M. MacElrea, "Restorative Justice": 53.

p. 21   "Our needs for acceptance …" Ibid., p. 47.

p. 22   "… Navajo culture approaches …" Philmer Bluehouse and James Zion, "Hozhooji Naat'aanii: The Navajo Justice and Harmony Ceremony," *The Mediation Quarterly* 10(4) (Summer 1993): 328.

p. 23   "This unique method…" Zion 1983, qtd. in Ibid.

p. 23   "In the traditional Navajo way ..." Robert Yazzie, "Healing as Justice: The American Experience," in *Justice as Healing: A Newsletter on Aboriginal Concepts of Justice,* Native Law Centre of the University of Saskatchewan, Spring 1995, p. 7.

p. 24   "The English words *mediation* ..." Bluehouse and Zion, "The Navajo Justice and Harmony Ceremony": 333-34.

p. 25   "Peacemaking is generally ..." Diane LeResche, "Editor's Notes," *The Mediation Quarterly* 10(4) (Summer 1993): 321, 322.

CHAPTER 2   HEALING INSIDE THE WHIRLWIND OF SEXUAL ABUSE

p. 31   "the completion of the Healing Contract...." Valdie Seymour, "Hollow Water First Nation Community Holistic Circle Healing," unpublished paper, nd.

p. 36   "that as we both ..." Hollow Water First Nation, "Position Paper on Incarceration," Hollow Water First Nation, MB, September 1994, pp. 41–42. (The "Position Paper on Incarceration" was a portion of an interim report made by the Hollow Water First Nation to the Departments of Justice for both Manitoba and Canada in September of 1994.)

p. 37   "an already unbalanced person ..." Ibid., p. 43.

p. 37   "rather than making the community ..." Ibid.

p. 37   "courtroom and process simply ..." Ibid., p. 46.

p. 38   "Our children and the community ..." Bluehouse and Zion, "The Navajo Justice and Harmony Ceremony": 328.

p. 50   "A small whirlwind..." Edward Benton-Banai, *The Mishomis Book: The Voice of the Ojibway* (Hayward: Red School House, 1988), pp. 52-54.

CHAPTER 3   DIGGING FOR THE ROOTS OF THE HEALING VISION

p. 56   "The dynamics of mediation ..." Bluehouse and Zion, "The Navajo Justice and Harmony Ceremony": 328-39.

p. 58   "The call that he ..." Basil Johnston, *Ojibway Heritage* (Toronto: McClelland and Stewart, 1984), p. 61.

p. 58   "Leadership was predicated ..." Ibid.

p. 58 "Even when circumstances ..." Ibid., pp. 61-62.

p. 60 "forsake their manitous and ..." Basil Johnston, "Introduction," in Rupert Ross, *Dancing with a Ghost* (Markham, ON: Octopus Publishing Group, 1992), p. vii.

p. 62 "Basil Johnston also speaks ..." Johnston, *Ojibway Heritage,* p. 21.

p. 63 "[T]he methods of [Western] science ..." Milton M.R. Freeman, "The Nature and Utility of Traditional Ecological Knowledge," *Northern Perspectives* 20(1) (Summer 1992): 9-10.

p. 65 "wording of these principles..." *The Sacred Tree* (Lethbridge, AB: Four Worlds Development Press, 1984), pp. 25-30.

p. 69 "[This denial] is expressed ..." Kaplan and Johnson, 1964, pp. 216-17, qtd. in Bluehouse and Zion, "The Navajo Justice and Harmony Ceremony": 331.

p. 69 "Peacemaking is more conciliation ..." LeResche, "Editor's Notes": 321.

p. 70 "CHANGE. Everything is in ..." *The Sacred Tree,* p. 27.

p. 71 "The highest compliment ..." Johnston, "Introduction," in Ross, *Dancing with a Ghost,* p. xii.

p. 72 "In ... preferring ..." Ibid., p. vii.

p. 74 "Coyote, Coyote ..." Peter Blue Cloud/Aroniawenrate, *The Elderberry Flute Song: Contemporary Coyote Tales* (Buffalo, NY: White Pine Press, 1982), p. 131.

CHAPTER 4 TOWARDS A FLUID REALITY

p. 79 "From the last to ..." Johnston, *Ojibway Heritage,* p. 21.

p. 80 "... pest ... waste ..." Ruth Beebe Hill, *Hanta Yo* (Garden City, NY: Doubleday, 1979), p. 14.

p. 81 "Modern textbooks ..." Anne Pausto-Sterling, "Is Nature Really Red in Tooth and Claw?" *Discover* (April 1993): 24.

p. 81 "Strikingly, those ..." Ibid.

p. 87 "no other authority except the force of ..." Johnston, *Ojibway Heritage,* p. 61.

p. 89 "To foster individuality ..." Ibid., p. 70.

p. 98 "Today for the majority ..." Frank Brown, "Heiltsuk Rediscovery Project: Goose Island Proposal," Bella Bella First Nation, British Columbia, p. 12.

CHAPTER 5 WATCH YOUR LANGUAGE

p. 111 "The Navajo never appeals ..." Clyde Kluckhohn, "The Philosophy of the Navajo Indians," in *Ideological Differences and World Order*, ed. F.S.C. Northrop (New Haven: Yale University Press, 1949).

p. 112 "For Anglos, answers to questions ..." Susan Urmston Philips, "Some Sources of Cultural Variability in the Regulation of Talk," *Language in Society* 5 (1973): 81.

p. 113 "[I]n all of this,..." Ibid.: 93.

p. 114 "How many of you out there ..." Danny Moonhawk Alford, "God Is Not a Noun in Native America," Hayward, California, 1993, p. 5.

p. 119 "Indigenous people view ..." Sákéj Henderson, "Algonquian Spirituality: Balancing the Opposites" (forthcoming), pp. 10-11.

p. 123 "I am brother to the Gee-thee-ba-sun ..." Benton Banai, *The Mishomis Book*, p. 52.

p. 127 "The Peacemaker wonders ..." Bluehouse and Zion, "The Navajo Justice and Harmony Ceremony": 330.

p. 128 "He that is good will ..." Charles Caleb Colton, *Globe and Mail*, 17 February 1995, p. 1.

p. 133 "Admit, assume, because,..." Hill, *Hanta Yo*, p. 7.

p. 134 "As a Mi'kmaq ..." Sasheen Gould, Eskasoni First Nation, unpublished essay.

CHAPTER 6 THE FIRST STEP TO RECONNECTION

p. 139 "All things are interrelated ..." *The Sacred Tree*, p. 26.

p. 148 "It is ... possible to understand ..." Ibid.

p. 152 "Is it *hashkeeeji* ..." Bluehouse and Zion, "The Navajo Justice and Harmony Ceremony": 330.

p. 158 "There are four dimensions ..." *The Sacred Tree*, p. 29.

CHAPTER 7 THE HEALING PATH HAS POTHOLES TOO!

p. 170 "In Navajo culture ..." Bluehouse and Zion, "The Navajo Justice and Harmony Ceremony": 330.

p. 172 "When Gladys shares her story ..." Lisa Tyler, *NeWest Review* (April/May 1995).

p. 176 "Chief Justice Robert Yazzie, in one of his papers. Robert Yazzie, "Healing as Justice: The American Experience," *Justice as Healing: A Newsletter on Aboriginal Concepts of Justice,* Native Law Centre of the University of Saskatchewan, Spring 1995, p. 8.

p. 178 "Our tradition, our culture ..." Hollow Water First Nation, "Position Paper on Incarceration," p. 42.

p. 178 "People who offend against another ..." Ibid., pp. 42-43.

p. 179 "Sacred justice is going ..." LeResche, "Editor's Notes": 322.

CHAPTER 8 THE WHIRLPOOL VISION OF CRIME

p. 183 "By the time MOVE approached ..." David Owen, "Pre-sentence Mediation Proceedings Benefit N.B. Crime Victims and Offenders," *The Lawyers Weekly* 27 January 1995, p. 12.

p. 184 "We are no longer enemies ..." Ibid.

p. 193 "Criminal trials tend ..." Braithwaite and Mugford, "Conditions of Successful Reintegration Ceremonies," *British Journal of Criminology* 34(2) (1994).

p. 195 "Human beings can ..." *The Sacred Tree,* pp. 29-30.

p. 196 "Our children and the community ..." Hollow Water First Nation, "Position Paper on Incarceration," p. 46.

p. 201 "Rationale ..." Ibid., pp. 12-15.

CHAPTER 9 AT THE CROSSROADS: RESPONDING TO THE ABUSE OF POWER IN SMALL COMMUNITIES

p. 212 "Crown Attorneys, to make their case ..." Hollow Water First Nation, "Position Paper on Incarceration," pp. 45-46.

p. 214 "Control issues were also ..." Grand Council Treaty Number 3, "Final Report of the Community Consultations: Aboriginal

Family Violence Strategy" October 1992, Kenora, ON, pp. 19-20.

Regarding Grand Council Treaty Number 3: This Ojibway treaty area, negotiated in the early twentieth century, is distinct from the Oji-Cree Treaty Number 9 area, which covers the northern portion of northwestern Ontario.

p. 220   "born into networks of ..." Sasheen Gould, Eskasoni First Nation, unpublished essay.

CHAPTER 10 CHOOSING THE HEALING PATH

p. 228   "Funding for the development ..." Grand Council Treaty Number 3, "Executive Summary," "Final Report of the Community Consultations: Aboriginal Family Violence Strategy," October 1992, Kenora, ON, Recommendation no. 22, Section C, p. 11.

p. 229   "Healing is also about taking ..." Patricia Monture-Angus, "Justice as Healing: Thinking about Change," *Justice as Healing: A Newsletter on Aboriginal Concepts of Justice,* Native Law Centre of the University of Saskatchewan, Summer 1995, p. 3.

p. 235   "Indeed, the group over whom ..." Carole LaPrairie, Ph.D., "Exploring the Boundaries of Justice: Aboriginal Justice in the Yukon, prepared for Department of Justice, Yukon Territorial Government, First Nations, Yukon Territory and Justice Canada, Ottawa, 1992, p. 111.

p. 236   "The potential for discrepancy ..." Ibid., p. 112.

p. 236   "There have been a number ..." Grand Council Treaty Number 3, "Final Report of the Community Consultations: Aboriginal Family Violence Strategy," October 1992, Kenora, ON, p. 38.

p. 238   "One woman that was interviewed ..." Ibid., p. 15.

p. 243   "The fact is, the criminal law ..." *Our Criminal Law,* Report of the Law Reform Commission of Canada (Ottawa: Queen's Printer, 1977), p. 27.

p. 243   "The criminal law should be employed ..." *The Criminal Law in Canadian Society,* Report of the Criminal Law Review Committee of the Federal Department of Justice (Ottawa: Queen's Printer, 1982), p. 59.

p. 243   "Those other avenues ..." Mr. Justice Doherty, *R.* v. *McDougall*
         (1990) 1 O.R. (3d) 247.

CHAPTER 11 GETTING STARTED ON THE HEALING PATH

p. 260   "The word *hozhoojigo* ..." Bluehouse and Zion, "The Navajo
         Justice and Harmony Ceremony": 334.

p. 260   "[Aboriginal peacemaking] brings ..." LeResche, "Editor's
         Notes": 321.

CHAPTER 12 AND FINALLY ... THE STARTING POINT

p. 267   "We realize ..." Grand Council Treaty Number 3, "Internal
         Report: Elders' Justice Conference," July 1994, p. 5.

p. 268   "As one elder emphasized ..." Emily Mansfield, "Balance and
         Harmony: Peacemaking in Coast Salish Tribes," *The Mediation
         Quarterly* 10(4) (Summer 1993): 341.

p. 268   "Children learned ..." Ibid.: 343.

p. 269   "Traditionally, the Dogrib ..." "Introduction," in Joan Ryan,
         *Doing Things the Right Way: Dene Traditional Justice in Lac La
         Marte, NWT* (Calgary: University of Calgary Press, 1995),
         pp. 1-2.

p. 270   "Justice in the English legal ..." Grand Council Treaty Number
         3, "Internal Report: Staff–Elders Consultation Conference,"
         Dalles First Nation, December 1993, p. 9.

p. 270   "European explorers often said ..." Robert Yazzie, "Healing as
         Justice": 7.

p. 271   "Why does your law ..." Ross, *Dancing with a Ghost,* p. 170.

p. 274   "For Anishinaabe people ..." Charlie Fisher, "A Treaty #3/Ontario
         Trapping Agreement: A One Man Lake First Nation Perspective,"
         pp. 1-11 passim.

p. 276   "Many of the *practices* from the past ..." "Internal Report:
         Staff–Elders Consultation Conference," Dalles First Nation,
         December 1993, p. 6.

p. 277   "I think it would have been *disgraceful* ..." "Traditional and
         Informal Dispute Resolution Processes in Tribes of the Puget

Sound and Olympic Peninsula Region," Northwest Intertribal Court System, Edmonds, WA, 1991, p. 72.

p. 278 "[T]he judges and lawyers of the Navajo Nation ..." Bluehouse and Zion, "The Navajo Justice and Harmony Ceremony": 327-29.

p. 279 "Identified values important ..." Marg Huber, "Mediation around the Medicine Wheel," *The Mediation Quarterly* 10(4) (Summer 1993): 357.

p. 281 "Listen, if anybody told me ..." *Report of Parliament's Standing Committee on Justice*, 1993, qtd. in Sean Fine, "Justice Committee Targets Poverty," *Globe and Mail*, 27 February 1993, p. 1.

p. 281 "If locking up those who violate ..." *Crime Prevention in Canada: Towards a National Strategy*, Twelfth Report of the Standing Committee on Justice and the Solicitor General (Ottawa: Queen's Printer, February 1993), p. 2.

p. 283 "If one follows respect ..." Grand Council Treaty Number 3, "Internal Report: Staff–Elders Consultation Conference," Dalles First Nation, December 1993, p. 9.